THE GREAT NORTH ROAD
THEN AND NOW

Improvement makes straight roads;
but the crooked roads without improvement are roads of genius

WILLIAM BLAKE

THE GREAT NORTH ROAD THEN AND NOW

Chris 'Wolfie' Cooper

Credits

ISBN: 9 781870 067799

Designed by Winston Ramsey,
Editor-in-Chief *After the Battle*

PUBLISHERS
Battle of Britain International Limited
Hobbs Cross House, Old Harlow,
Essex CM17 0NN
Tel. 01279 41 8833 Fax: 01279 41 9386
Website: www.afterthebattle.com

PRINTERS
Printed and bound by Ozgraf S. A., Olsztyn, Poland.

FRONT COVER
The Great North Road about to cross Girtford Bridge northbound at Sandy in Bedfordshire (see page 55).

BACK COVER
An abandoned section of the original Great North Road at Ayot Green, which is between Lemsford and Welwyn (see page 41).

FRONTSPIECE
This stretch of the Great North Road from Rainton up to Scotch Corner is known as Leeming Lane. This is the northern end where the modern dual carriageway comes around to rejoin the old alignment.

ACKNOWLEDGEMENTS

Thanks must go to all those who answered my newspaper appeals for information and those who helped me in many other ways. In no particular order: Bette Smith of Newark; Sally and Jane Cox of Stamford; J. Scott of Yaxley; Alan Edney of Newcastle-upon-Tyne; Don Whitfield of Darlington; Ivy Knox of Great Ayton; Cindy Todd of Brotherton; Peggy Skeggs of Hatfield; S. Laycock of Stockton on Tees; June Cooper of Sutton-on-Trent; Maurice Gunnell of Hatfield; David Oldham of Stamford; Joy Emerton of Hatfield, Terry Bend of Durham; Jim Page of Chelmsford; T. Adams of Little Berkhamsted; Brian Lawrence of St Albans; Barbara Davis and Bryn Jones; Robert Wade; Jo Cosme; Caroline Rawle; Andrew Jenkins of Colsterworth; George Hall of Lincolnshire; Suzanne Wallace of the Markham Moor Truckstop; Keith Hopkins of the Bypass Cafe at Cromwell; Albert Dean of Wokingham; Frank Nattrass and Carole Garbutt of Leeming Bar Garage. Plus all the library staffs up and down the country who could not have been more helpful.

A particular thank you goes to David Gregg of Tewin who spent a lot of time showing me around the southern end of the road. As a retired civil engineer, he was able to point out a number of things that I might otherwise have missed.

And last of all, my appreciation to the man in charge of the A1 upgrade at Brotherton who let me have the old road sign (the 1950's black and white type — see page 6) that stood next to the Fox. I repainted it and it now stands in my garden as a fitting memento.

ROAD TERMINOLOGY

I have tried to keep terminology to a minimum but there are a couple which need explanation. Officially, a road has a letter/number designation where the letter indicates how many carriageways, and the number how many lanes per carriageway. So a standard single carriageway road is referred to as an 'S2' road. If it has a 'suicide lane' up the middle it becomes 'S3'. If a central reservation splits the road into dual carriageway then it becomes a 'D2'. So a motorway with three lanes each way is a 'D3', occasionally with an 'M' added to show special (motorway) status e.g. 'D3M'. There are derivatives of these, but you don't really need to understand any more than S2, S3, D2, and D3.

The other terms I have used are 'GSJ' and 'multiplex'. GSJ stands for Grade Separated Junction. A GSJ is a junction where slip-roads or bridges exist so that traffic entering or leaving a road does not need to cross the opposing carriageway to do so. For example a right turn across a dual carriageway *is not* a GSJ, but leaving via a slip-road on your own side, then crossing under or over the dual carriageway via a tunnel or bridge *is* a GSJ. In general a fast free-flowing road with GSJs is far safer than one without. Junctions not GSJ'd are known as 'at-grade'.

A 'multiplex' is where two different road numbers share the same actual road. Imagine a hypothetical crossroads where the A1234 and the A5678 meet and cross. The roadspace in the centre of the crossroads is in fact shared by both roads. Now extend that to the A5678 joining the A1234 at a T-junction and then leaving it at another T-junction half a mile up the road. The half-mile between the two T-junctions is a multiplex. They can be much longer than half a mile. (Note that the two roads do not in reality meet, in fact the A5678 doesn't even exist!) As a road in Britain can only have one number, one is considered 'dominant' and so the other would normally be given in brackets on a sign. So the above half mile would be sign-posted as the A1234 (A5678).

SABRE

You may be surprised to find out that you are not the only one with a healthy interest in roads, and I believe a calendar consisting of photographs of roundabouts in the West Midlands was a best seller one Christmas. You are not alone; in fact there is a thriving web community of so called road-geeks, including engineers, truck-drivers and road planners. They are members of SABRE — The Society for All British Road Enthusiasts. (www.sabre-roads.org.uk)

This is a very comprehensive website, dedicated to Britain's roads, and if you cannot find the information you want on SABRE there is a thriving forum in which you will find experts on everything from the old London ringways plan to the disappearing road at Mam Tor. There are also links to a number of other websites where you will find all sorts of fascinating facts, and an ever-growing project to catalogue every single one of Britain's numbered roads.

PHOTOGRAPHIC CREDITS

Aberdeen University Library: 215. **Automobile Association:** 59 top. **Edinburgh & Scottish Library:** 214 bottom left. **Tony Fawcett:** 87 top right. **Francis Frith Collection:** 34 top, 42 top,43 top left, 44 centre, 51 top, 53 top, 77 bottom left, 83 top. **Getty Images:** Front Cover, 30 top left, 55 top, 78 top, 80 bottom, 86 bottom, 99 bottom, 107 top, 114 top, 142 top left. **David Gregg:** 33 top, 66 top and bottom left, 98 top, 108 bottom. **Brian Hodson:** 141 centre left. **London Metropolitan Archives:** 31 top. **National Motor Museum:** 100 top. **RCAHMS/Scran:** 211 top left and right, 213 top. **Tony Rook:** 21, 22 top.

Ordnance Survey: Maps credited to Ordnance Survey are reproduced by permission of HMSO Ordnance Survey Licence No. 100052053.

Contents

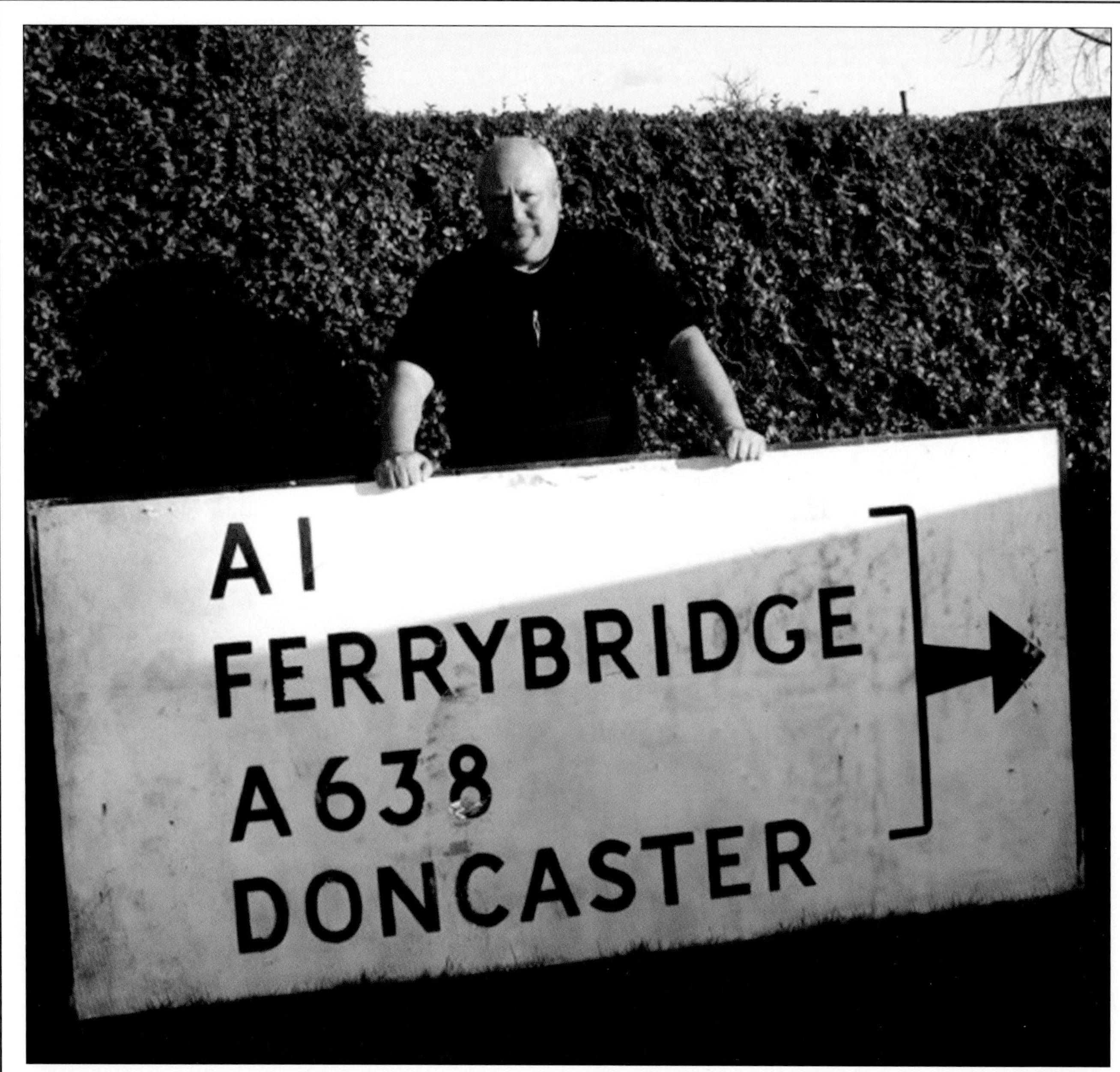
A1
FERRYBRIDGE
A638
DONCASTER

From the author

Some years ago the idea of researching a book on the Great North Road, illustrated with 'then and now' photographs, really appealed to me. I had my own lorry at the time and began choosing jobs that would take me up and down the road more often. Having studied Charles Harper's *The Great North Road* published in 1901, I explored every inch of the road — which now diverges in so many places from the A1 — and collected a mound of information and photographs.

It was sometimes a surprising journey, and at times for me rather sad, as parts of the road I knew as a child are now just a memory and even stretches I remembered as an adult lorry driver have now gone. And so utterly gone, too! I think the biggest surprise was how something could be so thoroughly changed, that not even a trace remains.

We take some things for granted: our house, our village, or town is just 'there'. It has been there forever and never changes, and we think that other things made of steel and stone are the same. Of course this isn't true; towns do change; a building disappears; a housing estate appears, but it is gradual and people don't notice. But the next time an old factory is knocked down and the site built on, wait a few months then go and see if you can remember exactly where it stood.

I learned this when exploring the changes in the Selby Fork to Bramham Crossroads area. If I had not been using this section regularly at the time of change, and following the alterations as they happened, even I would have lost track of where everything used to be. Multiply this by many times, up and down 'our' road over the years, and it is no wonder that memories fade and things get forgotten.

What I have provided in this book is a snapshot in time — the same as Harper did over a hundred years ago — but no doubt someone picking up this volume in 2113 may find that everything has changed yet again. Meanwhile, I hope that you will enjoy exploring the Great North Road with me, either in your driving seat or armchair, and find it as useful and interesting as I found Charles Harper's book.

But, even today the road to the north is changing and it was announced in November 2012 that the whole route of the A1 from the M25 to Newcastle is to be brought up to motorway standard.

I am a member of the Trucknet-UK forum, frequented by many lorry drivers both current and retired. A request for anecdotes brought some interesting — and occasionally unrepeatable — tales some, of which are included. Any old drivers who might wish to talk old times or browse the many photos going back many years should contact the website. (www.trucknetuk.com)

I will be very pleased to hear from readers regarding anything on the Great North Road. (gnrauthor@gmail.com)

This book is dedicated to the memory of my Dad, Clive Cooper of Malton (1937-2008), with whom I first saw the road, and to Bertie Powell, also of Malton, (1925-2004) who drove the road in the 1950s, '60s and '70s.

CHRIS 'WOLFIE' COOPER, 2013

The Great North Road . . . Then and Now. This is Wentbridge in Yorkshire, looking back towards the road from the Blue Bell public house.

Introduction

A road is something that most people use to get from A to B. How many of them actually think about that road while eating away the miles. Many people find driving a chore, something to be suffered, and the road a necessary evil. I can understand this on today's great motorways which are staggering under the strain of thousands of cars and lorries each and every day. However it wasn't always like that, there was a time when each road was different, when driving along them was a pleasure and the roads themselves had interesting quirks and places of interest. It is a curious trait of many things in Britain that they evolved in their own way, without a central plan until recent times. While centralisation in its way brought improvements, it also brought to an end the individual characters of many routes.

From a very young age I enjoyed looking at maps, and as a teenager all I wanted to do was learn to drive, which I did (taught by my mother), passing my test first time three months after my 17th birthday. I have also had a serious wanderlust, often wasting hours and miles having thought 'I wonder what's down here' and disappearing for an afternoon. Add to that the fact that I became a long-distance lorry driver at the age of 21 and you have a recipe for a lifelong exploration of Britain's roads, which is still ongoing. After many years it's easy to know the main routes across the country, and I have used them time and time again, north to south and east to west. You also have your favourites.

Mine came early. Having grandparents in both the Midlands, and North Yorkshire, a journey between the two was not uncommon even when I was a child in the late 1960s. I remember the M1 from Nottingham to the M18, and I remember the M18 in its rocky cutting between the M1 and the A1. But mostly I remember the A1. Northbound we would join it on the A1(M) Doncaster bypass where there was a huge dirty slagheap. Its still there, but you'd never know. It looks like any other green hill now. We'd follow it past Doncaster up to the Red House junction where the A638 out of Doncaster joined us. Past a curious little monument which we never really paid attention to until the day it appeared on the television and the whole family shouted: 'It's that thing on the A1!' Turns out it was called Robin Hood's Well and is one of the alleged burial places of Robin Hood (a Yorkshireman, whatever Nottinghamshire says!).

The next place was Barnsdale Bar services. A curious name, I often wondered what it meant. I found out many years later. Then for me the defining view on the whole stretch. Passing the turns for Wentbridge and Darrington you came over the rise and there below you was the majestic lay-out of Ferrybridge power station. That always told me I had come home. Even as a child I knew there wasn't too far to go once we had got to Ferrybridge. Soaring over the river on a great flyover I never really paid attention to a small stone bridge down below on the left-hand side. Gawping at the huge cooling towers I was dumbstruck to be told they weren't in fact indestructible because two of them had fallen in a freak wind only a year or two previously. Not far on there was a turning near a pub called the Brotherton Fox where we occasionally stopped to eat. Sometimes my father would carry on along this route for a change using the A162 that ran through Sherburn in Elmet and comes out at Tadcaster. Little did we know we had made a decision that had been made at that junction for around 2,000 years. Finally on past Fairburn, Micklefield and Aberford, mere names on road signs and at last Bramham crossroads where we turned off to head up the A64 through Tadcaster and York (both bypassed now) and finally up into the hills and home.

In later years working as a lorry driver I got to know the A1 and A1(M) from end to end, I always preferred it as a north-south route for a number of reasons. It's interesting for a start, plenty of history and old villages and buildings, none of which you will find on the sterile motorways with their overpriced service stations. Typically for me I soon started to explore the side turnings and bypassed towns out of sheer curiosity to see where the road went. I soon started to run into the name 'Great North Road'. What a name! What it conjured up for me. A Great Highway to the North. But where was it? I started to look at books to find out. Books about roads are not as common as I thought. It took me ages to work out how the road numbering system originated. It seems that not everyone has the same fascination as me. And then I realised. The Great North Road was the original incarnation of the A1. The first one, that ran through all the towns and villages. The one that carried the Roman legions. Well I was right and wrong. Indeed, that Great North Road is the A1 of the 18th and 19th centuries, but it wasn't the first one and the Romans would recognise very little of the present route.

In fact the A1 is both older and younger than you would think. Parts of the route date back to pre-Roman times, but the designation A1, has been around for less than 100 years — 1922 to be precise when the newly-formed Ministry of Transport first gave numbers to routes. Note the use of the word routes. Many roads existed mostly as ways from one town to the next. The designation A1 was the route from London to Edinburgh using a hodge-podge of many existing roads. For the sake of convenience I am going to use as a reference point the Great North Road of 1922 as designated by the Ministry with one exception that will become clear later. However roads, for many reasons, have changed and are changing, so a brief history is necessary.

'The defining view on the whole stretch'. This always told me I wasn't too far from home . . . or at least in the right county!

3
Meas.d Miles
Distance of each CITY & County Towns from LONDON.
Comp.d Miles
339 Barwick 260
108 Bath 87
47 Bedford 40
116 Bristol 94
60 Buckingham 44
301 Carlisle 235
50 Colchester 43
52 Cambridge 44
92 Coventry 74
28 Chelmsford 25
182 Chester 140
63 Chichester 50
56 Canterbury 43
122 Derby 98
262 Durham 200
123 Dorchester 97
63 Ely 57
172 Exeter 139
102 Glocester 81
30 Guildford 25
22 Hertford 20
57 Huntingdon 48
136 Hereford 101
66 Ipswich 55
256 Kendal 203
232 Lancaster 187
128 Lincoln 103
118 Litchfield 94
98 Leicester 78
215 Launceston 173
127 Monmouth 99
122 Nottingham 90
108 Norwich 90
66 Northampton 54
276 Newcastle 212
55 Oxford 47
96 Okeham 76
76 Peterboro 62
40 Reading 32
83 Salisbury 70
157 Shrewsbury 124
135 Stafford 106
97 Warwick 67
112 Worcester 85
127 Wells 102
67 Winchester 54
192 York 150
236 Bangor 180
241 Beaumaris 184
161 Brecknock 123
244 Cardigan 162
226 Carmarthen 157
269 St. Davids 207
209 Denbigh 160
204 Dolgelle 149
201 Flint 150
165 Landaff 128
158 Montgomery 122
149 Radnor 150
PART OF NORTH BRITAIN
THE GERMAN OCEAN
IRISH SEA
IRELAND
St. GEORGE'S CHANNEL
BRISTOL CHANNEL
THE ENGLISH CHANNEL
A Map of the Great Roads from LONDON. to all parts of SOUTH BRITAIN.
T. Badeslade delin.
Publish'd by the Proprietor W.H. Toms Sept. 29. 1742.
W.H. Toms Sculpt.

This is a general view of the remains of a Roman road on Wheeldale Moor in North Yorkshire. It is believed to be heading for signal stations on the north-east coast from a fort at Malton.

A History of Roads

Roads are built to provide a service — to provide a passage from one place to another which is defined. They show the way, and as time evolves and roads evolve, improve the passage and comfort of the traveller. Where roads actually go to is determined by the requirements of the time which is why some of today's roads in Britain do not make sense. However they probably did to the Saxon or the Viking or the Norman. For instance, why does that road have a great kink in it when it could be perfectly straight there? Look for the remains of a long gone farm, house or pond that once stood on that spot which the road had to avoid.

Before the time of the Romans, Britain had no requirement for a nationwide road system, although it is believed that a substantial local network existed. There was no national cohesion that necessitated the long distance movement of goods or people. Some of what was transported went by water. Most things were dealt with locally. Long distance trackways did exist although it's not clear how far they went in pre-Roman times, and natural features dictated their course, e.g. the need to ford a river or cross high ground. It is probable that the longer distances were covered by messengers and traders, but the requirement for a dedicated road

A couple of closer views of the same road. Note the ditches lying on either side with the middle raised up giving natural drainage. It is probable that at least some of our Great North Road started life like this.

system was not there. Reasons for the local roads in existence included routes to villages, markets, religious sites and ports. Roads could develop naturally, or be planned. (For a more in-depth look at the reasons for routes, the Institute of Civil Engineers has a useful document called *How Old is that Route* and it can still be found on the internet.)

With the arrival of the Romans the situation changed dramatically. They intended the military occupation of the whole country and as such built accordingly. Their method of fighting required a way for getting the Legions around the country quickly. A Legion on the move would soon turn the average track into a swamp so they planned and built Britain's first national road system. (Believe it or not, the next one to be planned would not be until the 20th century.) The Romans tended to use high ground for two probable reasons, first because it made sense, militarily, to be able to see for a long way ahead, and second that it avoided the scourge of all early roads: water. Where roads were much used, they became boggy quite quickly. The Romans made some excellent attempts at proper road building as opposed to just blazing a trail and some of their roads are still visible today in the remoter parts of Britain. There's a stretch near Goathland of *Heartbeat* fame. I wonder how many of the visitors to 'Aidensfield' know that! There's another stretch on Blackstone Edge near Littleborough in Lancashire. However it was easier to keep to the high ground wherever possible. They also built their roads on a raised bank called an *agger*. These also can be seen nowadays, on some quite modern roads too. If you are ever on the A19 between Chapel Haddesley and Eggborough, turn off by the power station one day, and stop and get out, and look back at the A19. It is quite clearly raised two or three feet above the surrounding countryside.

This photo taken on the A19 at Eggborough shows the road clearly elevated above the surrounding fields.

By the end of the Roman occupation, there was a quite substantial road system connecting up all Britain south of York, and still north of there to the Roman wall, although it's clear that due to the trouble they had subduing the northerners, it didn't leave much peacetime to build as big an infrastructure as further south. Here, however, we meet our first Great North Road.

Known as Ermine Street, it connected London to York. Quite a lot of it is still well-known and provides the alignments for some modern roads. Travelling north away from the City of London it followed roughly the route of the present A10 Cambridge road as far as Royston where it becomes the A1198 through Papworth and on to Huntingdon. From there it joined the present A1 at Alconbury Hill. This was a major junction in later years where the southbound traveller could chose to head for London via Royston or Cambridge, or could go straight on via Baldock, Welwyn and Hatfield. There was a large ornate milestone at the junction. The same decision is being made very near there today by southbound traffic using the A1(M), whether to stay on the A1 or divert via the A14/M11 route. And the milestone is still there if you know where to look. It stands in the hedge on the bank above the southbound carriageway of the A1(M), in fact before this stretch was upgraded to motorway, it stood in the central reservation of the dualled A1. The southbound carriageway of that road still exists as a 'B' road running alongside from Stilton to Alconbury Hill. The section of road from London to Alconbury via Royston and Huntingdon is now known as the Old North Road, and could be defined as a first incarnation of the Great North Road.

Coming back to Ermine Street, from Alconbury it headed north once more as far as Colsterworth. Just north of Woolfox, there are a couple of 'ox-bow' lay-bys, one on each side — given that term because they are lay-bys created by the straightening out of a sharp corner for modern traffic. This leaves a stranded piece of road often converted into a convenient parking area. In this case it must have been quite a curve in the road as can be seen if you stop in one lay-by, and follow its exit out across the A1 to the one on the other side, it crosses and recrosses the present dual carriageway. In fact the bend in the lay-by on the northbound side here was a bend in Ermine Street (or a change of alignment as they are known to scholars, because Roman roads were built as long straights with occasional bends). So the next time you are enjoying a bacon sandwich in that lay-by, remember you share the space with the ghosts of Roman engineers!

This is the ox-bow lay-by near Woolfox Lodge. It was created by ironing out a bend in the road on the Roman Ermine Street.

Volunteers uncover part of the Maiden Way Roman Road near the Roman fort of Epiacum (Whitley Castle).

At what is now Colsterworth roundabout, the Roman road leaves us for good and heads north-east to Lincoln and then north to a crossing of the Humber, probably by ferry, then up the present A19 to York. In fact there is evidence of an earlier route crossing the Trent at Littleborough, then going to York via Doncaster but that's beyond our brief.

For some reason, after the recall of the Legions and the fall of Rome, Britain alone amongst the Roman colonies descended back into barbarism and paganism. No one knows why but during the so called Arthurian age, from about AD450 to around AD700, very little is known about British history, with the exception of the generality that the Romano-British Celts of AD450 had been superseded by the Anglo-Saxons and Norsemen of later years. These peoples were seagoing and used rivers to gain the interior and had little use for roads. This allowed the Roman highways to disintegrate. Local people used the already cut stone to build houses rather than quarry their own, and bridges eventually collapsed so that in the end many of these roads were lost to history as the Anglo-Saxon and Norse settler made his own tracks much in the earlier way of the Celt. And by the easiest way, avoiding swamps and other obstacles. Also, some centres of population changed. London was central to the Anglo-Saxon while York gained in importance as the capital of Norse England. Others such as Silchester disappeared completely. And then the Normans came.

Contrary to popular belief, the Normans weren't really French. By the end of the first millennium, there was a loose affiliation of Norse kingdoms in Northern Europe: Norway; Denmark; Norse Britain, Ireland and Scotland; Anglo-Saxon Britain and Normandy. Men who were related by marriage or ancestry ruled a number of these kingdoms. Much in the same way that during the First World War, the King of England, the Kaiser of Germany, the King of Romania and the Tsar of Russia were all grandsons, or married to grand-daughters of Queen Victoria! Notwithstanding, the Norman invasion sealed one fact. The Anglo-Saxon rulers of England had all but secured the northern half of England from Viking rule. There were still various battles going on, especially in the two halves of the Kingdom of Northumberland (Deira and Bernicia, roughly corresponding with today's Northumberland, Durham and North Yorkshire). However Harold's victory at Stamford Bridge, followed by William of Normandy's victory at Hastings more or less put a stop to that. For the first time there was a unified England.

And for the first time there was a requirement to have a countrywide road system. William wanted to know what his new holdings were right down to the last lamb. He divided the country's estates amongst his earls, and went visiting with his entourage, as well as setting in motion the Domesday Book's account of England's wealth. He set the precedent of later kings of travelling around the realm, not least when there was trouble to be dealt with, first from rebellious northerners and afterwards usually from the Scots who were fooled by the French into making attacks on England on more than one occasion. From here we get the earliest mentions of kingly dissatisfaction with the highways, usually wanting to know why some earl or other had not spent time on the upkeep of a bridge. Now, as before, the most important parts of a road were where it crossed a river, and crossing points became important places. Initially the overlord of the area was usually charged with its upkeep, a burden not universally enjoyed. Henry I for instance in 1135 decreed that a road should be 'wide enough for two carts or six armed knights'.

Things stayed this way for a few hundred years, mainly because there were no advances in modes of transport. There was either the horse, or the foot. Occasionally horses pulled carts but they were terribly slow and unwieldy and apparently very uncomfortable. They were also liable to sink into any waterlogged ground.

Away from bridges and high ground, when a marshy area was crossed, travellers generally went round it in ever-wider arcs so that the track could be hundreds of yards wide at that point. Roads had a terrible reputation in the 16th and 17th centuries and planning a long journey was a major task and sometimes servants were even sent on ahead to reconnoitre the route! Eventually, with increases in agricultural expertise allowing expansion of the population with wider trade opportunities, and the industrial revolution making inroads in technology, traffic increased and the condition of roads worsened. There are some horrendous accounts of the state of late 17th century roads. As a result, the government got involved.

This is simply a lane in North Yorkshire that has never been upgraded to anything. The Great North Road probably looked a lot like this along much of its length until the turnpike era which began to transform roads in the 1600s.

Turnpikes and the Coaching Era

Back in the 1700s, travelling at seven miles per hour, and with 30 post stops, the 400 miles between London and Edinburgh would have taken up to six days.

Although a 1555 Act of Parliament had been passed imposing a duty on all parishes to maintain its roads, the Surveyor of Roads for a parish was an unpaid and highly unpopular position and consequently very little improved. Finally, in 1663, the Turnpike Act was passed and trials began. These trials took the form of three gates across the Great North Road in Hertfordshire, Cambridgeshire and Huntingdonshire. They do not appear to have had auspicious beginnings, but by 1700 private companies called Turnpike Trusts were being given charters to maintain stretches of road and were then allowed to collect tolls for the use of that road. Usually a gate or 'bar' was built across the road to stop people and collect the money and a small house was built adjacent for the toll-keeper. Known as toll-bars, they are still to be seen in many places around the UK and the name also lives on in such place names like Potters Bar, Leeming Bar and Toll Bar. As travel had been free up to this time, so the turnpikes were highly unpopular with local people, and time and time again toll-bars were destroyed until Parliament decreed that anyone caught destroying a toll-gate could be transported or even executed. No surprise then that those in Parliament were also often those who had invested in the Trusts! During this period some highly respected engineers made their names building turnpike roads, notably Thomas Telford and John MacAdam.

The condition of the roads improved concurrently with advances in vehicle technology. Carts evolved into coaches — which were still pretty primitive — but by the mid-1700s they enjoyed a basic suspension and thus were able to cover long distances more comfortably and more quickly. It follows that as travel became easier, it became more popular and started to snowball. Journey times shortened considerably (having an effect on many coaching inns) and the 'Golden era' of coaching was about to begin.

This in turn had a direct result on the courses of roads. Coach companies started to run between places of importance. Coaches ran in 'stages' at the end of which horses would be quickly changed to prepare for the next stage. Then a man named John Palmer from Bath advanced a proposal to speed up the Royal Mail, suggesting that the mail be distributed the same way. This was eventually taken up by the Post Office in the mid-1780s. They also took fare-paying passengers, the only real difference between the 'Post-Coach' and the stage-coach being that the post-coach did not stop for any longer than necessary when changing horses whereas the stage-coach would have refreshment breaks.

The coaching era gave rise to a sight that is still visible today by the sides of Britains roads: the coaching inn. This was a large inn, usually with an arch in its façade, which led through to a stable area where the horses were kept. They sprang up all over the country and there was much competition between them to secure the patronage of the various coaching companies. There could be a number of available inns, even in the smallest of places, and by 1800 competition was fierce.

The nature of the way in which these companies operated meant that nearly everything was contracted out — the horses, the driver and even the coach itself. It was the big business of the time. The inns provided horses and refreshments for the travellers and acted as way stations for the post with the innkeeper often being the local postmaster. There is even a case of the Great North Road's entire course being shifted in 1766 so that a nearby town would get the benefit of the coaching trade! Many of these inns are still in existence although not all still in the catering trade. They have become private dwellings and hotels, offices and shops, and many a house is called 'The Old Coach House'. Sadly some have gone forever.

One result of road improvements and shortened journey times was that horses were able to pull a carriage further before needing to be changed. And therefore the stages became longer, cutting some stops, therefore eliminating the requirement for coaching inns to be closely spaced. In the late 1700s, London to York took between four to six days but by 1830 it took just a day. And today I can do the same journey in four hours!

As usual, once a Victorian engineer put his mind to something it improved in leaps and bounds, but now those same engineers were working on something else. Something that was to cause a great slump in the use of roads for nearly a hundred years. In 1825 a Tyneside engineer, George Stephenson, opened a railway line between Stockton and Darlington. Almost immediately 'railway mania' erupted and within 20 years, around 100 railway lines had been built or being built, and by 1900 there were thousands of miles of track in Britain.

YORK Four Days Stage-Coach.

Begins on Friday the 12th. of April. 1706.

ALL that are desirous to pass from *London* to *York*, or from *York* to *London*, or any other Place on that Road; Let them Repair to the *Black Swan* in *Holbourn* in *London*, and to the *Black Swan* in *Coney street* in *York*.

At both which Places, they may be received in a Stage Coach every *Monday*, *Wednesday* and *Friday*, which performs the whole Journey in Four Days, (*if God permits.*) And sets forth at Five in the Morning.

And returns from *York* to *Stamford* in two days, and from *Stamford* by *Huntington* to *London* in two days more. And the like Stages on their return.

Allowing each Passenger 14l. weight, and all above 3d. a Pound.

Performed By { *Benjamin Kingman*, *Henry Harrison*, *Walter Baynes*,

Also this gives Notice that Newcastle Stage Coach, sets out from York, every Monday, and Friday, and from Newcastle every Monday, and Friday.

From the Black Swan in Holborn to the Black Swan in Coney Street, York. Both inns have since disappeared. A hundred years after this handbill was printed, the four-day journey had shrunk to a single day but, in spite of the increase in speed, it was the coming of the 'iron horse' that dealt the death knell to the coaching era.

The Fall and Rise of Roads and the Ministry of Transport.

Within a short space of time, road use had plummeted as the train could carry more people and faster and in more comfort than at any time before. The burgeoning long distance routes that had been evolving suddenly returned to become local byways with no more than a local farmer on them. However, toward the end of the 19th century, the road struck back! Other engineers, this time in Germany (and other parts of Europe) had been trying to make steam road vehicles. Steam engines proved too big to be efficient so they turned to other possibilities and eventually came up with the internal combustion engine.

While the so-called 'horseless carriages' were initially little more than a distraction, the invention of the automobile was another thing entirely. To begin with only the rich could

Top: **This has to be the most decorated milestone on the whole of the Great North Road as the flower beds extend quite a lot further than in my photo!** *Above:* **Yet another signal of past greatness.**

afford them yet, apart from giving them the capability of long distance travel, there was one added factor: convenience. On the train you had to mingle with everyone else and go where the train was going. The car gave the freedom to go where you wanted, when you wanted, and with whomever you wanted. (Still the same things that make car use attractive today, take note! Until anti-car groups address those issues, they will never woo people to public transport.)

All of a sudden the road system became the focus of a new group — the motorists. With the leap forward in automotive technology created by the First World War and the mass-production technologies of Henry Ford and others, many prosperous people were able to exercise their newfound freedom, as did ordinary folk in buses and coaches. Also industry took advantage of the new methods of transport. Roads that had previously seen nothing more than local traffic and the occasional passing stage-coach were now busier with cars that went faster and further than anything before.

However, it should be understood that nothing like what we now know as a road, existed even at the turn of the 20th century. As we have seen, earlier roads went through an evolutionary process but most were still little more than gravel tracks, in some cases with metalled surfaces. These dusty lanes show up clearly in old village photographs and, but for the rise of the motor car, they would have stayed that way.

It was not until 1919 that the government set up a body to specifically cater for all forms of transport. The Ministry of Transport Act of 1919 transferred powers and duties in respect of roads, railways, trams, canals and inland waterways, bridges and ferries, from a number of local authorities. And the remit covered all the traffic that used them.

One of the first things the Ministry of Transport did in 1921 was to classify roads for vehicle use. Class I roads were those connecting major towns and cities, while Class II covered roads that were links between Class 1 roads and the smaller centres of population. Classes I and II were soon changed to 'A' and 'B', long-distance routes being allocated the first 'A' road numbers, radiating from London in a clockwise direction. The Great North Road was rightly given the designation A1, the others being London-Dover (A2), London-Portsmouth (A3), London-Bristol (A4), London-Holyhead (A5) and London-Carlisle (A6). (The A7, A8 and A9 are all in Scotland.)

It should be noted that these were not the purpose-built roads we use today. The route to the north in 1921 could just as easily be described as the road from London to Hatfield, where it joins the road to Stevenage via Welwyn and Knebworth, then the road from Stevenage to Baldock, and so on all the way to Edinburgh. A route linking up separate roads if you like.

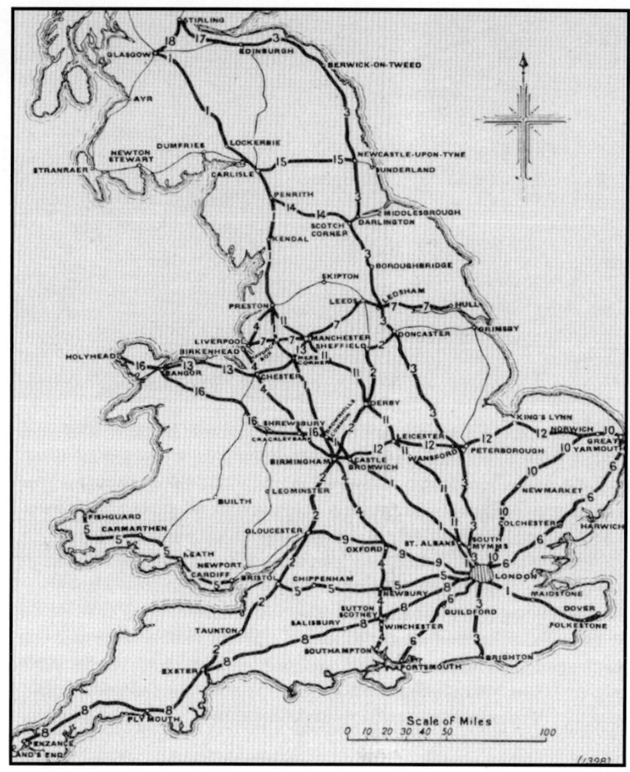

The Royal Commission on Transport in 1929 proposed a national scheme of 'arterial' and trunk roads but following the construction of 'motor-roads' in Italy and Germany, in November 1937 the Automobile Association put forward their own programme for the co-ordinated treatment of 18 highways of major importance and that 'each of these should be in charge of a road engineer, appointed by and directly responsible to the Minister of Transport, with duties and functions analogous to those carried out by Telford a century ago'. In November 1937, the Automobile Association proposed a provisional scheme for the development of the main highways of Great Britain in order of their importance as traffic arteries. All the roads are numbered on the accompanying map. The first six, in order are: [1] Dover-Glasgow; [2] Exeter-Doncaster, [3] Brighton-Edinburgh; [4] Southampton-Birmingham; [5] London-Bristol (across the Severn)-Fishguard; [6] Portsmouth-London-Yarmouth.

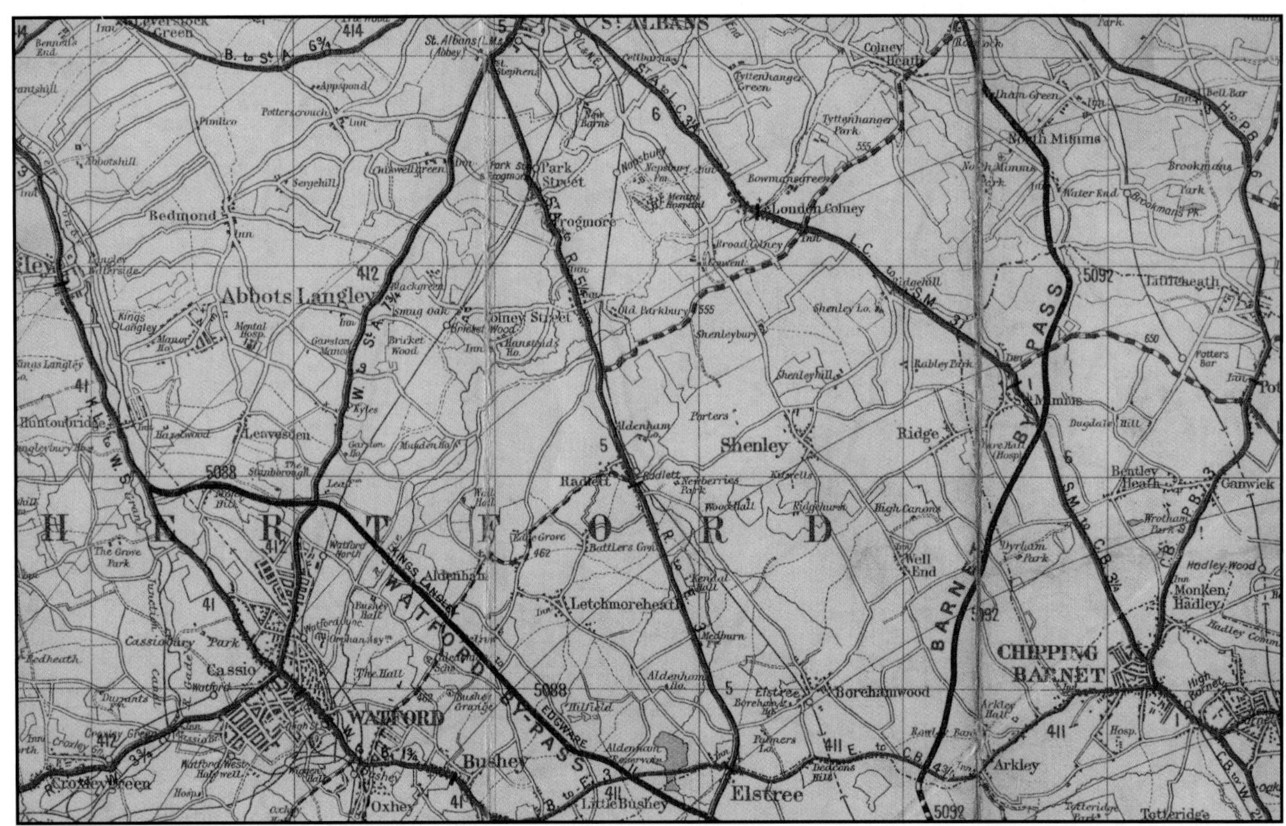

The passing of the Trunk Roads Act in 1936 provided for the building of bypasses comprising duplicate carriageways, cycle tracks and footpaths, although concern was voiced that they should be made as attractive as possible to lorry drivers so that they would follow the new route. The design of each trunk road was based on a speed of 70mph allowing for 720 vehicles per hour.

Even in the 1920s it was soon clear that a modern approach to highway construction was required. These took the form of so called 'Arterial' roads, which were mostly located around London to improve traffic flows and ease congestion in the suburbs, although there were some built in other parts of England. They also created the first bypasses and were built very wide to S3 status: a two-way road with what is today called a 'suicide lane' in the middle. They were even dualled in some places. As far as the A1 is concerned, it created the first major route change with the building of the Barnet Bypass which ran from the north end of the Archway road all the way out to Hatfield and continued out past Welwyn to Oaklands. Much of this road north of the M25 has changed again or has been destroyed by the A1(M), but a really early village bypass can be seen at Welwyn along with the remains of one of the earliest GSJs in the country — a semi-cloverleaf built on that same Welwyn bypass in 1927. It is believed that these road designs were copied from American examples being built at the time. It should be understood however that the description of 'heavy traffic' then would be nothing like what we mean by that term today!

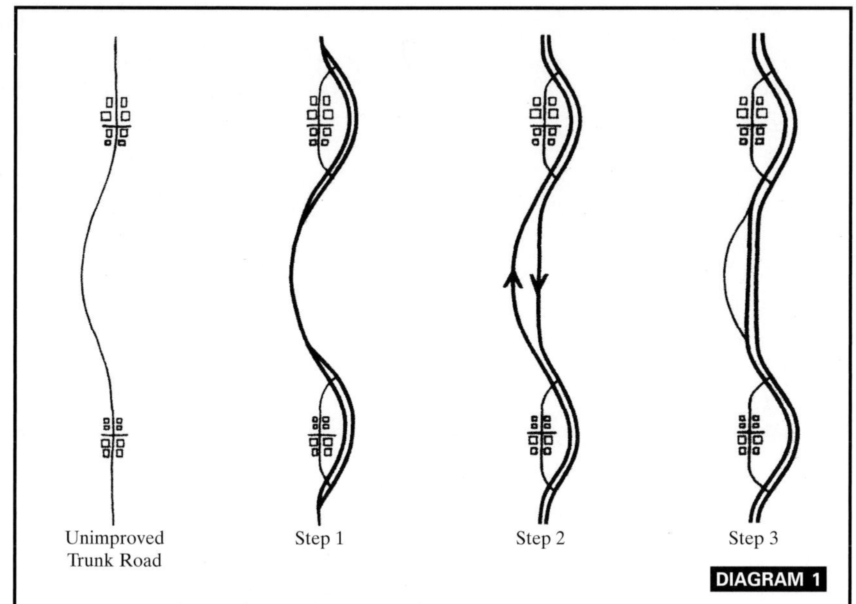

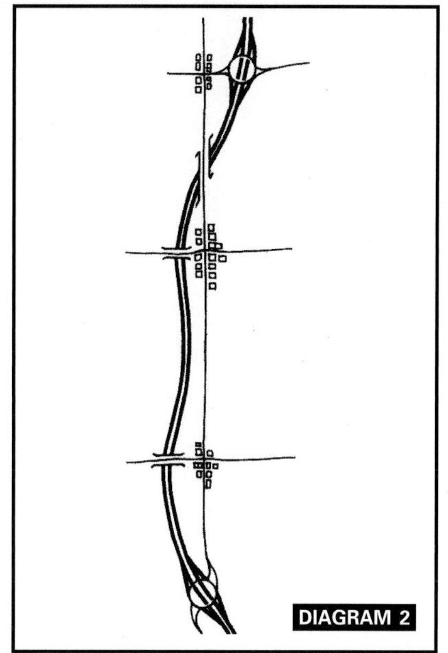

Further changes were planned for the late 1930s and 1940s but the Second World War intervened and it was not until the 1950s that things got underway again. By this time, people had been disrupted and moved all round the country, and car use was expanding hugely. Some of the towns through which main roads ran were literally staggering under the strain. In the case of the Great North Road, Stamford was a well-known bottleneck and also the road was still subject to such indignities as level crossings and pedestrian crossings.

The Ministry, influenced by what had been seen in Germany and the USA, was now planning Britain's first purpose-built 'motorways': roads that were intended for fast long distance travel and could be built totally from scratch. Instead of having to rely on trying to improve old routes, now the intention was to build using a scientific approach to road engineering, much as had been learned from the construction of railway track.

Roads can be improved in two ways. **Diagram 1** shows how a road is gradually improved over time and this is how most of the A1 was first updated. I will call this a *Type 1 Upgrade*. Step 1 shows where bottleneck towns such as Stamford or Newark were bypassed leaving S2 stretches in between. This arrangement can be seen north of Tyneside where Morpeth, Alnwick and Berwick are bypassed with dual carriageway, but the intervening stretches remain much as they did in the 1950s (although they are being upgraded in stages). Step 2 is where the in-between parts are upgraded to allow for faster travel along the whole road. Some parts of the A1 in Scotland still show this configuration but it is fast disappearing. And Step 3 is where the entire route has been upgraded leaving the towns to one side and creating local roads and 'ox-bow' lay-bys out of the remains of the old route. This is the status of most of the A1 between Baldock and Doncaster and, up until recent years, from Doncaster to Darlington. This stretch however has been radically upgraded in the last 10 or 15 years by the second method of improvement as shown in **Diagram 2**. I will call this a *Type 2 Upgrade*. This shows where a road is totally replaced by a new one on a different alignment. The original road usually still exists as a downgraded road for local use, and through traffic is generally discouraged from using it by appropriate signage. A clear example being what is now the B1164 between Tuxford and Carlton-on-Trent in Nottinghamshire. Go and look at that minor 'B' road one day; it's a lovely wide sweep of deserted road (usually). Why is it so wide? Because it was once the A1!

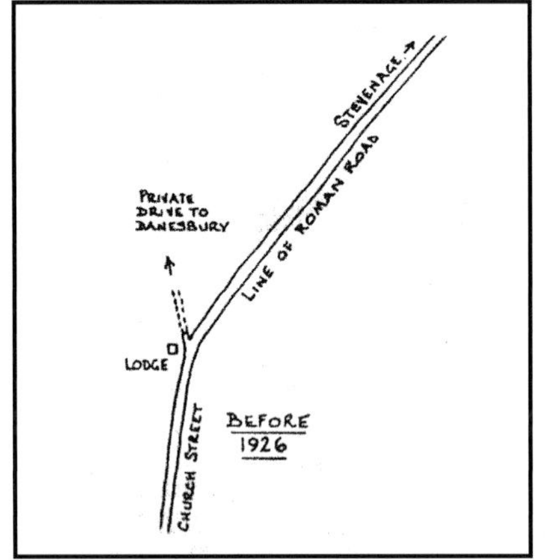

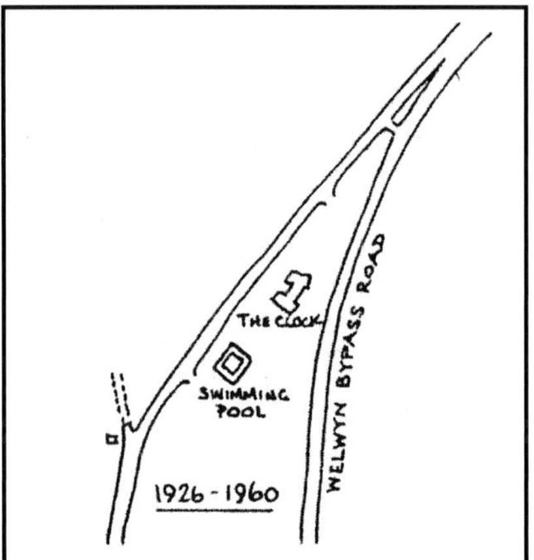

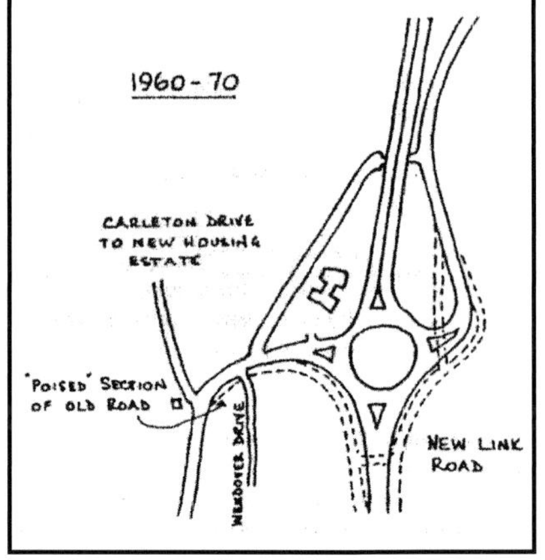

Tony Rook's sketches showing the changes to the Great North Road at Welwyn, Hertfordshire.

Sometimes the new road obliterates the original road in places. New bits are made to link up sections, and dead ends are created. This can make it difficult to trace the original alignments. In Hertfordshire, the A1(M) between the M25 and Stevenage has done exactly this to the old road. It was built in stages over a period of about 25 years and as short stretches were linked up, junctions changed more than once to accommodate first, the termini of the motorway parts, then proper junctions to allow access to the continuous motorway, especially as part was built in a deep cutting. Near Ayot Green, even the land that the Great North Road stood on no longer exists in places. In fact by recent times some places have had both treatments, being gradually upgraded in the 1960s, then again in the '80s and '90s. Welwyn again is a good example as is Bramham in North Yorkshire.

By the 1960s, the A1 was being upgraded along a large part of its length. To begin with this was mostly by the Type 1 method; bypassing towns, and then adding another lane alongside the existing one therefore making it up to dual carriageway standard. The second method was used in three main instances known as the Stevenage Bypass, the Doncaster Bypass and the Darlington Bypass. The first ran from the present Junctions 6 to 8 of the A1(M); the next ran from Blythe to Red House, and the latter from Barton to Brafferton. This was later extended all the way to Tyneside in the late 1960s. In more recent years further sections of A1(M) have been added reducing more stretches of original road to local status, and destroying some of it altogether.

The Clock Tower junction was modified again when the A1 was upgraded to motorwary standard.

It is interesting to note that the importance of this road was creating discussion in parliament as far back as the 1940s as these excerpts from this House of Commons debate from May 30, 1956 clearly indicate.

Mr Barnett Janner (then MP for Leicester North West):

'England's premier highway is, or should be, the Great North Road, which is designated A1. I am not altogether sure that we ought not to have a Roads Marks Act, in the same way we have a Merchandise Marks Act, because the term A1 is hardly applicable to this road in the circumstances which prevail. It is one of the principal routes for traffic between London and the North, but for three-quarters of its length, about 300 miles, it is wide enough for only one line of traffic in each direction.

'What is even more important, this overloaded highway has all the hazards to be found on the worst of British roads. There are blind bends, hump-backed bridges, congested towns, bottlenecks. Zig-zag turns, inadequate sidelines — everything calculated to promote the maximum delay and inefficiency. In such circumstances. I feel justified in asking for information of what the Government are doing about providing an up-to-date highway, and providing it quickly in a scientifically planned manner.

'I would briefly describe the present position on the A1 between the Barnet bypass and East Retford, in Nottinghamshire. After the Barnet bypass, which itself is adequate for only one line of traffic in each direction, the road is wide enough for three lines of vehicles only to the north of Baldock in Hertfordshire, a distance of less than 20 miles. From there to as far as the county boundary of Rutland and Kesteven, it is only wide enough for two lines of traffic, that is, for a distance of about 60 miles. On this length there are the usual hazards which one would expect — blind bends, hump bridges, villages and towns, including Stamford, which is notorious for its congestion. In places, there is a lane fenced off for the building of a second carriageway. North of the junction of the Great North Road with the A14, in Huntingdonshire, for a distance of 4½ miles, the road, in places, is along a narrow causeway made because earth has been taken away on both sides to make way for the foundations of the dual carriageways which have not yet been built. When one crosses the boundary into Kesteven one finds a road reconstructed recently to 30 feet width for a distance of 14 miles. It then reverts to two-lane width, then back again to three-lane for 1,300 yards south of Grantham. In the open it continues, as two-lane until just this side of the Nottinghamshire boundary. Near the village of Long Bennington, half a mile has been widened to about 30 feet. It is something like Joseph's patchwork coat of many colours but not as effective. Just at the boundary the road has been widened recently to 28 feet in two places, totalling under one mile."

However Arthur Molson, MP, was better informed:

'The present Minister has given considerable priority to works on A1. If the Hon. Member had looked in the Library, he would have found deposited there a map showing all the announced schemes. For Al, 23 schemes costing more than £100,000 each are to be authorised in 1955–56, 1956–57. 1957–58 and 1958–59. There is Page Street to Mill Hill, widening; between Apex Corner and South Mimms bypass, widening; Browney Bridge to Farewell Hall, Durham; Allerton Station; Wetherby bypass; between Leeming and Catterick, widening; Alconbury Hill to Woolpack Cross Roads; Doncaster bypass; East Retford bypass; Wansford Bridge to Stamford Borough Boundary, widening; East Retford bypass — Five Lanes End to the North of Checkerhouse, widening; Colsterworth diversion; Grantham bypass; Stamford Inner Relief Road; Woolpack Cross Roads to Norman Cross; Sandy to A428, Bedfordshire, widening; Norman Cross to Water Newton bypass; Biggleswade bypass; Wansford-Water Newton bypass, Huntingdonshire.'

Clearly this was not a job that was going to be completed in one sweep!

As can be seen therefore, the course of a long-distance road is by no means an exact science and not only *has* it changed in places, but *is* changing as we speak. It is therefore necessary to choose a moment in time as our reference point. As no changes of great significance had been made up to the time of the Ministry's A1 designation in 1921, I have used this date for the Great North Road.

The A1, as older drivers will remember it during and after the upgrades of the 1950s and 1960s, was pretty much in place by 1970 and stayed that way for some 25 years. It was subject to various planned upgrades in the mid-1990s, and although two sections were built north of Wetherby to Dishforth, and at Sawtry/Stilton, the project was cancelled and it is only since 1999 that building has started again. Most of this work is in Yorkshire because, with the extension of the M1 to terminate on the A1 near Aberford, upgrading those last parts between there and Tyneside to motorway standard will give a continuous motorway link via the M1 and A1(M) from London to the Tyne. An announcement was made in 2012 that it is planned to upgrade key sections of the A1 to bring the route from the M25 to Newcastle up to motorway standard.

(I am indebted to Tony Rook and a retired civil engineer, David Gregg of Hertfordshire for help on this section and for the use of his road upgrading diagrams from an article of his in Planning History *journal.)*

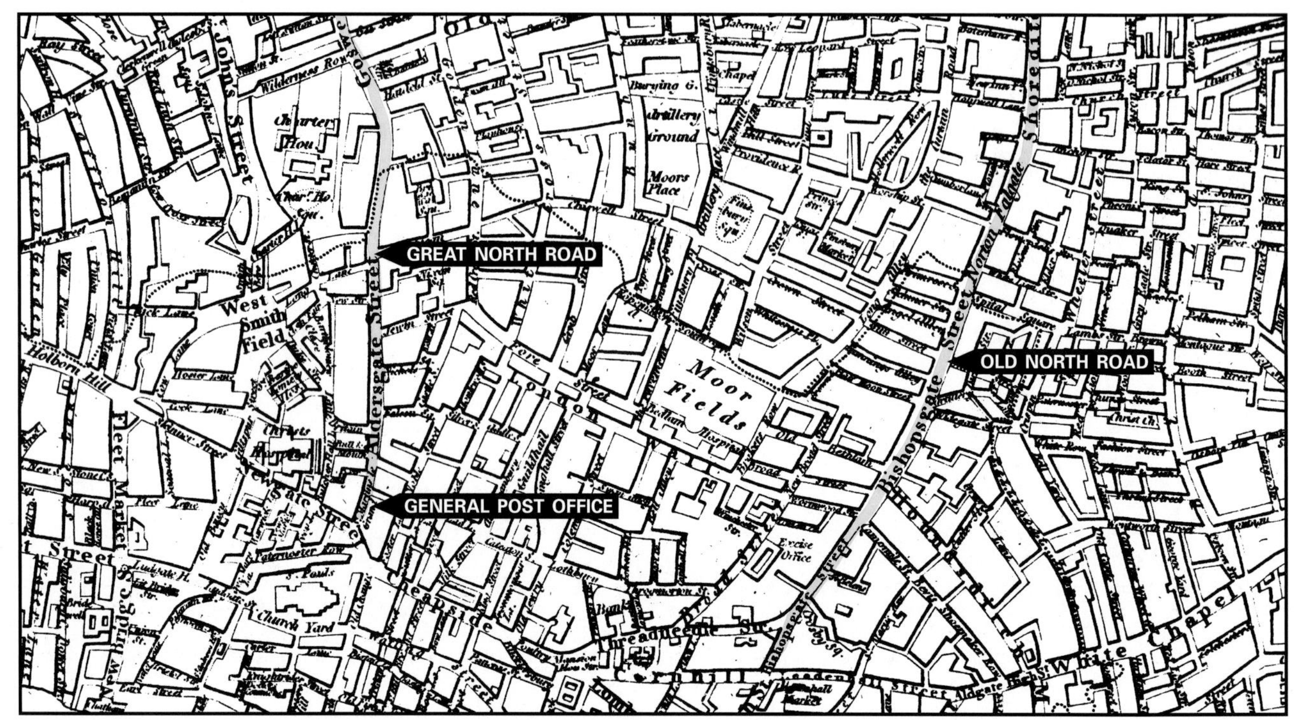

London to the M25

Of the two main routes to the north, the Old North Road began at Bishopsgate while the Great North Road — our road — started at the General Post Office building in St Martin's-le-Grand at the southern end of Aldersgate Street.

So where do we start? Any road has two ends, in this case one in London and one in Edinburgh. Either would suffice as a starting place but I will go with convention solely because I consider the Great North Road to be the major route to the North, and so we begin at its southern end.

In former times, the original City of London stood in the area now considered the financial heart of Britain, and was therefore the area that people travelled to and from. Since that time London has expanded far beyond its original borders and the social heart has moved westwards. During the war the City area was almost totally destroyed by the Luftwaffe and, for this reason, the Great North Road appears to peter out in the new steel and glass canyons of the 'Square Mile'. Its route though is still clear.

So where is the Great North Road's southern end? Mileages to or from London in earlier times were measured from a number of different sites — Hyde Park Corner and Charing Cross to name two — and there appears to be no stipulated common starting point. Fortunately, however, the main roads have generally survived the post-war reconstruction and old maps show two running north from the City of London: Aldersgate Street and Bishopsgate.

These two recognised routes were the Great North Road and what is now called the Old North Road. The latter began from Shoreditch Church and followed the line of Ermine Street along the present day A10 and A1010 via Bishopsgate, past Liverpool street station and on through Stoke Newington, Tottenham and Edmonton to Waltham Cross. This road then continued through Ware and Royston, on the present A10, where it turns onto the present A1198 to Huntingdon before rejoining the Great North Road just north of Alconbury.

Several authors including Charles Harper, the tireless traveller who cycled round Britain at the beginning of the last century, all use Hicks's Hall at Smithfield as a starting point for the Great North Road. This was a magistrate's court built in around 1610 by Lord Hicks, a one-time Lord Mayor of London. It is long gone, but is believed to have been somewhere on the lower end of St John Street just to the west of Aldersgate. During the coaching era, the start was fixed at the bottom end of St Martin's-le-Grand as that was the site of the main post office from where the post

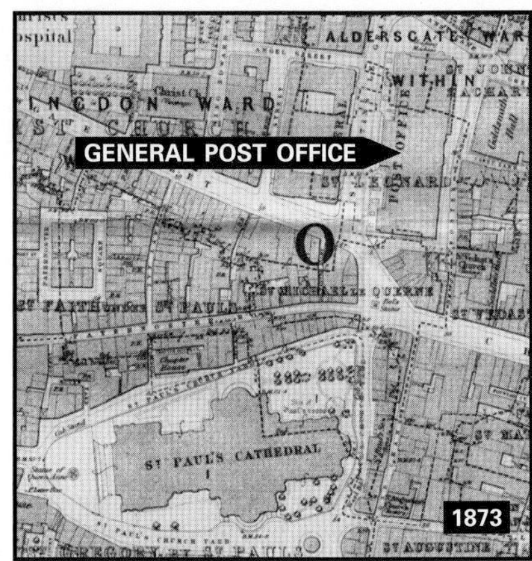

The old General Post Office building on St Martin's-le-Grand, marking the beginning of the Great North Road.

coaches all departed. Discussions to the starting point of different eras could continue, but for our purposes the Great North Road and the A1 will be considered to begin at the junction of St Martin's-le-Grand and Cheapside. Incidentally, in *Hollar's Survey of the City of London 1667* the last few yards at the west end of Cheapside have the name Blow Bladder Street. The mind boggles!

Between 1825 and 1829, Sir Robert Smirke built an all-new Post Office headquarters on the eastern side of St Martin's-le-Grand. Post Office buildings were also built on the west side of the street and from here the post coaches left for the whole country. Unfortunately the buildings are no longer extant but BT's headquarters building stands on part of the site. A painting by James Pollard shows the early morning mayhem as the post coaches left for their various destinations. The coach to Edinburgh would turn north up toward Aldersgate Street and pass the site of the old city gate, the Alders Gate, which stood at the junction with London Wall. A little further on Aldersgate gives way to Goswell Road where in 1682 you would have been out in the sticks. Today the architecture on the section from St Paul's to the Angel is almost entirely modern and very high making any kind of comparison meaningless.

Left: **Apart from the GPO building marking the traditional starting point of the Great North Road, it was also where the North Road Club's annual cycle ride to York began.** *Right:* **The original post office building was demolished in 1912.**

The first toll gate on our Great North Road stood here at Islington, depicted in this print of 1809.

It is said the driving through present day London is like driving a succession of High Streets. There is a reason for this. In the main, you *are* driving a succession of High Streets. In the 1700s, Islington was a village north of London. Like any present day dormer town, it grew in its own right with its own shops and taverns on its own High Street. Eventually like many others, it was overtaken by the urban sprawl and became an integral part of what is now Greater London. So the mail coaches of the 1800s would still have been in the city when they got to one of the first stops on the northern road, the Angel at Islington. The present building with its distinctive cupola has stood on the corner of Islington High Street and Pentonville Road only since 1899, but an earlier building is first recorded in 1665. It served as a coaching inn for many years and was in the food and drink trade until 1959.

The first turnpike gate stood at the far end of Islington High Street, where it becomes Upper Street at the junction with Liverpool Road. On passing through, one had left London behind. Incidentally, the area off to the west of the Great North Road and Liverpool Road here was called White

Then this was the gateway to London from the north; now just a busy high street.

In 1813, Archway was constructed to avoid the steep hill at Highgate. The initial idea was to drive a tunnel through the hill but when the workings collapsed, a cutting was substituted. This meant that Hornsey Lane had to be caried across on an arch supported on massive brick piers.

Up until 1812, the Great North Road ran straight on up Highgate Hill into the village. This was a real trial for horses pulling a heavy coach when even small hills were a real obstacle. Highgate Hill was an exhausting climb for horses that had already done the four miles from St Paul's. In 1813 a plan was made to drive a tunnel through the hill but there were problems and the tunnel collapsed, becoming the deep cutting visible today. After 1813, the new road ran straight through the cutting past Whittington College to the right and under the Hornsey road arch. It cut 100 feet and half a mile off the route through the village before meeting back up with the old road at the bottom of North Hill.

Reaching Highgate, the horses were rested at the Woodman inn, another well-known coaching halt. The view back into London from here was apparently quite famous but today's high-rise buildings and the growth of London have long since spoiled it. Having started his journey at St Paul's, the traveller is now higher than the cross at the top of the cathedral. A right turn as you go into Highgate is Hornsey Lane. This road crosses Archway road on the very archway that gives it its name. The present Archway is not the original but was built in 1897.

Conduit Fields, and it was used in the 18th century as a venue for cricket matches by a certain Thomas Lord. Lord went on to open another ground further west, which was named after him. Islington, a 'pretty, neat town' according to Oliver Goldsmith, stretches along Upper Street as far as Highbury Corner. It stood on the edge of Islington Common off to the east and had a semi-rural air. Although Upper Street hasn't changed much in over 150 years, you won't find sheep wandering along it, and the remnant of the Common — Islington Green — is now just about 200 yards long.

At Highbury Corner our route takes a turn to the north-west along Holloway Road. It is believed to have got this name because, like many old roads, it was subject to wear and water damage and eventually sank into a cutting made by constant usage . . . a real 'hollow-way'. As you go north, on your right-hand side just before Upper Holloway station was the site of the West London Union Workhouse, a huge institution built in 1864 to house 500 inmates! When we arrive at the Archway junction, we come to the first of our diversionary routes.

As this arch severely restricted the increase in traffic, it was demolished in 1900 to be replaced by the present bridge, but in doing so London lost the landmark proclaiming where town and country met.

Charles Harper was born in London in 1863 and by the time he died aged 80 he had researched, written and illustrated over 60 travel guides covering various locations in Great Britain although his speciality was roads which he travelled by cycle. The first book, published in 1892, covered the Brighton Road with the theme 'Old Times, and New on a Classic Highway'. His two-volume history of the Great North Road appeared in 1901 from which this illustration of 'the great common of Finchley' is taken. Harper described the area thus: 'Between 1700 and 1800 the great Common of Finchley was a parlous place, and not one of the better-known highwaymen but had tried his hand at "touching the mails" as they went across this waste; or patrolled the darkest side of the road, ready to spring upon the solitary traveller. Indeed the child-like simplicity of the lonely travellers of those days is absolutely contemptible, considering the well-known dangers of the roads.'

Leaving the village of Highgate, now no longer an isolated hilltop village, we take North Hill towards Finchley. And here we come to our first major parting of the ways of the A1 and the Great North Road. As mentioned in the previous chapter an entirely new road was built here to 'arterial' status. This road began at the junction of North Hill and Archway Road. Known alternatively as either the Barnet Bypass or the Great North Way it runs north westward, briefly multiplexing with the North Circular as far as Five Ways Corner where it turns more or less northward paralleling the M1. A 1955 photograph shows clearly the D2 (dualled) status. It also shows the old-style metal lampposts being replaced by newer concrete ones. Albert Dean who lived on the Great North Way in the 1950s relates that *'during the next five years [after the replacement] about a dozen people doing 60-70 mph hit the concrete lamp-posts and died. So, about 1960, they were all replaced with a tubular steel version that bent, but in the next five years only a couple of people hit them. As far as I know no one had ever hit any of the old iron gas lamps at all, even going back to when they were put in during first construction of the road circa 1930. It was probably down to higher vehicle speeds and more traffic, drink and fatigue, but perhaps also to colour; the concrete posts maybe "vanishing" against the background buildings. However, it was peculiar that serious accidents seemed to only start happening on our length of the A1 when the experts started making the road "safer"!'*

Albert also told me of the beautiful trees that lined the road although clearly someone at the Ministry disagreed.

'Around 1965, a coach-load of the first Japanese tourists to visit the UK since before the war screeched to a halt in front of our house, and about 50 of them caused chaos milling around for over an hour taking hundreds of photos of half a mile of beautiful trees in full bloom. Practically the next day the UK Ministry of Transport ripped out all the trees and lamp-posts to grab the cycle track for a third lane and the tree space for a sunken service road for us, leaving us with a fine new view from the front room of the four-foot concrete wall supporting the road, topped by its four-foot protective grey steel railing. It was strange they did that at the very moment the zoos were beginning to develop the non-bare natural environment enclosures for their animals; presumably the government thought we were the wrong type of animal so could use us to keep the otherwise redundant cage making industry going at full steam. 'It was all done to relieve the jams at Staples Corner where the M1 terminated and turned the Great North Way into the rush-hour car park.'

Five Ways Corner used to be where the Great North Way joined up with the A41 for a short multiplex. It is now Junction 2 of the M1 built in 1967 and for ten years this was the beginning of the M1. The Barnet Bypass runs north on the east side of the M1 for nearly two miles to Apex Corner in Mill Hill where the A41 leaves to the west, and the A1 finally heads due north, clear at last of traffic lights and roundabouts with the exception of one last roundabout for Borehamwood and Elstree (Stirling Corner). We are at last out in the countryside and three miles north of Stirling Corner the Barnet Bypass goes under the M25 and becomes the A1(M) at Bignalls Corner.

This however is a modern and therefore somewhat boring stretch of road. To go and see the Great North Road as it was, we need to again retrace our steps and go back to the bottom of Highgate Hill. At the junction of North Hill and Archway Road, the A1000 was the Great North Road up until the Barnet Bypass was built. In fact it is actually called Great North Road at this point. It heads almost due north, crosses the North Circular on a flyover, and becomes Finchley

From 1800 . . . to 1900 . . . to 2000. The High Road now marches across the former common as it approaches North Finchley.

High Road. Immediately before the North Circular on the right is the Islington and St Pancras cemetery which is the largest in London and predates most of the buildings in this area. A tree opposite the cemetery on the corner of Oak Road was reckoned to be an old hiding place of highwaymen, and was called Turpin's Oak. A map of the mid-1870s clearly shows the cemetery, but the area just north of the North Circular where Finchley Hospital now stands was just a tiny hamlet called Fallow Corner. In those days, barely 130 years ago we were well out in the sticks by now.

Nowadays however we are back amongst suburbia, where there are houses set back amongst leafy gardens while the road, wide at this point, stretches gently uphill. It doesn't pass through Finchley but heads due north through the outskirts leaving the town to the left. The road is wide but it is impeded and harassed by innumerable traffic lights and bus lanes. Shops and businesses line the edges but don't quite seem to have that local feeling as the shops did in Islington and Highgate — possibly because they aren't as old.

The roof on the right belongs to Christ Church although sadly Dick Turpin's oak no longer stands.

Left: **A drawbar trailer has clearly become unhitched from its lorry and come a cropper while travelling down Prickler's Hill just south of the High Street in Barnet.** *Right:* **The trailer sat in the garden of No. 53 not far from the unique and well-loved 'Hole in the Wall cafe** *(below).*

As one approaches the main junction in Whetstone, where the A109 crosses the road, there is a lane just before it on the right called Friern Barnet Lane. This is the other end of a road that comes up from Highgate, now known as the B550. There is evidence that this was an early alternative route between Highgate and Whetstone via Muswell Hill and Friern Barnet.

Leaving Whetstone there is more suburbia, but becoming a little older again as we approach the last great town on the road swallowed up by London. Barnet is more of an area than a town, comprising a number of villages that have grown together all with the suffix Barnet like Chipping Barnet, New Barnet, and East Barnet. The Great North Road approaches the area, coming down Prickler's Hill from Whetstone. At the bottom of the hill on the left-hand side is a large fence with advertising hoardings on it. A small barely noticed door in this fence leads into the Hole in the Wall cafe, known to drivers for many years and still sells a mean bacon buttie to which I can attest.

Running up Barnet Hill, we arrive in the only Barnet to have its town centre directly on the road: Chipping or High Barnet. This is obvious as the roadside buildings are much closer to the street, and older. Today it simply marks the final built-up area on the way out of London. At the junction with Wood Street, the High Street turns due north and runs up to another junction now signposted the A1081 to St Albans. This road is actually another of the Great Roads and where the Holyhead Road or Watling Street branched off the northern route. In fact it is not the original but one built by Telford in 1826. The original Holyhead Road is now unclassified and called Kitts End Road that branches off a little further up.

The main claim to fame of this area is the Battle of Barnet fought in 1471 as part of the Wars of the Roses. Edward of York marched down the Great North Road and met the Earl of Warwick on Hadley Green, now part of the town. It was a comprehensive victory for the Yorkists, and Edward went on to become Edward IV. A stone marks the site of the battle just beside Kitts End Road. After passing this we are finally out in the countryside and two miles up the road at Ganwick Corner we pass under the M25 and into the outskirts of Potters Bar.

Here, on Easter morning in 1471, the bells were ringing for morning service as the Battle of Barnet began and by evening the power of the barons had been broken for ever. The obilisk, erected in 1740 by Sir Jeremy Sambrooke, is supposed to mark the spot where the Earl of Warwick made his final stand.

The M25 to Baldock

This is probably the most interesting stretch of the road for the simple reason that it is the most altered. It has been subject to a motorway upgrade that took place in stages during the 1960s, '70s and '80s. Parts of the road were totally bypassed while other sections were altered, and then altered again, as another stage of motorway was built.

If we go back to Bignalls Corner, the Barnet Bypass arrives from the south at a huge roundabout which includes exits to the east and west M25, the A1081 back into Barnet (and the Great North Road), South Mimms services and the A1(M) north. This is quite a recent addition. The stretch of A1(M) between here and Junction 2 was the second to last to be built in 1979. It does in fact bypass the Barnet Bypass! If you take the turn into the services, but turn immediately left as if going into the truck services, you drive around a one-way system where you can turn left or right at the end. If you turn left onto Swanland Road, you are back on the Barnet Bypass. It runs up immediately to the east of the A1(M) and was the old southbound carriageway of the bypass. The original northbound lane now lies under the newer southbound lane of the A1(M). You can no longer travel the entire bypass route as some of it between Tollgate Road and Hatfield has disappeared under the A1(M). It reappears half way along Roehyde Way and crosses Junction 3 of the A1(M) to become the A1001. On an 1880 map of the area none of these roads exist except Tollgate Road on a slightly different alignment.

At Junction 3 of the A1(M), the roads reverted to the old A1 until quite recent times. The stretch of A1(M) between here and Junction 4 at Stanborough was the last to be built (in 1986) linking the motorway out of London to the Welwyn Garden City and Stevenage bypasses. The A1 ran along Comet Way which was named after the de Havilland Comet which was built in the huge factory which was established on Hatfield airfield in 1934. It later became part of British Aerospace and built aircraft well into the 1990s. Latterly however production has been moved elsewhere and the University of Hertfordshire now uses much of the site. It has also been rented out to film companies and it was here that much of *Saving Private Ryan* and *Band of Brothers* was made.

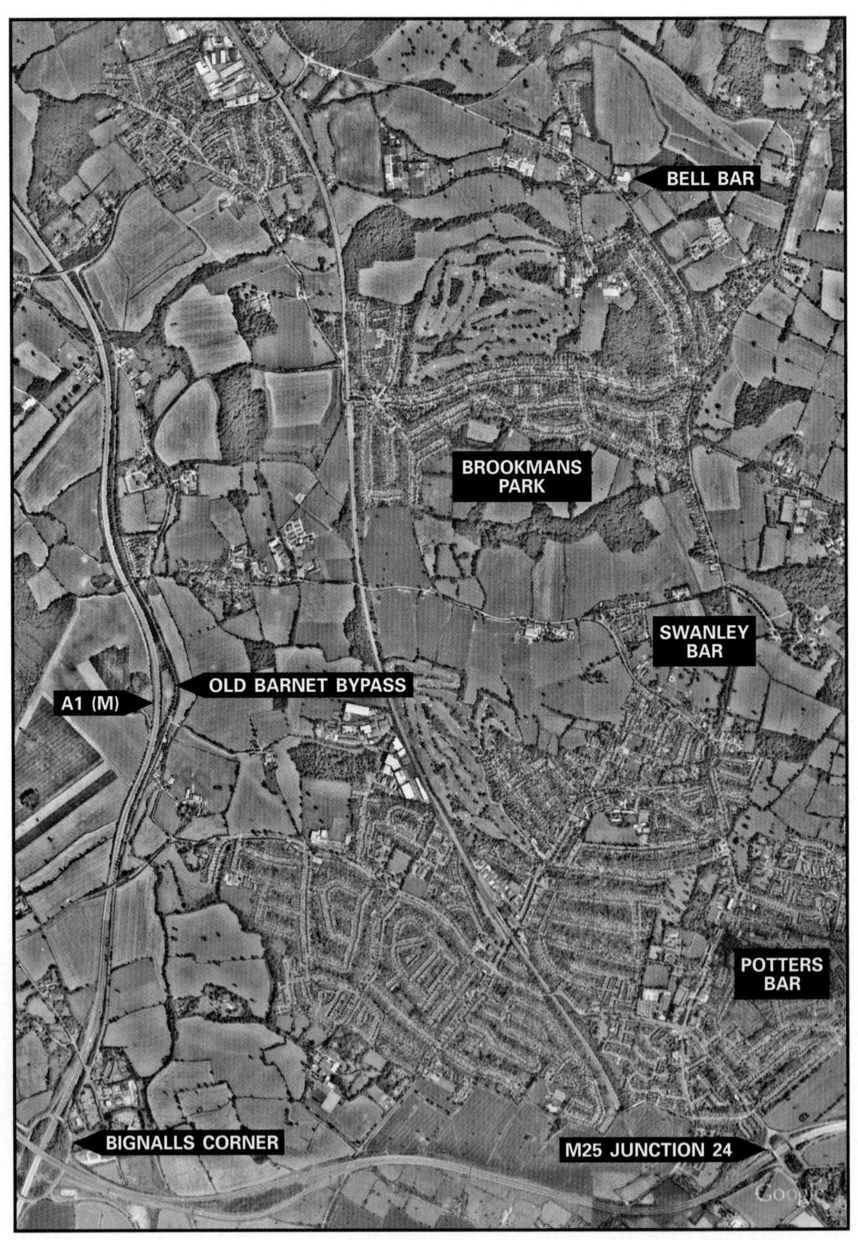

In 1978 David Gregg, a retired civil engineer, took this photograph from the newly-constructed bridge on Dixons Hill Road showing the conversion of the prewar Barnet Bypass into the A1(M).

The roundabout just to the south of the factory is where the Barnet Bypass finished up and leaves us with only two routes to trace. The next few hundred yards is the only place where the old A1 lies *above* the more modern route. When the Galleria shopping arcade was built, the A1 was realigned slightly as it lay where the shopping centre now stands. The A1(M) runs under the shopping centre in the Hatfield Tunnel. Incidentally, there is a spot of controversy surrounding this tunnel as I have been told that it was originally intended to run the A1(M) over the old A1 Great North Road at this spot. However de Havilland protested vigorously, pointing out how much it would disrupt their business, so eventually, at a cost of many millions, the Hatfield Tunnel was built. Shortly thereafter, British Aerospace shut their operation down!

My comparison in 2013 shows how the old bypass has been rebuilt as the southbound carriageway of the motorway.

At Potters Bar, the Great North Road passed through the town as the High Street.

From here to Stanborough, Junction 4, the A1(M) runs on a totally new course, but to find the Great North Road we have to go back to the M25 where we left it approaching Potters Bar. The word 'Bar' in the place name indicates the site of an old toll-gate although Potters Bar did not really benefit from passing coaches as it was midway between the main halts of Barnet and Hatfield. In fact it didn't really grow until the advent of the railways made it somewhat more convenient for commuting to London.

Our Great North Road approaches up Barnet Road and at the junction with Southgate Road, changes its name to High Street. This runs due north and, at the far end, the Great North Road forks to the left. There is a reason for this. Prior to 1804, there was no Hatfield Road and the Great North Road made a major dog-leg here, first forking to the right, then turning left and travelling west for a short distance before turning almost back on itself and rejoining the present road to Hatfield at Billy Lows Lane. This was the site of the turnpike gate that was moved back to the top of the High Street, where the present fork is, after the kink was straightened out.

By way of interest, half-way up the High Street on the right is Oakmere Park where Zepppelin L31 crashed on the night of October 1, 1916. Kapitänleutnant Heinrich Mathy was shot down by 2nd Lieutenant Wulstan Tempest. The combat took place high up, lit by searchlights, and was witnessed by many thousands. When the 'Zep' caught fire, the roar of triumph from an exultant crowd who had suffered under the hated Zeppelins was heard for miles.

Going back to our route to the north, we leave Potters Bar on Hatfield road running through the suburb of Littleheath, once a village in its own right. Leaving the built-up area, the road, while numbered here the A1000, is once more called the Great North Road.

At Swanley Bar Lane (another turnpike reference), we find some early changes. The road between here and Hatfield actually used to be straighter than it is now. Today the road describes a huge double curve, some three miles long, past the villages of Brookmans Park, Bell Bar and Welham Green. However, an earlier route departed from the present Great North Road at the B157 to cut across an area now covered in housing, across the grounds of Chancellors School and into Bell Lane at Bell Bar. It then

The garage on the right has gone to be replaced with a pub.

From 1840 . . . to 2012. Bell Lane at Bell Bar was an early forerunner of the Great North Road.

rejoined the present road where Bell Lane does today. If you go straight across the present road into Woodside Lane, it continued up to the boundary of Hatfield Park where there is a fork in the lane. This is because at different times the North Road followed different paths across Hatfield Park. The northernmost fork is the earlier path that was diverted in 1784 to the slightly more southern route across the park. Some 70 years later, the owner of the estate took the chance to divert the route out of the park altogether. When a railway was being planned in the area, he donated some land for it with the agreement that the turnpike road was also diverted to its present course.

As for the Great North Road, it curves to the west past Brookmans Park and the mighty Brookmans Park wireless station, built in the 1920s, bisects Bell Lane and Woodside Lane (the original route) and then curves back north passing Welham Green and approaches Hatfield. It also has the distinction of being the last road built for a Turnpike Trust in England, and possibly the last main road built for some three-quarters of a century.

Left: **In 1900, Charles Harper pictured himself in this sketch cycling north at the point where Bell Lane crosses the Great North Road.** *Right:* **From a pencil sketch to my camera. I took this comparison at the same spot on Woodside Lane in 2012.**

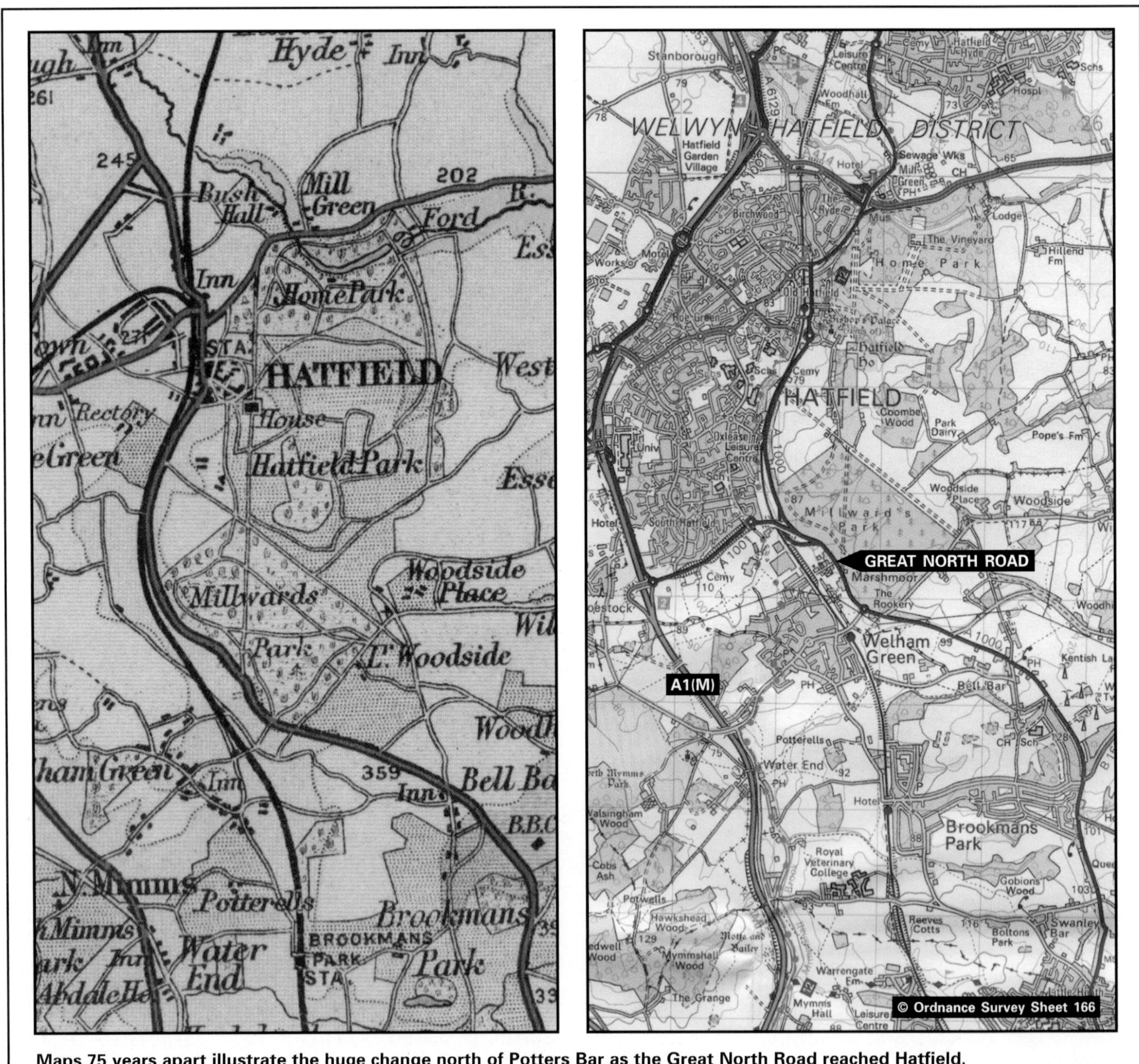

Maps 75 years apart illustrate the huge change north of Potters Bar as the Great North Road reached Hatfield.

This is where an early route entered Hatfield Park at the top of Woodside Lane. Hatfield House was the seat of the Marquis of Salisbury and was built by the first earl in the early part of the 17th century. During the First World War, a mock battlefield with trenches, craters and barbed wire was located in the grounds to test the first British tanks. A Mark 1 could be seen there until moved in 1970 to the Bovington Tank Museum.

On the left, just before Welham Green, stands the Rookery — a transport cafe that must have seen better days. It was certainly a tea shop as far back as the 1920s.

Now we come to the start of an area that has changed vastly over the last 50 years. The earlier two roads approached Hatfield past the church and the Great North Road arrives alongside the railway line a few hundred yards to the west. It curved away from the track to become the London Road through the village and curved back to rejoin the line by the station before heading to the junction with the Hertford and St Albans roads by the Red Lion Hotel. Just north of here it crossed the railway on what was known as Wrestler's Bridge and disappeared off back into the countryside.

The Rookery at Welham Green was a transport cafe for many years and appears to have been a tea shop for years before that.

Hatfield has changed dramatically — this is where the Great North Road originally entered the village.

If you were to try and follow the Great North Road through Hatfield today, you would soon become disorientated, as it was designated as a 'New Town' in 1948 and has grown dramatically since that time, infilling the space between the Great North Road and the A1 (M) with housing and industry. The old route begins where the Great North Road arrives at a roundabout to the south of Old Hatfield. The A1000 goes straight on, but a slight right fork takes you onto the Broadway (which was the London Road) and into the old village. The Salisbury hotel still stands, but where Fore Street joins the Broadway, the road disappears. It took a left-hand bend here back towards the station but it is gone. An office building and a grassy area now occupy the spot but there is no sign of the old road.

To pick up the tale again we have to go back by the roundabout and go up the A1000 to the station where the Great North Road would have emerged opposite where the station car park is now. Once more we follow the A1000 up to a large crossroads junction where the St Albans road leaves to the west, and the A1000 turns right. We need to go straight on and we do so for a couple of hundred yards when we are faced with a brick wall with the entrance to an alleyway. This alley is a footbridge over a railway and we are at the point where, after climbing Wrestler's Hill, the road crossed the railway line where there was a road bridge here until 1966. Brian Lawrence describes here what happened:

'It was a few minutes before eleven o'clock on the morning of Sunday, February 20 when I realised that something was wrong. I had been sitting reading the newspaper at home and decided that it was time for a coffee. I went into the kitchen and turned the tap but the flow of water soon became a trickle. I turned on the gas but the supply was not there. From the lounge window it was clear that things were not normal, it was so quiet with the absence of the usual steady stream of traffic. Word soon spread that there was a major problem up at the Wrestler's Bridge. In fact the bridge had collapsed and a busy road had suddenly become a cul-de-sac.

'Wrestler's Bridge had been built in 1850 and, until the A1 was diverted away from Hatfield old town, it had formed vital part of the premier trunk road from London to the North-East and on to Scotland. Although the road was then reclassified as the A1000,

Utterly transformed, this was one of the most amazing comparisons I took. The only clue was the church tower. Eventually I discovered the building on the right with the distinctive brickwork which once looked onto the Great North Road.

it continued to bear the name of the Great North Road and was still very heavily used as it linked with the new A1 only a few hundred yards further north, close to the site of the present Tesco store. Beneath the bridge ran the six tracks of British Rail's East Coast Main line to York, Newcastle and Edinburgh.

'The last northbound train had passed under the bridge at 10.30 and the last southbound train went through just a couple of minutes before the dramatic collapse. Prompt action by the men working on the track nearby prevented any other trains entering that section of the line but it was little short of a miracle.'

The decision was taken not to rebuild the bridge and a footbridge was installed instead. Nowadays, one has to turn right at the junction onto the A1000 and follow it for a short way, turning off left again to head along the A414 toward the A1 (M). Assuming we could drive over a ghostly Wrestler's Bridge, we would pass the Wrestler's pub and drive through modern housing to emerge onto the A414 at a roundabout near the huge Tesco's store at Stanborough.

The next roundabout up is Junction 4 of the A1(M) and also meeting the road here is the other end of Comet Way from the Barnet Bypass. The Great North Road has been obliterated here by the motorway junction but, if you run up alongside the motorway for a few hundred yards to the next roundabout, you can turn left under the motorway to another small roundabout. The first exit off this roundabout is a small lane with a cul-de-sac sign on it. However, look at the road name: Great North Road. You can follow this lane back down the western side of the motorway until reaching the point where it ends at a fence. This is where it would cross and if you could look over the fence, you would find you were looking across the motorway and straight down the road past Tesco's and back towards the Wrestler's bridge.

The A1 has changed many times and in many places yet we can still find examples of every previous age; from the original hollow-ways . . . to the paved turnpike roads and the great coach roads . . . and on to the arterials and wide motor roads of the early 20th century.

After the key Wrestler's Bridge collapsed in February 1966, it was never rebuilt as a road bridge and now just a footbridge stands in its place.

Leaving Hatfield to the north, we would once have arrived at a fork in the road by the East pub. This fork is now a roundabout and we approach it not from the south but from the east over the motorway. We can turn south though back down the old Great North Road but, if we do, we arrive quickly at this dead-end. If you could see through the trees past the motorway signs you would see the road approaching straight at you. If we head back to the roundabout we are on the original route.

If we then take the left fork, which is signposted as the B653 for Wheathampstead, after a half a mile we turn off towards Lemsford village. There, in front of the church on the corner, we find a suspicious curved offcut of road which tells us that at one time the right turn was probably part of a fork rather than a minor road turn-off. From there, we then drop down into the village. This shot was taken looking back up towards the church.

Now things start to get a bit more complicated. Going back to the small roundabout we see another two exits, the B653, and the B197. As it happens, these are *both* previous incarnations of our road. The B653 called here Brocket Road heads for Wheathampstead. However barely a mile along it is a right turn to Lemsford village. Turning right here, the road drops into Lemsford, a quiet village seemingly in a backwater of time. At the bottom of the hill, just past the bridge over the Lea, is a pub called the Long and the Short Arm. If you stand looking at the pub, there is a gate on the left at the rear of its car park. If you look over the gate there is an overgrown track leading away from you, a unique original stretch of the 1820s Great Road. The track that starts behind that gate runs along the edge of Brocket Hall estate and meets the motorway opposite the Welwyn Garden City golf course.

Arriving at the bottom of the hill, the old road veered to the left of the Long and the Short Arm pub.

David Gregg pictured the pub today for me — the old road ending at a five-bar gate in what is now the car park.

This is the Waggoners pub which once sat squarely on the Great North Road.

When the road was cut by the motorway this became a back-water. You may notice a cat's eye or two on the bend.

This whole stretch from our roundabout at Stanborough was the Great North Road until 1833 when Lemsford was bypassed with the other road leading from that roundabout. Now called the B197, it straightens out the dog-leg of Lemsford village and joins the A1(M) at Junction 5. On your left, shortly before that junction, is a small row of three newish houses next to a garage. They stand on the site of the Lemsford truck-stop which was certainly serving food in the early 1970s. To stay on the Great North Road we need to cross under the motorway at Junction 5 and follow again the B197.

We are now ascending Digswell Hill and the A1(M) at this point is in a large cutting to ease the gradient up this slope. This has cut the original road in a couple of places and it does not settle back to its original course until we are on the way down the hill just past the Red Lion pub. To follow the original road we need to take a left turn across a bridge over the A1(M) to Ayot Green. Just on your left here is another turn that leads back down the western side of the motorway with a pub nestling in the trees.

Following this lane you come to a dead end and, much like the one at Stanborough, you can look over the gate and see the lane align with the B197 coming up from Junction 5. In fact the Great North Road went up the hill on the present line of the A1(M) then veered off to the west slightly to come up this lane. With the Waggoner's pub still open there, it then curved back to the east over the A1(M)s cutting, past the front of the Red Lion, and rejoined the present B197. For proof you need look no further than the Red Lion. Go and look at the car park in front of the pub. It has a line of cat's eyes across it!

***Left:* A bit further round the bend you are faced with a gate and more cat's eyes. Judging by the pattern of the cat's eyes I spotted here I suspect the road at this point was three-lanes, the so-called 'suicide lane' type of road. Traffic approaching from either direction could use this centre lane to overtake, hence one took one's life in one's hands as you could end up racing towards an oncoming vehicle!**
***Right:* Not far from the Waggoners on the other side of the motorway is another pub. It once sat squarely at the roadside but is now set back with a car park in front. Go and have a look at the car park. There are more cat's eyes. The road from the Waggoners passed the front of the Red Lion and went off down the hill. With the changing of alignment the Red Lion has acquired a car park.**

Welwyn: looking north up London Road. The Great North Road turned right into Church Street in front of St Mary's.

From here down to Welwyn, the B197 remains the exact course of the Great North Road. When you approach Welwyn there is a left turn into the village which was the original course of the road. It's called London Road, something that is always a bit of a giveaway. It goes straight down the village High Street and takes a right turn into Church Street and leaves to the north-east emerging near the present Clock Hotel. It may come as no surprise to you that Church Street is not its original name. It is shown on a map as late as 1884 as North Road!

However Welwyn may lay claim to some of the earliest modern style road alignments in England. If we go back through the village — all the way back to where we turned off the B197 — and instead stay on the B197, we are on a 1920s arterial road built to bypass the village. Unfortunately it has been disturbed by the building of the A1(M) and is no longer in its original form. It also joins the two parts of Junction 6 of the A1(M). This area is the

meeting point of two parts of the A1(M) that were built some 11 years apart, hence the confused state of Junction 6 with its slip-roads and roundabouts seemingly all over the place. The motorway section north of here is much older, having been constructed in 1962, with the area around the Clock Hotel being its southern terminus. The stretch to the south was not built until 1973 and necessitated further changes to an area which had been altered already.

The stretch of B197 between the two junction parts is actually a multiplex with the A1000, coming from Welwyn Garden City. Midway down this stretch is a GSJ built in 1927 with the Hertford Road. This is believed to be the earliest known GSJ in Britain.

At Junction 6, the original line of the Great North Road actually runs along the rear of the Clock Hotel and under the A1(M) to join up again with the B197 at Oaklands. This gives rise to one question, does this mean that present day visitors to the Clock Hotel approach it from the rear? The building is believed to pre-date the 1920s arterial upgrade and therefore must have originally fronted onto the Great North Road, now at the 'rear' of the building.

Left: **The Clock Hotel with the comparison that I took in 2007** ***(right)*** **on the Welwyn Bypass. I am told that the hotel was built in the 1920s.**

One can understand my amazement when I went back to take a colour shot in 2012 only to find that it had burned down in 2010!

Still complete with cat's eyes, the old road still runs behind the site of the hotel.

Left: **Harry Macdonald set up his woodcarving business in a barn beside the Great North Road at Woolmer Green.** ***Right:*** **Sadly no trace of it remains to be seen today.**

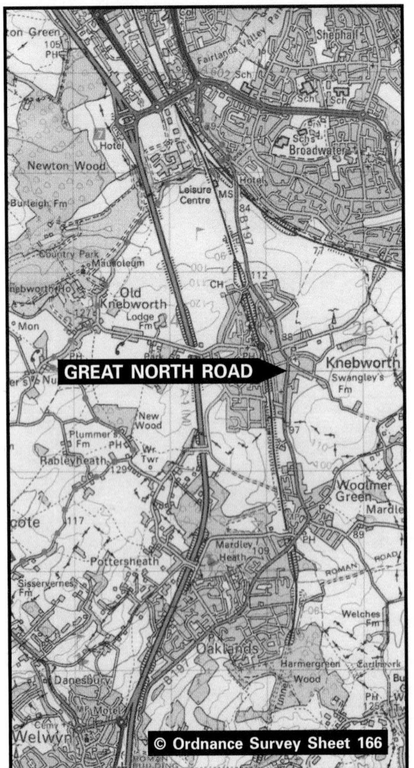

The Great North Road looking north in Knebworth village . . . then and now.

On an 1884 map, there are no buildings at all between Welwyn and Woolmer Green but this is now quite a built-up area. The road, still numbered B197, leads away north-east from the motorway exactly on the line of the 1884 road, only a bit wider after being upgraded to arterial status. There is one small deviation at the bottom of Mardley Hill. The bend in the road here was quite severe and was straightened out slightly leaving a stranded ox-bow stretch at the bottom of the hill. This road is called Lower Mardley Hill. Our Great North Road mounts Mardley Hill which must have been a fair climb in the early days.

Over Mardley Hill we come to the village of Woolmer Green. Lisle's Vauxhall garage here has been aiding the motorist of the Great North Road since around 1900 and had a petrol pump as early as 1910. Another landmark in the village was the so-called 'Woodcarver's Cottage' — a cottage covered in carved wooden animals and birds. It was on the right-hand side as you rounded the bend in the village and was well-known enough to feature on a Pathe newsreel.

Still on the original course, we then pass from Woolmer Green into Knebworth. Surprisingly enough, the present village of Knebworth is not much more than around 125 years old as an 1884 map shows nothing here whatsoever. The original village, built up around Knebworth House, is a mile to the west and is now called Old Knebworth. It would appear that people started settling on the Great North Road site in the late 1880s, possibly around the railway station that was built there. It is noteworthy here that as the road passes through the village, it reverts from arterial status to pass through, and then regains its width at the other side of the village

From Knebworth we still follow the original line of the Great North Road down the hill to Broadwater. The Roebuck Inn here, now an hotel, has been serving travellers on the road for a very long time and is believed to date from the 15th century.

You have to be a little careful to stay on the original Great North Road. A hundred years ago there was nothing on the road between Broadwater and the present Fairlands Way. Old Stevenage was a market town dating back at least 900 years, but became a casualty of Lord Abercrombie's plan, formulated in 1943, to house those who had been bombed out during the war. He called for a ring of 'New Towns' to be built around London and Stevenage was one of the first, earmarked in August 1946.

Charles Harper's sketch of the famous Six Hills — a row of burial mounds — now classified as an ancient monument. They stand right next to the road. Depending on which account one believes, they date from either the Iron age or Roman era.

To follow our course we need to stay on the B197. At the first roundabout past Broadwater take the first exit which is called London Road (this is always a bit of a hint as to a road's history). Pass under Broadhall Way, over another roundabout and up to the junction with Six Hills Way. Here things get really confusing. The Six Hills are a row of six Roman burial tumuli in a line along the road. They were a real landmark to coach travellers and very well-known but when I was first looking for them I couldn't find them. Old engravings clearly show six largish mounds on the right-hand side of the road. I knew they lay south of the Old Town and looked up and down the old London Road without success. Eventually I spotted them: on the *left-hand* side of the road by the junction with Six Hills Way. In their time they were no doubt the largest objects around but, dwarfed by present-day constructions, they are now very insignificant and much smaller than I was expecting.

The Great North Road now branches off just before one reaches the Six Hills.

One of the better finds I had during my research was discovering a short cine film showing the Great North Road in 1939 and, best of all, it is in colour! Someone had clearly been driving north on the road and stopped to take a minute or two of footage in a number of places between London and Grantham.

I have been able to identify most of those places and have taken comparison photographs. This is Stevenage Road between Knebworth and Stevenage. It must have been a popular place to stop and take photos but unfortunately tree growth has spoiled the present day view.

This is one of the first places on our journey where our Great North Road no longer exists. To follow its path, we back-track a few yards from the junction with Six Hills Way to the start of the line of mounds. Then take the small left turn which takes you to the correct side of the mounds and there is the road although now it is a dead end. It allows access to one or two factories and ends in a grassy area eventually cut off by Six Hills Way. We need to go on foot for the next few hundred yards as the actual course is under the grass immediately to the right of the factory access road, between there and the mounds. You can see it on aerial pictures. Follow it to where it is cut off by Six Hills Way immediately west of the roundabout. Carefully crossing the road we come to another grassy area with a cycle path in a subway under the roundabout. Right in front of you the cycle path goes under a bridge but on top of that bridge is just grass. No path, nothing. What used to go over that bridge was the Great North Road! It sits there abandoned and forgotten. If you stand on the bridge, lining yourself up on it, you will see our next landmark: Lytton Way, crossing at an angle to arrive at Six Hills roundabout.

The Great North Road in Stevenage south of the old town has been extensively disrupted by the modern town. We can however follow it on foot for a short way as most of it is still there, albeit in different guises. We start at the Six Hills and cross over Six Hills Way. Although another new road — Lytton Way — bars our route, you can see a straight road running away from you — the old Great North Road.

Left: **Cross Lytton Way on foot and then follow the road north. It is no more than a service road and has in fact been built on in a couple of places but as a pedestrian you can follow it until you come to the road that serves Tesco's car park** *(right)*. **The Great North Road runs in front of the store to where a footbridge now crosses the modern Fairlands Way.**

And on the other side, another small factory access road that just happens to line up with you on the bridge, and the grassy area back over by the mounds.

Cross over to this lane and look along it. Although the road markings indicate that it is only a series of side roads, note how they are all in a line running away from you. This is indeed the old course of our road. For the next 200 or 300 yards it is part of a factory service road and, believe it or not, part of a supermarket car park! The large Tesco's store here has used it as access to its car park and in fact the course of the Great North Road runs right up the front of that store. You will see a footbridge at the far end of the car park which crosses Fairlands Way. It is on a direct line with our route and if you stand on it, a straight road clearly stretches away from you both north and south.

Walking over the footbridge, we can rejoin the route as a road — Ditchmore Lane to be precise. This is where the old town began, an area then called Brick Kiln End. The 19th century brickworks were to the west of the railway and there is still a Brick Kiln Road in about the right place.

Left: **This view is from the footbridge looking back south.** *Right:* **From the footbridge looking north. The straight road can clearly be seen stretching away from you, first as Ditchmore Lane, then as the High Street of the old town.**

Now on Stevenage High Street, this view looking south down the Great North Road with little change over the years.

The far end of Ditchmore Lane crosses straight into the High Street which was the centre of Old Stevenage. We can now follow the route of the Great North Road more easily. At the northern edge of the street there is a small one-way system and our road once more becomes the B197. It heads north as North Road and, after crossing Martins Way, the last of the new roads to bar its path, heads out of town on its long journey.

As we leave Stevenage to the south, we are once again on the exact course of a road that would have been familiar to coachmen in the 18th century. Half a mile after leaving the built-up area, we join a road coming from Junction 8 of the A1(M). None of the roads to the west of this junction existed before the mid-1960s. Although we have to turn right at a T-junction, it is our road that is the older. The new road just joins up with us; in fact old maps show a small kink in the road here so earlier travellers may have had to turn sharp right, too, to carry on their northern progress.

Another mile or two and we come to the village of Graveley. This village does not appear to have changed at all since the 1800s, which is surprising considering the massive transitions only a short distance away. It was a busy place when the A1(M) finished at Junction 8 and all the traffic came back onto the old Great North Road, but when the A1(M) was extended beyond Baldock, Graveley became a backwater.

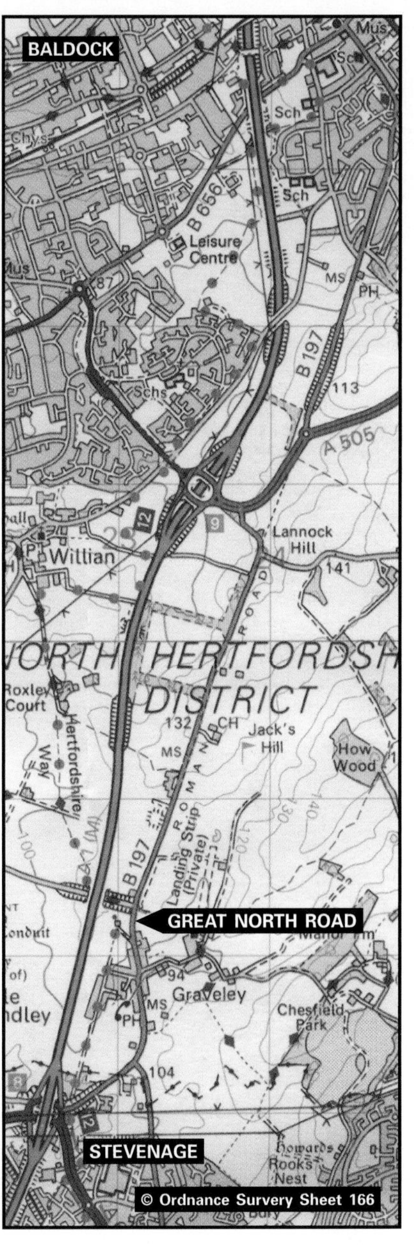

We carry on north and barely a mile further on we arrive at Jack's Hill Cafe, a watering hole that would have been very well-known to the long distance users of this road. It stretched along the road for around 200 yards with fuel and garage facilities as well as the cafe. Behind the buildings was another facility not quite so welcome — a wrecked car dump. The original cafe building is a chain pub nowadays but, by a stroke of luck, I was able to get into contact with the original owners, Peter and Gillian Cave. They still own the caravan site which stands on part of the area. They told me that they had owned other cafes, all of which were given the name Jack's Hill after this, their first one. So if you are eating in the Jack's Hill truckstop on the A5 at Towcester, the name comes from a 'caf' on the Great North Road.

Top left: **The old Jack's Hill truckstop is now called the Hungry Horse** *(top right).* **The building behind the cafe** *(above)* **may have been driver's accommodation in the early post-war years before lorries had the facility of sleeper cabs.**

Once again heading north, we take a small deviation to accommodate the roundabout for the road coming from Junction 9 of the A1(M). In this case the original stretch was straight whereas the modern road is on a curve. The opposite of an ox-bow lay-by, an ox-bow straight! Its path can be traced on aerial photographs and on an old map there is a milestone marked on that small stretch.

Rejoining our route a couple of hundred yards further up, after having gone around the roundabout, we find that the B197 has finally expired, and the road is now renumbered A6141. It runs into Baldock through a chalk cutting which was dug in coaching times. A truly tough job by hand.

The road runs past housing and at the bottom of the hill we reach a Tesco store . . . but this time it is one with a difference! With its very ornate frontage of pillars and dressed stone, this was once the Kayser Bonder stocking factory. Apparently, when Tesco asked for planning permission to open there, they were required to keep the original frontage. And very striking it looks too! But why did a stocking factory have such a striking frontage? Many years ago, this stretch of the Great North Road was home to a number of film-makers and film stars. They had homes here because it was handy for the studios at Elstree and Borehamwood which became Britain's Hollywood. A studio was built in Baldock, allegedly by Mary Pickford's company, but it was only used for a short while before being taken over by Kayser Bonder. I have since discovered that this may be an urban myth but it's a good story all the same.

Baldock has a lovely wide High Street reminiscent of many other towns with a coaching history. Even today, beyond the boundaries of the road, there are wide verges leading up to Georgian houses. The whole stretch between Tesco's and the church must have been a very bustling place when full of horses and coaches. We are in fact on a junction with an east-west route, partly known today as the A505 which connected Oxford with Cambridge which resulted in a lot of congestion. Even today White Horse Street is full of vehicles although Baldock has not been directly on the north-south route since 1967.

At the far end of White Horse Street we take a left turn to head north again on the aptly named North Road which, for a short while, takes on the number A507. I say for a short while because a mile and a half north of the town, the old road takes a detour to accommodate a large roundabout upon which our single carriageway road ends. The route of the old road is visible south of the roundabout, but on the other side it is swallowed up by the southbound slip-road.

This roundabout is Junction 10 of the A1(M), and for now its last one. So far we have looked at three separate routes: the Great North Road, the Barnet Bypass and the A1(M) but at this point the latter terminates. From now on until we get to Stilton, the Great North Road and the A1 are one and the same, and are on the original route with no changes bar the odd village bypass.

Entering Baldock, one would turn right at the junction, now a mini roundabout. This is called Whitehorse Street and was in fact a multiplex with the A505 coming from Royston through to Hitchin and Luton which now bypasses the town. At the far end, we turn off left again to head north. This is Whitehorse Street, looking west.

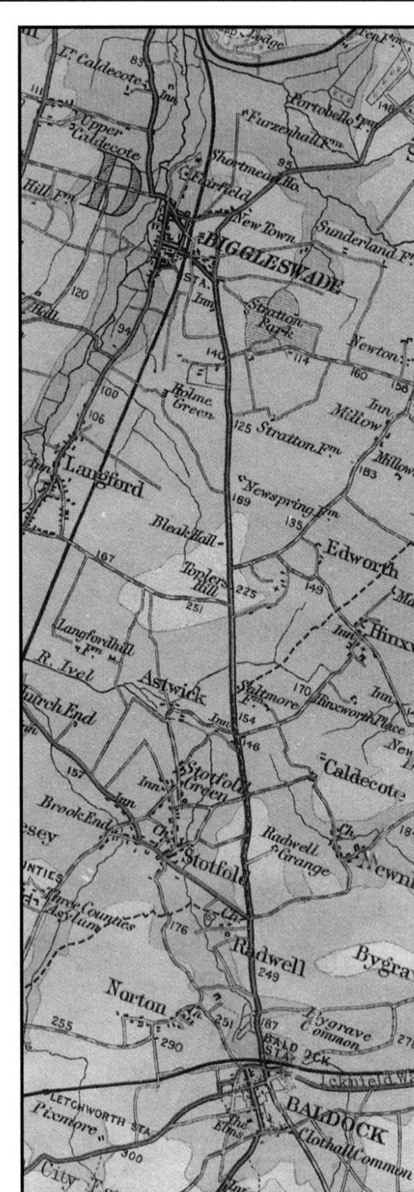

The road at the turn of the century.

Some stretches of the road do not change, even 22 years apart. At this point near Astwick, pictured by David Gregg, the southbound carriageway was the original Great North Road.

Baldock to Alconbury

Once we go around the roundabout and up onto the dual carriageway, the old two-lane Great North Road has been transformed for many miles for, in the 1950s and early '60s, the whole road between here and Markham Moor was dualled in the last stages of a Type 1 upgrade (see pages 21-22). In general the original S2 road is one of the carriageways of the dual carriageway, but there are places where it switches from side to side and it's not easy to tell which is which. Some giveaways are alignments and gradients. In general a newer stretch will have easier curves and shallower gradients than the original road. If you can find a place where there are bridges then it is usually easy to tell by the architecture, and bridges are often dated. A good example of this is just south of the Black Cat roundabout (see page 56) where the River Ouse is crossed. One carriageway has an old stone arch bridge, and the other a far more recent concrete structure.

This shot, taken looking east down the High Street at Biggleswade, shows another lovely wide town market place, reminiscent of Baldock. I'm guessing that lots of coaches and horses needed room to manoeuvre. Nowadays its full of parking spaces and pedestrian areas. On the day I turned up it was market day which made it even more cluttered than usual.

For the next five miles, our A1 from the terminus of the A1(M) runs in a straight line believed to be of Roman origin. A comparative study of the field shapes on a map of 1891 and modern satellite photography indicates that the Great North Road on this stretch is entirely underneath the southbound carriageway. The modern A1 takes a turn to the north-west at a roundabout south of Biggleswade and here is our first bypassed town. A right fork at the roundabout keeps us on London Road, Biggleswade (the A6001).

A hundred years ago the road from this roundabout to the junction with Drove Road was open country with only the Biggleswade Union workhouse (demolished 1972) and the Yorkshire Grey Inn (still there) for coach passengers to look at. Today it is built up all the way into the town. At the junction with Drove Road, there is a lane on the right called Eagle Farm Road. This was the site of Spreadeagle Farm and denotes where the Great North Road turned to the left to enter the town centre. After a short distance it becomes the High Street, which used to be a wide open market space. The market area is now paved over and the road is no wider than anywhere else, but the Old Market Hall still stands although converted to modern uses.

At the end of the market place the Great North Road turned north into Shortmead Street. The original is another still from the cine film

At the far end of the High Street is a T-junction where our Great North Road turns north again to leave the town. Here it is called Shortmead Street. There is some evidence that through coaches that didn't need to stop left the town via Crab Lane and Sun Street without travelling down the High Street. Sun Street and Shortmead Street meet up a quarter of a mile out from the town centre and the road turns sharp left to cross the River Ivel.

Over the bridge, the road goes straight on toward Upper Caldecote, and to stay on our Great North Road we would have taken a right turn 100 yards after the bridge. However, times having changed, the right turn leads only to a small ox-bow stretch where there is a Sainsbury's store and a municipal skip site because this is where the bypass rejoins. There is an at-grade roundabout where we turn right back onto the dual carriageway. The small ox-bow stretch terminates in a dead end up against the dual carriageway a hundred yards north of the skip site.

We are out in the countryside and again a comparative study of maps is required to tell exactly where the Great North Road ran. Between Biggleswade and Lower Caldecote the original course was still the southbound carriageway except where another ox-bow stretch runs through Lower Caldecote and crosses the northbound carriageway to enter the village. It is believed there was a transport cafe here called the Tower Cafe.

Just north of the village is another ox-bow stretch on the left used as a large lay-by, and another on the right a little further on which is not a lay-by but access to a farm. This is a good example of where a road has been upgraded to avoid villages and twists and turns.

Shortmead Street turns west to cross the River Ivel and nowadays carries straight on to meet the dual carriageway at a roundabout by a Sainsbury's supermarket. However, in earlier times, after the bridge it cut north again the other side of what is now Sainsbury's. The stretch still exists as an access to the supermarket and a skip site further up. It is then blocked off as can be seen in this photo.

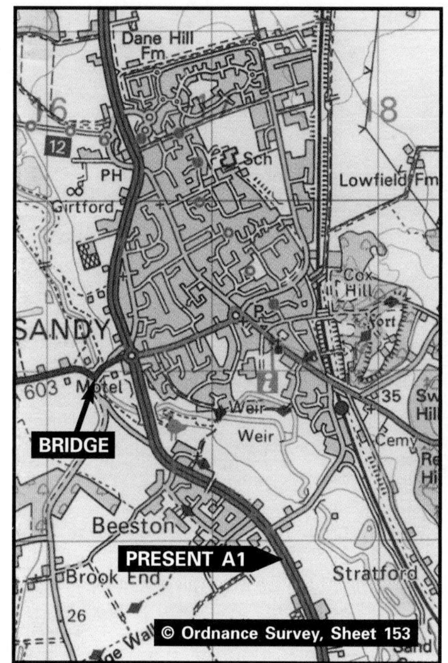

The bridge at Sandy. Over on the far side the Great North Road turned north. The turning still exists but now exits onto the A1 dual carriageway.

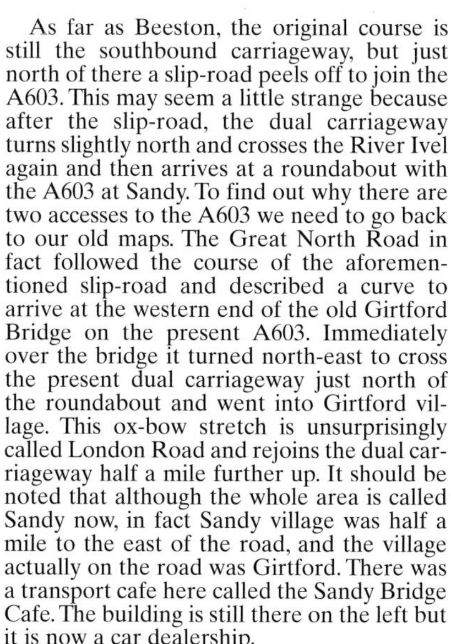
As far as Beeston, the original course is still the southbound carriageway, but just north of there a slip-road peels off to join the A603. This may seem a little strange because after the slip-road, the dual carriageway turns slightly north and crosses the River Ivel again and then arrives at a roundabout with the A603 at Sandy. To find out why there are two accesses to the A603 we need to go back to our old maps. The Great North Road in fact followed the course of the aforementioned slip-road and described a curve to arrive at the western end of the old Girtford Bridge on the present A603. Immediately over the bridge it turned north-east to cross the present dual carriageway just north of the roundabout and went into Girtford village. This ox-bow stretch is unsurprisingly called London Road and rejoins the dual carriageway half a mile further up. It should be noted that although the whole area is called Sandy now, in fact Sandy village was half a mile to the east of the road, and the village actually on the road was Girtford. There was a transport cafe here called the Sandy Bridge Cafe. The building is still there on the left but it is now a car dealership.

North of here as far as Tempsford, it is difficult to say which of the carriageways formed the original Great North Road. Suffice to say that it is under one or other of the carriageways of the present dualling. As we approach Tempsford, our road peels off the dual carriageway to head down Church Street, Church End, to emerge back onto the dual carriageway half a mile later passing Tempsford village to the east. The Great North Road then appears to alternate between carriageways of the D2 until we get to the River Great Ouse. There is no doubt of the original course here because the dual carriageway crosses the river on two separate bridges. One is modern, but the other on the northbound side is a much older stone bridge, and the northbound carriageway twists and turns around the river to arrive at the Black Cat roundabout, the junction with the A421 from Bedford.

This well-known landmark on the A1 was named after a garage that stood here back in the 1920s. It was called the Black Cat Garage and had a silhouette of a black cat as its logo. The original garage is long gone, and the junction was the subject of a major reconstruction in 2005/6 but a silhouetted black cat still resides there.

Just north of the roundabout is yet another ox-bow lay-by where a kink in the old road was ironed out. The old road at the moment is under the northbound carriageway as far as Wyboston, a village split by the present road. However our Great North Road was the small lane through the village, east of the dual carriageway that rejoins it 200 yards further up. Then it peels off again almost immediately to become the southbound slip-road from the A428 onto the A1. You can't drive it northwards but if you could you would come to the roundabout where the A428 joins it from the

The Black Cat roundabout was named after the silhouette of a black cat which was the sign for a garage which once stood at the junction. The roundabout was much altered and upgraded in 2005-6 and in fact moved slightly. They have however reinstated the rather startling silhouette on the roundabout itself.

This is a particularly nice find. A still from the 1939 colour cine film showing the Crown pub on the Great North Road looking north toward Eaton Socon. As luck would have it, this small stretch, pub and all, was backwatered when the dual carriageway was built and the road into Eaton Socon diverted to accommodate a roundabout. So it is still there just as the unknown cameraman saw it.

Another still from the film shows a tea stop a few hundred yards north of the previous photo. Interesting to note that the building is more half-timbered in 2012 than it was in 1939! It is another venue which has become an Indian restaurant.

east. There is a stranded bit of Great North Road just south-west of the roundabout which would have joined up the slip-road with the B1428 into Eaton Socon, which is, at this point, called Great North Road.

At the turn of the 20th century, Eaton Socon was a small village but it grew rapidly in the 1960s and is now part of St Neots. As you pass through the village on the B1428, it retains a little of its old character. At the far end of the street there is a roundabout with a left and a right fork. The right fork is St Neots Road and the left fork is the B1048 which runs through a mile of suburban housing. This was the old Great North Road, and in 1900 there wasn't a single house between the roundabout and the present Cross Hall road.

As we reach the T-junction with Cross Hall Road, we need to turn left to find a slip-road back down onto the dual carriageway, but not so fast! Look straight across the road. There is a small lane that serves a few houses and is a dead end. Again, this is a stretch of original Great North Road and terminates up against the side of the dual carriageway like so many others. We have to turn left and then right to continue our northbound journey.

The old road is actually called Great North Road along its entire length in Eaton Socon. At the northern end you turn left onto Cross Hall Road to get back to the dual carriageway with a right turn just after you turn left. This is also called Great North Road and was where our road used to leave town. Now it's a dead end.

This is yet another brilliant 1939 shot of what is believed to have been an inn on the road near Southoe. This is now a busy dual carriageway and I ended up having to get a passenger to take the comparison from the window of my car as we passed by. Stopping on this dangerous bend like the 1939 cameraman did was out of the question.

Half a mile to the north we reach another deviation. A fairly long ox-bow stretch leaves to the right and brushes the village of Little Paxton. We cannot leave here because, as in other places, the old road has become the slip-road onto the dual carriageway. We have to pull off at the slip north of the village which curves back on itself and crosses the A1 to become the north end of the ox-bow stretch. If we were to follow it all the way back, we would find ourselves travelling southbound on the A1. So we have to turn around, but just before we cross back over the A1, note the right fork which incorporates the southbound off slips. This is the original course rejoining 200 yards further up but we cannot use it going north; we have to go by the modern route.

The next three miles via Southoe to Buckden manages to stay almost entirely on the original route with the exception of a small ox-bow lay-by on the southbound side at Southoe. The road doesn't actually go through Southoe but passes just to the side of the village. Years ago, this stretch of the modern road was used to test different road markings.

In the old days, there was a notorious speed trap on the outskirts of Buckden. Note the garage on the left.

Another garage in the town was Robinsons — or the Buckden Motor Depot — photographed here by Mr Flint in 1906/07.

What started out as a cycle business is now a beauty parlour.

Arriving at the roundabout at Buckden, we need to drive through the village to stick to our original route. It follows the High Street past a pair of coaching inns and Buckden Palace before emerging back onto the dual carriageway a mile further on. Half a mile out of the village, we go over a bridge

over a slip-road to the B1514 into Brampton. If you have time, go and look at the bridge from below. It is clearly not a road bridge because the slip-road is built on the course of an old railway track.

The Great North Road didn't actually go through Brampton village, but instead it met the Huntingdon to Thrapston road a little west of the village where there was a well-known coaching inn called the Creamer's Hut. This later became the Brampton Hut Hotel as can be seen here at the crossroads in 1939.

We cross the GSJ with the A14 — a major east-west route nowadays — but even 20 years ago, this was the much more minor A604 between Kettering and Huntingdon. Just beyond here there are a pair of ox-bow lay-bys one on either side. From the one on our northbound side you notice a factory building surrounded by barbed wire fencing. This is Huntingdon Life Sciences, much loved by the animal rights fraternity.

And now we reach the end of this stage of our journey for we have arrived at another stretch of A1(M). Our dual carriageway glides effortlessly into a four-lane motorway joined by a spur from the A14 bringing traffic from the M11. This is actually a fairly important junction in the history of our road. Back in Chapter 5, you may remember that I described another route out of London heading north, the present A10. Well this is the meeting point of the two.

To reach the original road we must backtrack a small distance to where the A1(M) starts. There is a slip-road here which we must take to visit the villages of Alconbury and Alconbury Weston. The road takes quite a wide loop to the west here leaving Alconbury between present and past roads and goes through Alconbury Weston,

When the road here was dualled, the old road became the northbound carriageway and a roundabout was installed here. Then it was upgraded again, the junction was made into a GSJ and then realigned slightly, presumably to remove the curve in the road. So the old northbound carriageway, and thus the Great North Road, is still to be found lurking between new road and Brampton services. You can see the yellow lines across the old road surface that signified the approach to a roundabout. You can also see the modern roundabout through the undergrowth more or less in the same place as the earlier one. The hotel stood the other side of the wooden fence.

re-crossing the A1 on a bridge. You will notice a small road next to the A1 as you cross, and if you go around the factory you can get onto it. You find yourself on a bank above the motorway, looking down onto it. You may notice a large monument with a small railing around it at the top of the bank above the motorway. This is the famous Alconbury Milestone. Southbound travellers came to a fork in the road at this point and the stone indicated that from here there were two routes into London.

Going back to the bridge that we used to cross the A1, on the Alconbury side there is a fragment of old road off to your left, just as you start to cross the bridge which lines up with the monument over the motorway. When the dualling took place in the 1950s, the Great North Road became the southbound carriageway and for many years the monument stood in the central reservation. The present arrangement is very much different with the motorway lying some 30 feet lower than the old road. The small road which was originally the Great North Road, then became the southbound carriageway of the A1, and is now the B1043 allowing non-motorway traffic to access Alconbury, Sawtry and Norman Cross.

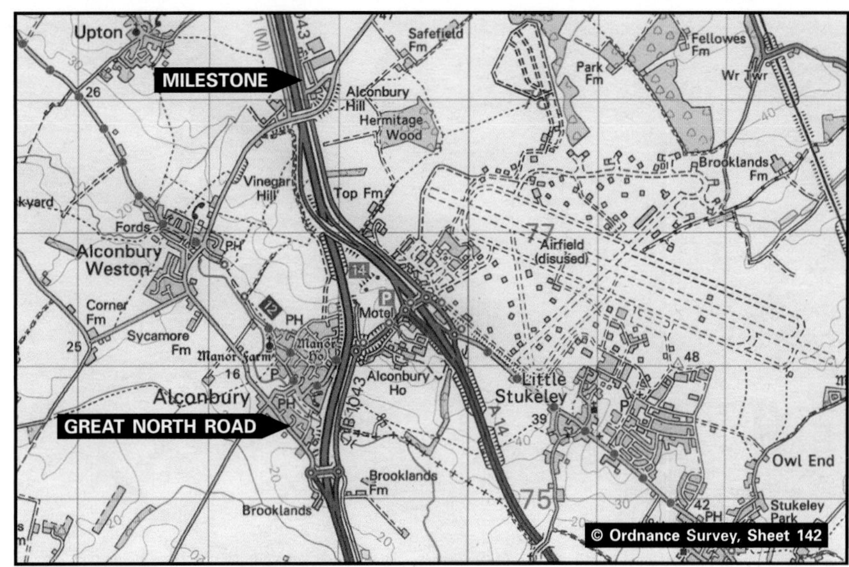

At Alconbury the road didn't actually pass through the village but went through Alconbury Weston, a little further on.

This is the famous Alconbury Milestone which once marked the southbound fork in the road. It has stood alternatively at the fork in the old road; in the central reservation of a dual carriageway, and now above the motorway, all without having been moved.

Looking south at the point where the Great North Road and the Old North Road once met. From here, we finally leave the succession of villages that mark the lower part of our great northern journey as the road now passes through much lesser populated areas with the exception of a few larger towns.

Alconbury to Little Ponton

Up until now, there seems to have been a village every couple of miles, but from now on the distances become greater and the villages fewer. However the deviations are clearer and stretches of the old road can still be found.

Some years ago I worked out of a yard in a village just north of York, Sutton-on-the-Forest. Occasionally I did a run to a factory in the East End of London and back to the yard. I could just about do this in a day bearing in mind that we are only allowed to drive lorries a certain amount of hours a day, so in effect I did this in around ten hours, not counting loading and resting time.

On the return trip I would come to the top of Alconbury Hill and see the four-lane highway stretched out in front and feel that I'd cracked it. As an aside, this widened motorway was part of an ambitious plan to upgrade the A1 to motorway standard along its whole length. This was the only part built before the project was cancelled and, in my view, a good job too! Hence its lonely splendour. Anyway, upon seeing it, I knew I had escaped the crowded south and all I had to do now was make my way back up my favourite road.

Others clearly felt different. Even today Alconbury Hill is a fairly lonely spot. Here stood the Wheatsheaf coaching inn, apparently a very busy spot at one time. According to Charles Harper it sent out 30 pairs of horses a day but with its trade wiped out by the railways, the inn is now under the southbound A1(M).

The down slope on the northbound side is known as Stangate Hill and the woodland around was apparently a haunt of highwaymen although we don't need to worry about highway robbery as we have enough to do with tracing the old route. To do so, we need to leave the present A1 as described at the end of the last chapter, pass through Alconbury and Alconbury Weston and once we have crossed the motorway, pass the factory and turn left behind it. This brings you to a T-junction. Turn right onto the B1043 and

Stangate Hill was the original route north of the Alconbury Milestone. In later years it became the southbound carriageway of the A1. When they built the motorway it was again relegated to a single carriageway. Nevertheless, the 1939 photo and the 2012 comparison are remarkably similar.

Although the village of Sawtry, just south of Stilton, was not directly on the road, Sawtry's Royal Oak Inn stood here opposite the entrance to Fen Lane.

we are again northbound on our journey. And on a very old route as from here for a fair distance we are on the Roman alignment called Ermine Street.

Inspection of an 1890 map clearly shows that we are on the original route and when the dualling took place in the 1950s, this became the southbound carriageway. However it was changed back when the current motorway was built alongside it! A dead giveaway is the name of a couple of cottages on the right: Toll Bar Cottages.

All gone now, obliterated by the motorway behind the hedge on the left.

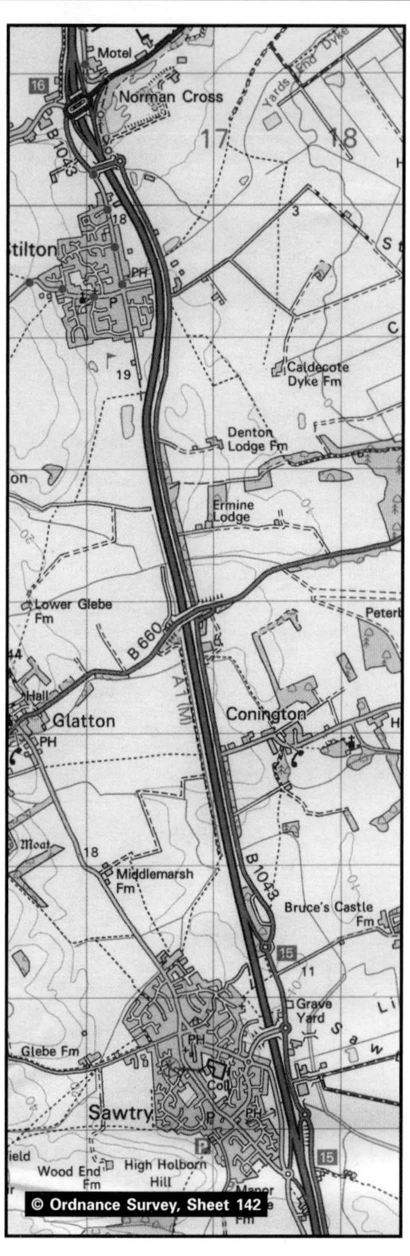

We carry on past Sawtry until we reach the point where the road suddenly bears to the right, still alongside the motorway that is deviating to bypass the village of Stilton on the line of the earlier dual carriageway. Here the Roman influence is clear: the straight road through the village joins perfectly at both ends with our Great North Road. However we can no longer drive it although I understand that this was possible before this stretch was a motorway.

We have to follow the B1043 to its end at a roundabout beyond the village and re-cross the motorway to a T-junction. This is the old north road out of the village and so we can turn left into the village and drive straight through to where a gate stops you from going any further, This is the other side of the motorway to where we deviated to the right. So retracing our route and facing north again has us firmly back on track. In fact, as the 1950s dualling also bypassed Stilton, we can now imagine ourselves for the first time on a nostalgic pre-1950s drive as this stretch has never been altered

Stilton was another busy old coaching centre and this is borne out by the wide village street and the inns on both sides of the road, particularly the Bell with its highly ornate wrought iron sign. The village is famous for Stilton cheese which was sold at the inns there, but it originated from Leicestershire. Now a backwater, we leave it behind and head north out of the village.

The Bell Inn in Stilton was sketched ***(above)*** **by Charles Harper in 1900, and captured** ***(below left)*** **by our unknown cinematographer in 1939.** ***Below right:*** **Now bypassed by the A1, the main street reflects the passing of the years.**

A lovely shot of the northern end of Stilton in 1960 showing where the village road emerges on to the new dual carriageway. Taking the comparison here was difficult because the bridge is obstructing the view, but this is almost the exact spot. The village road joined the dual carriageway at the right-hand end of the bridge.

A report in 1955 described the A1 as the 'ugliest and terrifying country lane in the world' on which in the course of a year over 2,000 people are injured and nearly 100 killed between London and Scotch Corner. Here a Bedford TK lorry has come to grief on the Stilton bypass in 1964. It appears to have the name 'RV Chandler' on the side and maybe 'Portsmouth'. Today the road is motorway status.

Ermine Street formed the basis for the Great North Road at this point. This aerial view shows the course of the old road as it approaches from the south, through the village, and arrives at the site of the Norman Cross in the foreground.

Left: **The monument at Norman Cross commemorates the thousands of French prisoners incarcerated here during the Napoleonic Wars, one Charles Bonchew being executed there in 1808 for wounding a sentry.** *Right:* **The nine-room Norman Cross Hotel was one of the 175 inns in Great Britain managed on temperance lines by the People's Refreshment House Association. In 1937 a room with breakfast cost 7/6 (37½p).** *Below:* **At that time Norman Cross was a simple crossroads, but later a roundabout was added. Now it is a motorway junction and the hotel has been lost for ever.**

We arrive very quickly at a site of a well-known landmark. Although the area is vastly different these days, this was Norman Cross. A motorway junction now all but obliterates the original lay-out which was home to a couple of landmarks. Here traffic for Peterborough and parts of Lincolnshire branched off and many folks will have stopped at the Norman Cross Hotel.

The road up past the Premier Inn is the continuation of our road although just a short stub is left. When the road was initially dualled, there was a roundabout here and just past the roundabout on the left was a curious monument — an eagle on a plinth. The area between the Great North Road and the road to Peterborough was the site of a Napoleonic prisoner of war camp. Apparently it was a place of great hardship and many Frenchmen never made it home and the eagle commemorates some 1,800 men buried in the nearby fields. In 1990 the eagle was stolen and it was not until the new motorway was built that the monument was moved and a new eagle installed. It now stands in a small lay-by on the Peterborough road.

Kate's Cabin is a well-known stop on the A1 and has been a transport cafe for as long as I can remember but I discovered during my research that the current Kate's Cabin is not the original.

Early maps show a place called Kate's Cabin a few yards north. It turns out to be the building just the other side of the A47 slip roads and beautifully shown *(left)* in this still from 1939.

From here we have to return to the motorway for a short distance. Our old road is buried under the southbound carriageway, and there is no longer a way through, but from Norman Cross to where the motorway terminates at another junction it is only about a mile. Here the A1139 branches off to the right into Peterborough, the A605 going left to Northampton. Both of these roads are recent, neither shows up on a 1970 road map.

However once we pass under this junction, the four-lane motorway suddenly ends and we are back on the dual carriageway of the 1960s. Almost immediately, we come across a small GSJ junction next to a very well-known transport cafe called Kate's Cabin. At one time there was a crossroads here and Kate's stood directly on the corner. The A605 on the west side of the A1 has been diverted to the other junction now, but the road into Peterborough is still as it was.

Kate's Cabin has been a transport cafe as long as I remember so I was surprised to discover that it is a relatively recent addition. Nineteenth century Ordnance Survey maps mark a building as Kate's Cabin a couple of hundred yards north of the current one. This is the original Kate's and is the white building on the left immediately past the A605 junction which is reputed to be named after a lass named Kate who dished out gin to coach passengers in the 18th century. There is some evidence that this building was not the first Kate's but does stand close to the site of it. And the position of Kate's shows that our old road at this point was the northbound side of the dual carriageway. So we are right back on course.

When I stopped to photograph it in 2012, I found it empty and locked up. Has its time finally come?

I have talked a lot about ox-bow lay-bys created by straightening the road and just north of Kate's Cabin is a classic one on the southbound carriageway just north of the Chesterton junction.

Continuing north, the road makes a diversion to the north-west, separating from Ermine Street, possibly to avoid the remains of the Roman town of Durobrivae which lies between the A1 and the River Nene. In fact there is some evidence that in medieval times the whole route shifted westwards to get away from the wetlands of the Fens but as our 1920 Great North Road followed this route, that is the way we will go.

There is a small ox-bow lay-by on the eastern side of the bend implying that our original road has changed sides again. This is borne out by the village of Water Newton a mile further on which is in fact an entire ox-bow village! On the southbound side, you can leave the dual carriageway and meander through this small village before rejoining the fast road again. There is even an old milestone still in place.

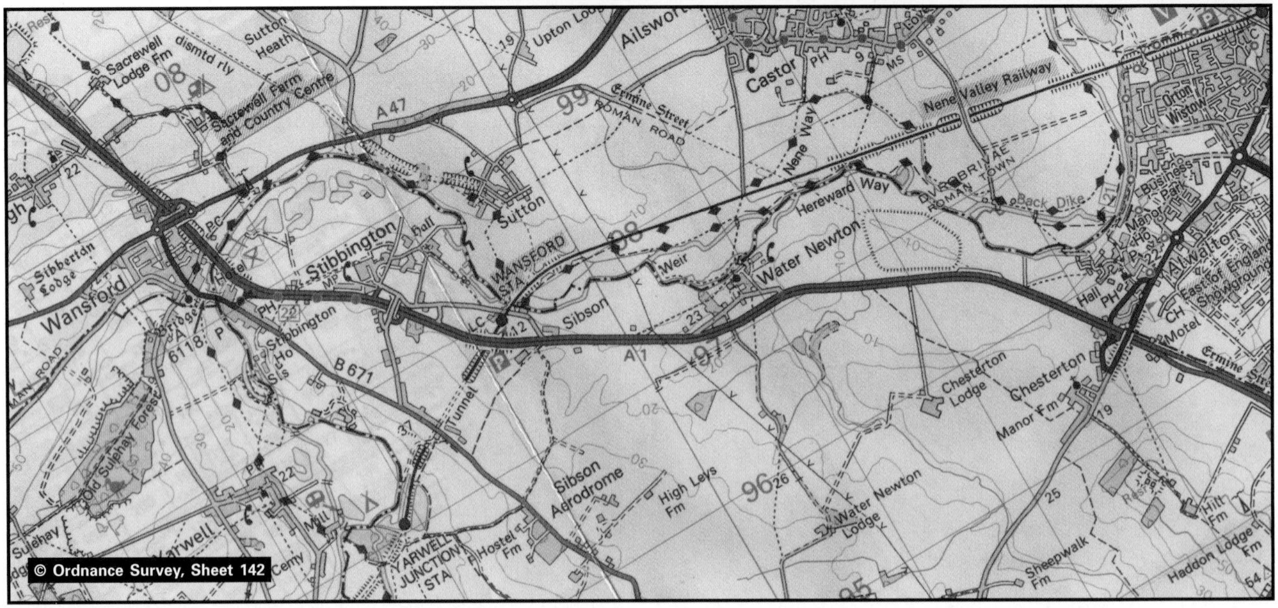

© Ordnance Survey, Sheet 142

At one time a single carriageway, now the Great North Road from Chesterton to Wansford has been dualled.

Timeless Water Newton — then and now. Writing at the turn of the last century, Charles Harper wrote that Water Newton comes in sight standing dry and secure in its knoll above the water meadows of the River Nene. The church faced the highway before Wansford Bridge was built and the road diverted. Even the same milestone still stands against the wall.

This is one of my favourite comparisons and I just couldn't believe my eyes when I finally worked out where this was.

The 1939 footage illustrates admirably how the S2 road of the early days has now been converted into a dual carriageway.

On the left, just past Water Newton, is the Sibson Inn. Originally it was a farmhouse, and later yet another coaching inn, a small part of our old road can be seen in front of it. It dives under our dual carriageway and pops out on the other side where it follows our old road away from the dual carriageway, past the Nene Valley Railway and skirts the edge of Stibbington before recrossing the dual carriageway and going into Wansford. Another classic case of the curves in old roads being straightened out. Going through Wansford by the old road, we cross the Nene by a very narrow old stone bridge with recesses and a three-ton weight limit. This bridge was notorious for being dangerous and was the reason for an early bypass of Wansford. Just before the bridge is the Haycock, another ex-coaching inn.

At the far end of the village we come to a roundabout where the A47 crosses over the A1. This is completely new. Originally the road from Leicester emerged into Wansford via the Old Leicester Road and crossed the

Taken from an upstairs bedroom of the Haycock Inn *(right)* which is still a hotel today, the view of the bridge at Wansford has hardly changed at all in over 100 years.

Great North Road in the village before heading off to Peterborough. Nowadays both roads have bypassed the village and they cross at a large GSJ just north of the village. We take the northbound slip-road, but if you look to the left there is another small remnant of the old road that terminates up against the dual carriageway. Interestingly, this is known as Black Swan Hill. One presumes it is named after yet another inn and in fact there is a building that could well have been an inn just past the junction with the slip-road.

Once clear of Wansford, apart from a small ox-bow stretch opposite the turning for Thornhaugh, the way is clear to Carpenters Lodge roundabout just past RAF Wittering. At this point in earlier times there was no roundabout, the road merely turned slightly north and ran along the boundary of Burghley House. Now, however, the dual carriageway goes straight on and the old road is a right turn at the roundabout, the B1081. As you turn right at the roundabout, again you can see the fragment of road that was left over when the dual carriageway was built. In 2008/2009 this roundabout, along with five others, was removed so that the dual carriageway now has no major junctions on it between Peterborough and the Tyne.

Another great shot from 1939. This is where the road from Wansford rejoined the early S2 bypass.

The same shot today, the slip road came out where the section of wooden fence can be seen just beyond the bus stop.

'Stamford compels enthusiasm, from the first glimpse of it on entering, to the last regretful backward glance on leaving', wrote Charles Harper in 1901. 'It is historic, picturesque, stately, aristocratic, and cleanly, all at once. Its stone-built mansions and houses chiefly of the Renaissance period, from Elizabeth onwards to the time of George the First, it is in this sort the most beautiful town in England, after Oxford and Cambridge, and even in some aspects surpassing them. Apart from its lovely churches, one seeks not Gothic architecture at Stamford, but in the stateliness of classic methods as understood in the 16th and 17th century revival. The entrance is of a peculiar stateliness, the broad quiet street descending, lined with dignified private houses, to where the river Welland flows beneath the bridge, dividing the counties of Northampton and Lincoln, and Stamford Baron from Stamford town. On the right hand rises the fine tower of St Martin's, its perforated battlements showing lace-like against the sky, just as when Turner painted his view.'

Now in the Usher Gallery, Lincoln, William Turner depicted the scene around 1828.

Harper: 'Lower down across the street straddles the sign of the great George inn. The "distracting bustle of the George, which exceeded anything I ever saw or heard", as the Reverend Thomas Twining wrote in 1776, has long since become a thing of the past, and a certain quiet dignity now belongs to it. The George is an inn with a history. Charles the First slept under its roof on August 23, 1645, and 'Billy the Butcher,' (the vulgar nickname by which the people called William, Duke of Cumberland) returning from Culloden, stayed in the house and celebrated that victory. Distinguished foreigners without number have rested here and wondered at the habits of English men. The foreigner, it is to be feared, never, with every advantage, really understands us; sometimes, too, he is so perverse that we find a difficulty in understanding him. Thus, Master Estienne Perlin, who travelled the roads and sampled the inns of England so far back as 1558, says we were great drunkards then.'

Stamford was once a huge bottleneck on our journey to the north.

We continue on into Stamford on the B1081 London Road which looks very much as it did in 1890 and I suspect our 1920s motorist would still recognise the High Street as he drove down it to go under the large sign for the George Hotel crossing the street from building to building on an old wooden beam. The George is another very well-known coaching stop and could probably tell many a tale. Although the current hotel has seen many refurbishments, its possible that parts of the early buildings have stood here for a thousand years as records indicate some kind of monastic order owned a rest house there.

Just past the George is the bridge over the River Welland which replaced the old ford that was paved with stone which gives the town its name. Once over the bridge, our Great North Road — as the B1081 — follows a dog-leg course through the town via St Mary's Hill and St John Street.

Stamford is a pretty town, built of old stone but the streets are narrow and it was a notorious bottleneck on the Great North Road. In November 1955 P*icture Post* published an article which was entitled 'The Great North Road: 400 Miles of Death'.

After crossing the river, the Great North Road turned sharp left and then right again by the London Inn.

The street then narrowed down to one lane where vehicles had to take turns to pass each other.

Somewhat exaggerated, perhaps, but in 1955 we are talking about the time when roads were creaking under the strain of traffic and vehicles were nothing like as safe as they are today.

Picture Post describes Stamford thus:

'In Stamford, the signs read "Stay Awhile Amid Its Ancient Charm". You're not going to have any option. Here there are three dead-stop bottlenecks where larger trucks have to be guided through by policemen while the lines of traffic grow hundreds of yards long at each end of town.'

(Interesting to note the use of the word 'truck' in an English publication of the 1950s.)

Apparently the Postmaster-General threatened to divert Post coaches away from Stamford 100 years earlier after horses were killed in an accident there.So there is the first evidence that the old road could no longer handle its traffic and Stamford would be bypassed within five years.

From St John Street we pass through Red Lion Square and then take a turn up Scotgate. As we head north, the place and road names change as we are now leaving dedicated Anglo-Saxon territory and heading into areas that at one time were Danish. Old Norse–gata meant street hence many street names ending in the anglicised suffix 'gate' which is very common in Yorkshire and the north-east. Scotgate, the street of the Scots.

At the junction with Empingham Road, Scotgate becomes Casterton Road and in coaching times we would be leaving the town here. The road mounts a hill and then falls away on the other side leaving Stamford behind. Part way down the hill around the place where Perth Road goes off to the left, Ermine Street rejoins us having entered Stamford on a slightly different alignment. Towards the bottom of the hill, Casterton Road is left behind and the B1081 becomes the Old Great North Road and as such passes through the village of Great Casterton.

Another signal that the Romans are with us again, place names including the term 'caster' (or indeed 'chester') signify a Roman fort, e.g. Tadcaster and Doncaster. There is indeed the remains of a fort in Casterton.

Just through the village our old road meets up with the dual carriageway coming up from Carpenters Lodge roundabout. A close inspection of old maps reveals that it ran between the

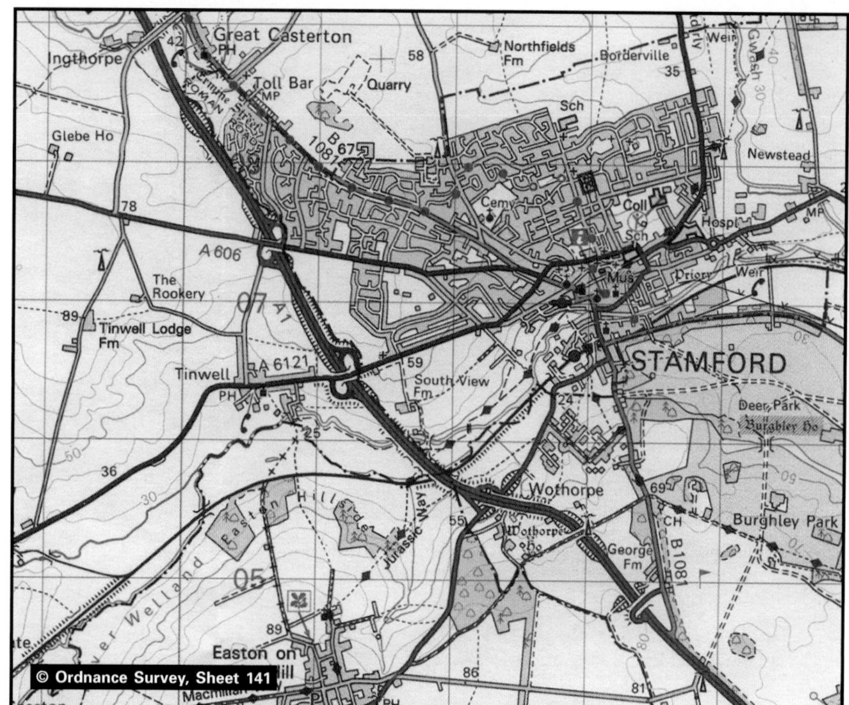

The bypass came in 1960 moving the road west as far as the village of Great Casterton . . . as peaceful then as it is today.

The dangerous bend at Woolfox Lodge evened out in later years leaving a section of the Roman road as a convenient ox-bow layby. The aerodrome which borders the road at this point was used by RAF Bomber Command during the Second World War.

current B1081 junction and Tickencote Lane so the old road is under the new. There is however a small ox-bow stretch for a couple of hundred yards after Tickencote Lane.

So we must rejoin the dual carriageway and head north again knowing that at this point the old road is right under our feet as it is under the northbound lane and stays there for some distance. On our left, on the other side of the dual carriageway, is a wood called Bloody Oaks. This is a reference to the Battle of Empingham which was fought across this ground during the Wars of the Roses and was another victory for the Yorkist cause.

Staying on a military theme, a mile or so further on, we will notice some old brick structures in the fields on the right. These are relics of what was RAF Woolfox Lodge, a WWII Bomber Command station. The control tower can be seen across the fields but its easy to lose against the trees behind it.

As we pass Woolfox Lodge the road which has been straight for a few miles takes a single turn to the north and straightens out again. Right on the apex of the curve on the left hand side is a long ox-bow lay-by which closely follows the curve although somewhat tighter. This is the original bend in Ermine Street which has been eased slightly with the building of the dual carriageway leaving this relic of the Roman engineers where you can share your bacon sarnie with the ghosts of the Legions.

Ahead of us is a section which gets a mention in *Picture Post.*

'The notorious straight run to the Ram Jam Inn. The road is still only 22 feet wide, but it seems you can see for hundreds of yards. Infuriated by the delays at Stamford, the clogged traffic attempts to sort itself out along this stretch. And overtaking cars crash, head-on with distressing regularity, with vehicles which pop like jack in the boxes out of the six hollows which do not seem to be there at all.'

The straight and the hollows are still there but now duplicated with two southbound lanes so that death and disaster are no longer as commonplace as in earlier days.

There is little of interest between here and Colsterworth, the road is almost straight as a die and our old road still lies under the northbound carriageway. The road passes close to Stretton but not through it. However two local inns shared the passing trade being sited on the road. The first coming north was the New Inn

A notorious stretch of the road; the driver lived for ten days after this head on crash.

In between Stamford and Grantham there is quite a long stretch without any villages directly on the road. This gave rise to the establishment of a handful of fairly large and well-known coaching inns. The New Inn is now a private house.

— well it was new in 1780 according to a board above the door! Along with many others it didn't survive the railways and became a private house for a long time. Latterly it was an antiques shop run by Ralph Cox and his daughter Jane sent me a photo of the Cottesmore Hunt there in 1964. It later became the Greetham Inn but is now a private house.

The other is the curiously-named Ram Jam Inn. As far as I can make out, the pub was originally called the Winchelsea Arms owned by a Charles Blake in the mid-18th century. He brewed a concoction called Ram Jam that he sold to passing travellers and the sign advertising this eventually gave the place its new name. How easily such places gain their odd names!

We are really motoring now, the road is straight as a die thanks to the Romans, although undulating. However there is a small conundrum to discuss.

The next junction, a couple of miles further on, is for South Witham. The side road goes under the A1 and is reached via a couple of small slip-roads. Go down and have a

The Ram Jam Inn was named after a brew served by the landlord. It is still in operation. This picture shows the southbound carriageway being built, proving without doubt that here at least the northbound carriageway was the Great North Road.

An interesting shot taken under the A1 at South Witham which shows two completely different styles of bridge: the arch and a concrete one built much later to support the second carriageway. Incidentally, this is another location where the road underneath has utilised an old railway line as the arch bridge once spanned a railway line, not a road.

look. The southbound carriageway is on a triple-arch stone bridge while the northbound is on a much more recent concrete affair. It should be noted that this is another place where a railway cutting has been utilised for a road. The original side roads met the Great North Road a couple of hundred yards south of the present bridges, in fact where the slip-roads are. A railway line passed under the stone bridge. When the A1 was dualled, the road underneath was straightened out and laid where the railway was, although as usual the cut-off parts still exist as tracks and the second concrete bridge was built.

Now this shows clearly that at this point our old road ran on the line of what is now the southbound carriageway, while a photo taken at the Ram Jam Inn, only a couple of miles south of here, clearly shows it being on the line of the northbound lane. Aerial photographs of this area in fact show up some curious crossover lanes between the two sides which could be relics of old roadworks, or could be orphaned stretches of Great North Road. My guess is that curves in the old road were simply ironed out and whichever carriageway was on a better alignment got that bit of the old road.

Just north of the junction is another old inn. The Fox, marked on the 1890 map, still stands right by the road on our right. Barely a mile further on stands Black Bull farm, also next to the southbound side, which was another old inn.

Barely half a mile on from the Black Bull there is an unmarked left turn just past the interestingly-named Honey Pot Lane on the right. You need to know where it is as it's not signposted at all with the exception of a weight limit sign. In 1890 the road that by now is heading pretty much due north, veered away from the course of Ermine Street and down this lane. Parts of Ermine Street still appear to exist at this point, but not as a continuous road. Our Great North Road follows this lane into the village of Colsterworth.

The present dual carriageway follows the old course of Ermine Street here and goes straight on to Colsterworth roundabout where it also veers off slightly to the west. On the southbound side, not far from the roundabout, there is an ox-bow lay-by which indicates that something was there before and was straightened out and an old map shows up a fragment

Also at South Witham is the Fox standing isolated at the side of the road. This has been a truckstop for many a year and is still just about open.

of Ermine Street here. Strange how sometimes the earlier road is ignored for a new route although in this case it has been reborn. And in fact reborn quite early on. Colsterworth was first bypassed in the 1930s, the bypass then being dualled with the rest of the road.

Back to our Great North Road. Following the left turn-off the A1, we come to Colsterworth village whose only real claim to fame is that Isaac Newton was born in a nearby manor house. Moving on, we soon arrive back at the dual carriageway a mile north of Colsterworth roundabout. This is another one which has been removed and turned into a GSJ in 2009.

From where the lane rejoins our modern road for the next three miles, the Great North Road manages to avoid every settlement except Great Ponton where there is the obligatory coaching inn called the Blue Horse. This is another inn that has moved. Although it appears to have old style architecture it was built when the road was dualled as the original inn lay right on the crossroads, about where the eastern end of the footbridge now stands. At Little Ponton, we leave the dual carriageway again.

Looking north at the crossroads in Colsterworth — once the Great North Road.

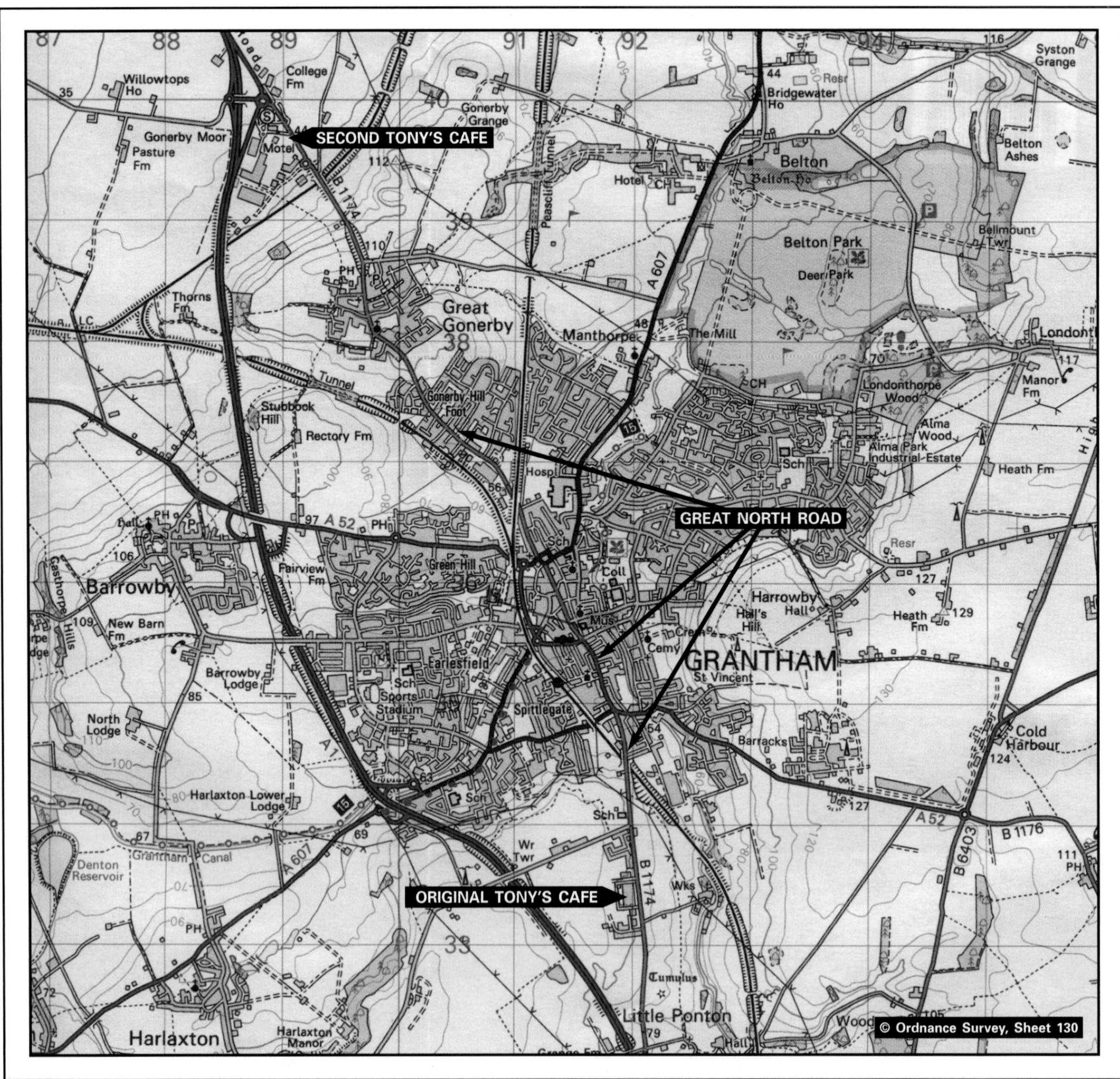
SECOND TONY'S CAFE
GREAT NORTH ROAD
ORIGINAL TONY'S CAFE
© Ordnance Survey, Sheet 130
Willowtops Ho
College Fm
Gonerby Moor
Pasture Fm
Motel
Gonerby Grange
Peascliffe Tunnel
Bridgewater Ho
Syston Grange
Belton
Belton Ho
Hotel
Belton Ashes
Belton Park
Deer Park
Bellmount Twr
Great Gonerby
Thorns Fm
Manthorpe
The Mill
Londonthorpe Wood
Manor Fm
Gonerby Hill Foot
Stubbock Hill
Rectory Fm
Alma Wood
Alma Park Industrial Estate
Heath Fm
Hospl
Tunnel
Green Hill
Fairview Fm
Barrowby
New Barn Fm
Coll
Mus
Harrowby Hall
Hall's Hill
Heath Fm
Cemy
GRANTHAM
St Vincent
Earlesfield
Barrowby Lodge
Sports Stadium
Spittlegate
North Lodge
Barracks
Cold Harbour
Harlaxton Lower Lodge
Grantham Canal
Denton Reservoir
Wr Twr
Wks
Cumulus
Little Ponton
Harlaxton
Harlaxton Manor
Wood
A 52
A 607
B 1174
B 6403
B 1176
A 1

Little Ponton to Markham Moor

If we take the off-slip for the B1174 signposted Grantham and cross over the current dual carriageway, at the point where the road becomes two-way, we are back on the Great North Road. The actual road is the southbound slip-road. There is in fact a building on that short stretch that could have been another coaching inn. It is shown on earlier maps, although does not have a name.

From here, all the way through Grantham and back to the dual carriageway, is another stretch of unchanged Great North Road. This part as far as the railway bridge, now called Spitalgate Level, is pretty much as it was in 1890 with the exception of the industry on the left and a decent surface. In fact after the railway bridge where it becomes South Parade, the 1890 map shows only some terraces on the right which may be the ones that are still there now.

At the north end of South Parade, we join up with the A52 coming in from the east and stay with it until it veers off to the west to avoid the town centre. We go straight through the middle, following St Peters Hill, High Street, Watergate, North Street and North Parade.

Once we go under the railway bridge on Gonerby Road, we are well on our way out of town. The 1890 map shows an inn, a brickworks and a few houses at the bottom of Gonerby Hill which we are about to climb, but a huge estate has now sprung up there, infilling the area between the road and the railway line. Of the Lord Nelson Inn there is no sign.

At the top of the hill, we pass through the village of Great Gonerby which as far as our road is concerned hasn't changed much apart from being more built up on the Grantham side. Once through the village we start dropping down again, quite steeply although it's called Newark Hill now. In earlier times, before a cutting eased the incline somewhat, Gonerby (or Gunnerby) Hill was a well-known trouble spot for coaches. Even in later years, after the cutting was made, lorries heading south struggled up the hill causing other vehicles to perform some dodgy overtaking manoeuvres which even gets a mention in *Picture Post*:

'And to watch the streams of traffic from the high banks of the cutting — where one can see both ways, even though the road users can't — is as hair-raising a spectacle as any that you can pay money to see.'

The High Street in Grantham looking north in 1939 *(top)* and 2012 *(above)*. This was a narrow section, almost like Stamford, which caused huge traffic jams before the bypass was completed in 1960.

Left: **This is another (and sadly the last) still from the 1939 footage. We are looking down Newark Hill having just left the village of Great Gonerby.** *Right:* **The view today is almost identical except for undergowth which in fact is a recurring theme.**

Some of my comparisons are spoilt by undergrowth and foliage which is far more extensive in this day and age. Hedgerows are also no longer trimmed which restricts the line of sight in some cases.

After passing through the village we go down the hill and pass the site of another transport cafe where the current services are now. This was called Tony's'. Apparently Tony had a cafe south of Grantham on the Great North Road at the top of the hill and, when the dual carriageway was built, he moved to the site now occupied by the services. I've also heard the name 'Little Green Hut' in connection with this cafe. Chris Webb remembers the old A1:

'Going through Stamford, Grantham and Newark, Tony's cafe was south of Grantham. And at Newark the old northbound A1 was three lanes just after the level crossing. The lane in the middle was every man for himself.'

This three-lane configuration was known to every motorist and commercial driver as the 'suicide lane' and for good reason. They are almost extinct in Britain now but then they provided an unrestricted overtaking lane for both directions. So vehicles hurtled towards each other in the centre lane, hoping they could overtake and pull over to their side in time before the inevitable head-on crash!

We catch up with the dual carriageway again at Gonerby Moor roundabout, another one that was ironed out in 2009. Although the configuration is pretty much the same, the dual carriageway simply passes by a hundred yards away, cutting a corner off, and we now have to join it via a bridge and slip-road rather than at the roundabout itself.

This photo is taken almost directly over the road from the last picture but looking south, back up the hill. The wagon on the right coming down the hill is a Bedford OL. The wall is still there today but covered in ivy.

Gonerby Moor. This Scania is actually southbound on the dualled A1 sometime around 1980 judging by the cars. It is negotiating the roundabout which was bypassed in 2009. Tony Fawcett pictured the roundabout for me today — the service station is Gonerby Moor services and it stands on the site of the second Tony's café.

Looking back up the same hill in 2012. Very little has changed and although my photograph shows an empty road, in fact it is still very busy here as I had to wait quite some time to get a car-free comparison.

Travelling north we are briefly back on the original track except for a small ox-bow stretch on the right where the lane goes off to Marston. This lane is called Toll Bar Lane recalling the presence of another toll-gate. A mile further on past two more ox-bow lay-bys, we have to divert again.

Here the old road took quite a sharp turn to the right just past the lane on the left for Allington. This has now been altered and we can go and look at another quite lengthy stretch of original road. However to do so, we have to travel a little further to get off the dual carriageway at a GSJ and cross over to a roundabout and turn back on ourselves to get into Foston village. Follow the road through the village and we find ourselves approaching the junction just mentioned where we could rejoin the southbound A1 should we want to. So re-orientating ourselves, we turn round again and we are now entering the village as we would have done 90 years ago via Main Street. In the village centre, the road makes a curve to the left and becomes Newark Hill indicating the road to Newark.

As you go down Newark Hill out of the village, you will note that it is nothing more than a lane. This would have been difficult for two-way traffic at the best of times, and in fact Foston is another place that was bypassed early on — sometime in the 1920s according to the village website. Possibly at the same time as Colsterworth. So what you are looking at is a unique piece of the original road as it would have looked in 1921, barely more than a track.

North of Gonerby Moor there are two villages which were once on the Great North road. The first is Foston.

As we follow it we come back to where we joined the road off the dual carriageway but this time, when we come to the roundabout, we head alongside the dual carriageway into Long Bennington. Curiously, the road here is wide enough to have been our Great North Road into the 1950s and indeed it was until the bypass was built as part of the dual carriageway in the mid-1960s.

Long Bennington was a long narrow village spread along a wide road and is not much different today although built up somewhat further away from the road. Today we pass through easily and half a mile further on the road joins the southbound carriageway of the A1. To carry on our northbound journey we have to go back into the village and take a side road to return us to the northbound lane.

After rejoining the dual carriageway, two miles further on there is a right turn signposted Claypole. We need to turn right here across the southbound carriageway. As we do so and join the side road, the B6326, look to your right at the side road merging seamlessly with the southbound carriageway. Again this is where the old and new roads diverge. The old road runs into Balderton and remains as it was with the exception of the spot where it crosses the current A1 as its path has been obliterated by the junction. After negotiating the two roundabouts that make up this junction we are back on track on London Road, Balderton.

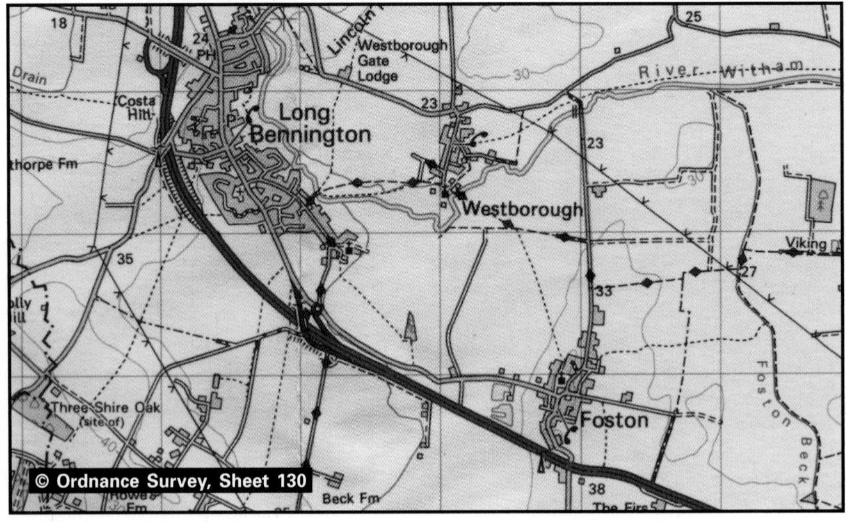

Apparently London Road is also a bypass having been built in 1767 as a turnpike bypassing the village centre. An 1884 map shows that Balderton was far smaller then, being clustered around the present Main Street. The same map indicates that the original road into the village probably ran down the current Sibcy Lane and Pinfold Lane.

Balderton has grown out of all recognition since 1900 the old and new parts of the village having grown together. In fact you can go all the way into Newark without leaving a built-up area but before we do, we should make mention of a very sad sight on the A1. If we had remained on the main road instead of going into Balderton we would very quickly have noticed the remains of an aircraft on the right-hand side. It is an English Electric

There is no trace of the garage today.

Lightning XN728 which was bought by a scrap dealer and placed in his yard next to the A1 sometime in the early 1980s. It's been there ever since, left to the ravages of the weather and graffiti vandals and it looks terrible — such a sad end to such a wonderful aircraft. It was finally destroyed on September 9, 2011.

The second is Balderton — this was the Great North Road which here is also known as London Road.

This junction was called Turks Head corner after a pub which once stood on the right.

However we carry on into Newark. In 1884 there was hardly a building to be seen between the present Halton Lane in Balderton and the fork with Baldertongate in Newark. In the past, if we were to go down Baldertongate, we would have headed straight as a die into the large market square in the centre of the town where stage-coaches would find inns and passengers refreshment. They would then have left by either Kirkgate or Stedman Street to head for the Trent Bridge below the castle.

Our Great North Road however could never have managed the tight lanes around the market square and instead follows the route of the present B6326 London Road which multiplexes with the B6166 where Portland Street joins and goes into Lombard Street. The junction of London Road, Portland Street and Lombard Street is known as Beaumond Cross after an ancient market cross that stood there for hundreds of years. In the late 20th century it was moved to a nearby park where it still stands.

Portland Street is the continuation of the A46 from Leicester into town and therefore the original Fosseway, the Roman road upon which the A46 is almost entirely built between Leicester and Lincoln. Although the Fosseway has also diverted slightly coming in to Newark, the original route ran along Mill Gate. Lombard Street turns sharp right where Mill Gate joins us and it becomes Castle Gate, for obvious reasons as Newark castle stands here on our left. It is a picturesque ruin as it was partly demolished by Parliamentarians after the English Civil War. We turn left at the castle down Beastmarket Hill, once again the B6326, letting the Fosseway head off down Bar Gate to Lincoln.

At the bottom of the hill stands Trent Bridge although this branch of the river is called the Devon. Newark seems to have had the same reputation on the Great North Road as Stamford as a bad bottleneck with the locals getting more and more fed up with wagons being driven through by drivers who would far rather not be stuck there at all. Some things don't change. And then, when you finally escaped and went over the bridge out of town, there was one more obstacle: a level crossing! It was one of a few to cross the Great North Road but can you imagine a level crossing that stopped traffic on the M1 once an hour or so?

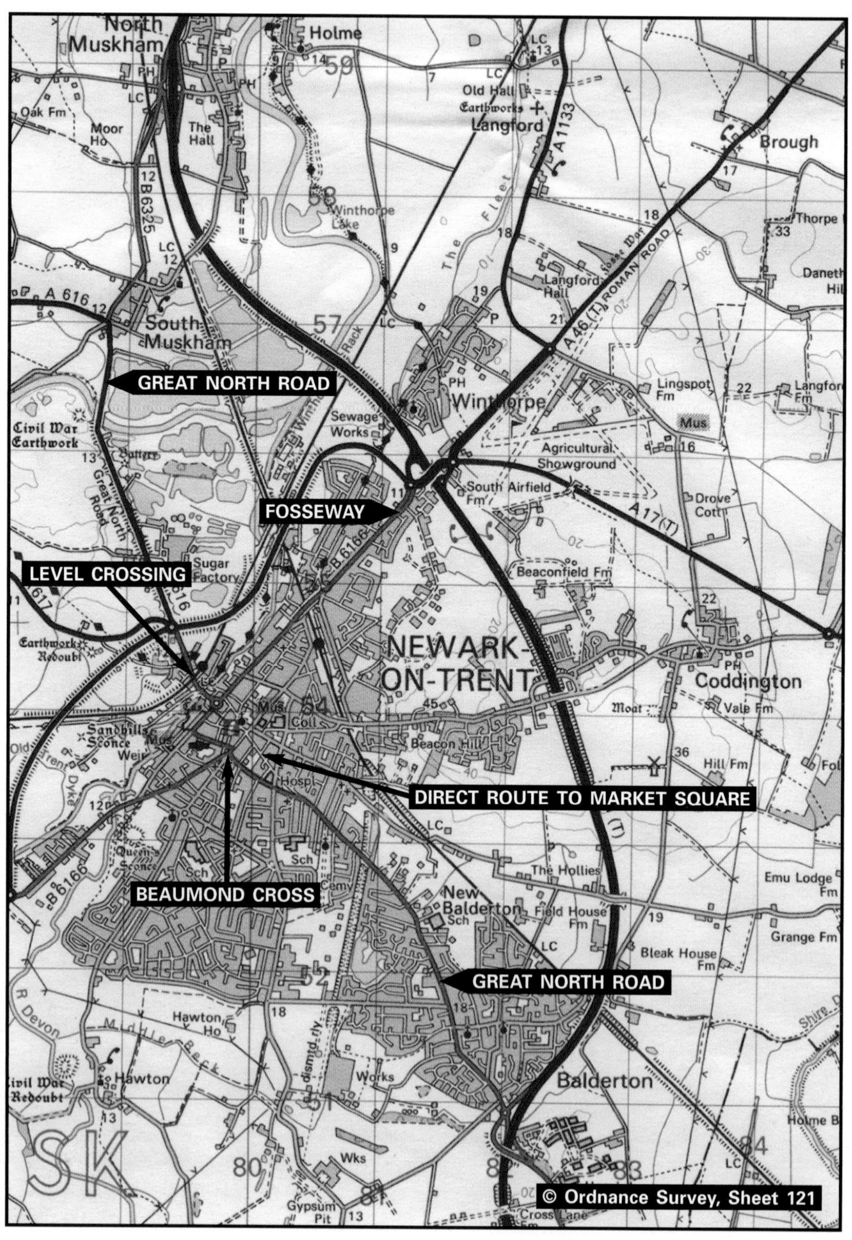

Lombard Street looking back south to Beaumont Cross.

The Royal Oak has stood on Castlegate for at least 300 years.

The Great North Road crosses the river via this bridge.

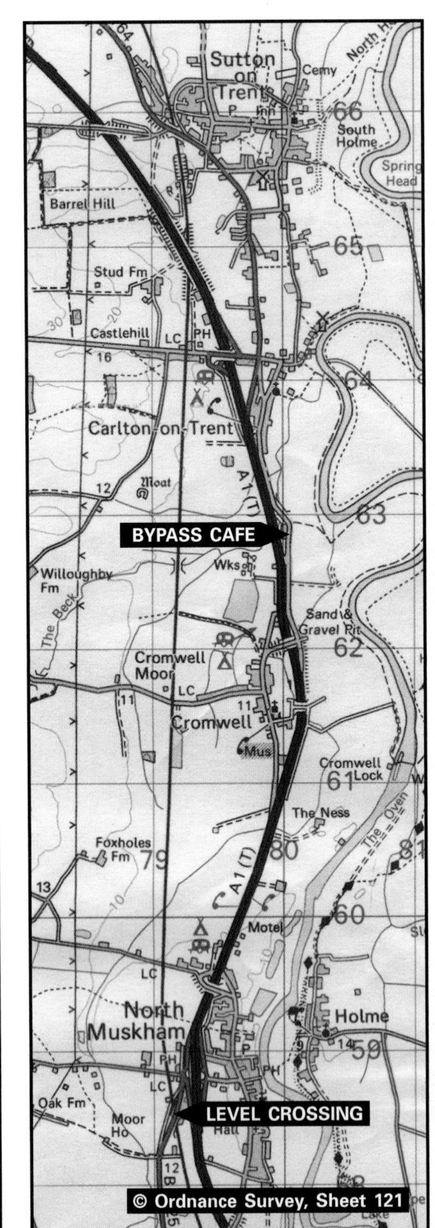

This is the site of another of the infamous level crossings which stood in the way of Great North Road traffic and caused huge tail backs. It lay a couple of miles north of Newark at North Muskham. The old road ran off to the left, now marked as a dead end as the new bridge has cut the corner slightly.

Free at last, we are actually on a flood plain between two arms of the River Trent which in earlier days created all sorts of trouble for travellers until in 1766 John Smeaton was called in to do something about the problem. He carried the road over the plain on a series of brick arches which can still be seen on this stretch.

We leave Newark behind crossing over the recent A46 northern bypass and heading up past the sugar factory towards South Muskham. We cross the Trent again just before the village which we skirt and here there was another level crossing just before North Muskham where we rejoin the dual carriageway.

The junction with the A1 was once a simple crossroads marked by the Lord Nelson inn which still stands although now an Indian restaurant. There is a short dead end stretch of the old road down on our left as we go up the slip-road to the dual carriageway and another on our right on the edge of North Muskham where the old road was cut by the junction.

The next eight or ten miles is quite interesting as the modern A1 simply straightened out the route leaving nearly all of our old road intact on one side or the other. We motor on up the A1 for only a short distance before coming straight off again at the next junction for Cromwell. At the far end of the village we are cut off by the dual carriageway again, but if we turn right just before that we can cross over the top and turning left head up alongside the A1.

For some reason there are two or three off-slips from the southbound A1 in quick succession where really none is necessary as the road from Carlton serves this area. It is not known why this should be but it is reminiscent of the area around the A1(M) in the Welwyn/Hatfield area where sections of new road were finished at different times leaving slip-roads to the then-existing old road still in place. So you can probably imagine that in each case the new dual carriageway once ended at that point with an access road to the Great North Road.

On this stretch stands the Bypass Cafe, a prefab style building that has certainly been there as long as I can remember. Some say that it had something to do with prisoners of war and an old concrete air raid shelter next to it could bear this out.

Although the village of Cromwell is reputed to have been the home of Oliver Cromwell, it is more reliably linked to Lord Cromwell, the Lord Treasurer of Henry VI. His residence, Cromwell House, is said to have been located on the site of the present rectory of St Giles. These days, Cromwell's claim to fame is the Bypass Transport Cafe although the original building *(below)* is due to be demolished and moved to a Portakabin, the corner of which can just be seen at the rear of the red lorry.

Carrying on north from here we arrive at Carlton-on-Trent where we take the left fork in the road for the neighbouring village of Sutton-on-Trent where the road becomes the B1164. From here to Tuxford we are in a small time warp. This stretch hasn't changed since the nearby A1 was built and is one of the most perfectly preserved stretches of 1950s motoring on this part of the Great North Road. Many a time I have enjoyed a clear run down here, looking across the fields at the transport on the A1 queuing up for some blockage or other.

In the village of Sutton we come to a cross-roads and then the road goes over a railway bridge. However look again at the cross-roads. There is a small right fork that runs almost alongside the bridge approach. It is small and easy to miss but if you take it you will note that it's called the Old Great North Road. This is another small section that included yet another level crossing which was replaced by the bridge.

For the next five miles we can enjoy the Great North Road until we arrive at Tuxford. Some accounts say that here one needed to turn left and then right to stay on the old road.

This is an interesting pair of illustrations as both of the cottages are still there but note how the road seems to be curving in the opposite direction and rising. This is because there was another level crossing here that had to be bridged. The road ran down to the crossing by the Nags Head pub. You can see on the comparison — the small lane going down the side of the bridge ramp — that is the old road.

Another garage which has disappeared since Sutton-on-Trent was bypassed was this one run by the Smith family.

In fact this is the case today as the Great North Road has been cut in two by the dual carriageway, However the 1887 map only shows the route straight in to Tuxford and no sign at all of a road on the current line of the B1164. This would imply that this is a later construction when the dual carriageway was built to allow access to Tuxford from the Sutton area.

If we stop at the point where the B1164 arrives back alongside the dual carriageway we left behind at Cromwell, you can look over and see the continuation of the road on the other side. In fact nowadays it is the A1 northbound off-slip into Tuxford, and you need to be aware that the slip-road very quickly becomes a two-way suburban street. We, however, have to continue alongside the dual carriageway for half a mile and turn left onto Lincoln Road and under the dual carriageway into Tuxford market place where we bear right. Our slip-road from the A1 joins us on the left and once again we are back on track. Tuxford is a small place and we quickly head north out of town on our Great North Road still numbered the B1164.

As we head up the hill, there is a windmill on the right-hand side. This is one of three that stood in this area giving the hill its name of Mill Mount. There is a lay-by on either side along the ridge and it is a favourite place of mine to park up for the night in my lorry.

June Smith, the girl in the doorway, showed me where the garage once stood when I took this comparison in 2007.

Crossing over the hill between East and West Markham but not touching either, we drop back down to the village of Sibthorpe. Here things start to get more interesting again, As you come into the tiny village, there is a sharp left-hand bend. Right on the apex there is a small lane straight in front which is gated. Once upon a time our road went straight through this gate and carried on in a straight line to reach the Markham Moor Inn where it was joined by the road from Lincoln (currently the A57). However when the A1 was upgraded, a large roundabout was put in here and the immediate area much changed. There was also another transport cafe here called Morleys but alas long gone. It lay where the petrol garage is on the northbound side, not where the current truckstop stands.

Markham Moor to Red House

Coming from Tuxford, we drop down to what is now Markham Moor, but on our right before we get there we reach this gate. Our road once went through here — note the roundabout ahead.

If you go and stand outside the Markham Moor Hotel which is a couple of hundred yards to the north east of the present Markham Moor dual carriageway junction, you are standing right on the spot where the Great North Road and the road from Lincoln — the A57 — originally merged. At each end of this short stretch, around a hundred yards long, was a fork in the road. We are at the southern end looking south and the left fork to Lincoln lay behind the motorcycle dealership that currently stands there. The right fork ran in an almost straight line across the current junction to join up with the spur in Sibthorpe mentioned at the end of the last chapter. This junction is another one upgraded in 2009 of which most traces have disappeared.

So now we look north again. You will notice a small section of road that runs parallel to the main road between the hotel and a cottage. This is the original carriageway and the northern fork was right outside the cottage. And here is where things start to get interesting as the left fork is named the Old North Road while the right fork is the Great North Road. So what is going on here?

In fact the left fork is the original road which ran from here via West Drayton across open countryside in a fairly direct line to Barnby Moor. It was apparently one of the only stretches of the whole road not turnpiked by the mid-18th century. Best of all, most of this can still be driven and it gives a great insight as to what the road must have looked like before modern times, and one small stretch remains virtually unchanged since 1750.

At the other side of the roundabout stands the Markham Moor Hotel. If we could see back across the junction, we would almost be looking straight at the gate in the previous photo.

Unfortunately the building of Gamston airfield has removed a length of the road so, apart from the stretch between Markham Moor and Twyford Bridge, we need to use the current dual carriageway to bypass the airfield. Then we turn right off it down Jockey Lane. About a quarter mile down this road is a farm called Jockey House on an old crossroads, the right turn of which would once have taken us back across the airfield to Twyford Bridge and Markham Moor, but the left turn is the continuation of the Old North Road from Markham and can be driven all the way to Barnby Moor. With one small exception. When we reach the B6420, the tarmac road would have us perform a dog-leg, turning right to come to the A620 out of Retford, and then turning left on the A620 coming back to our line and then turning right again down the side of Ranby Prison. However, where we come onto the B6420, there is a green lane which cuts out this dog-leg and traces the original route. It's rough and badly rutted, but it is driveable and it is probably the sort of road surface an 18th century traveller would have had to put up with. Its only about 300 yards long and comes out on the A620 which you simply cross over down the side of the prison. I suspect this is as close to an old coach road as you will get.

So how come this stretch is not our Great North Road? Well, you will notice that this route skirts the side of Retford, an old market town, without going into the town. This of course meant that Retford was not getting any of the commercial advantages of being a coaching stop. So the local corporation applied via their Member of Parliament to have the turnpike designated as the road from Markham Moor to Barnby Moor via Retford. This was eventually passed in 1766 and the new road became our Great North Road; thus the old one faded into obscurity. To follow it we need to go back to Markham Moor.

Standing again outside the Markham Moor Hotel, now look at the right fork. Currently signposted as the A638, this now becomes the route for our journey. We travel north leaving the dual carriageway behind and we will not meet up with it again for over 20 miles.

It should be noted that when the Great North Road was dualled at this point, it was not the A1 but the A638. This is because the route didn't go through any towns requiring bypasses — in effect the A1 and A638 swapped numbers as far as the Red House junction.

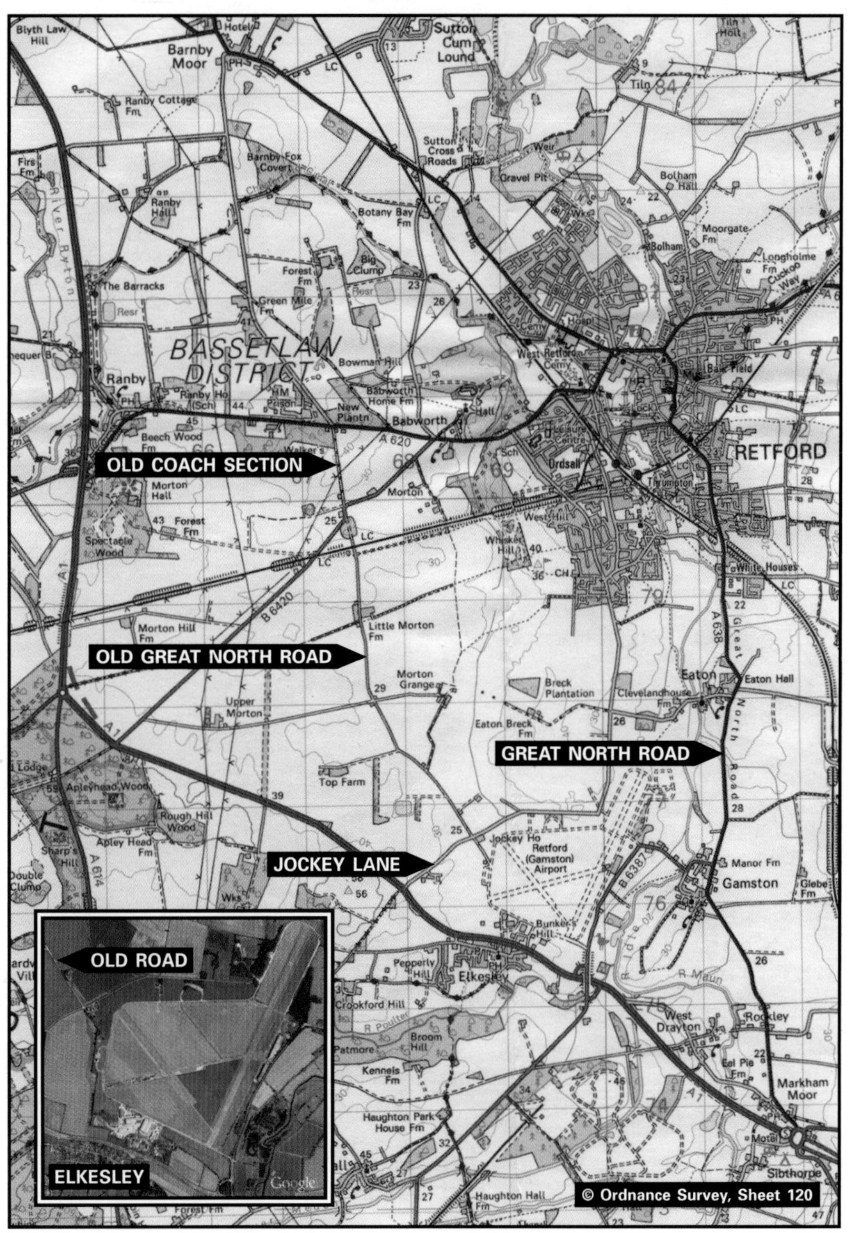

© Ordnance Survey, Sheet 120

In 1960, work was being finalised on the Retford bypass at Elkesley although when David Gregg took this photo there was a little bovine congestion to deal with on the southbound lane! Nominally, this is also the eastbound A57.

West of Retford town this short section of the original Old Great North Road serves as a flashback to earlier times. The contrast could not be greater.

Travelling north is similar to the journey from Cromwell to Tuxford (of which it is of course a continuation); a nice big wide road without too much traffic. We skirt the villages of Gamston and Eaton before arriving at the outskirts of Retford. Nowadays Retford is built up but at the turn of the 20th century there was very little habitation until you arrived at Bracken Lane. And even then it was mostly smallholdings and the building that is now the Elms Hotel. A public house, the Nags Head, also once stood opposite what is now Oaklands Lane.

Our road, at this point, not surprisingly called London Road, heads straight into the centre and, becoming Carolgate, traverses the town centre from south to north, becoming the market square at its northern end. North of the square at the fork our road heads off north-west as Bridgegate. At the junction with Hospital Road it becomes once again North Road. As the A638, we hurry on through countryside to Barnby Moor.

It just does not seem possible that this pedestrianised street in Retford between Carolgate and Bridgegate was once the Great North Road! Farrands, the grocers, on the left is now just a distant memory. Emma Caddy kindly took the comparison for me.

We are now approximately 150 miles from London and Ye Olde Bell at Barnby Moor was one of the most popular watering holes on the whole of the Great North Road. The German Baedeker's guide of 1937 gives the price of a room at 6/- (six shillings or 30 pence in todays decimal currency). Breakfast or lunch cost 3/6d (17½p) and dinner was another 6/-. The Royal Automobile Club guide of 1938-39 also gives us the phone number 'Ranskill 16'. The telegraphic address was listed as 'Motoring' and the weekly tariff was five guineas.

During the coaching era, Barnby Moor was an important stop between Doncaster and Newark. There were two large coaching inns here, the White Horse and the Bell both owned by the same man, a George Clark who also owned enough of the surrounding land to keep the many post-horses fed. Both inns still stand and are open for business, a nice change as so many of the old coaching inns are long gone. The small left turn signposted Ranby, just after the White Horse is the other end of our pre-1766 Great North Road.

Now Ye Olde Bell is a 4-star hotel with rooms from £80-£170 per night.

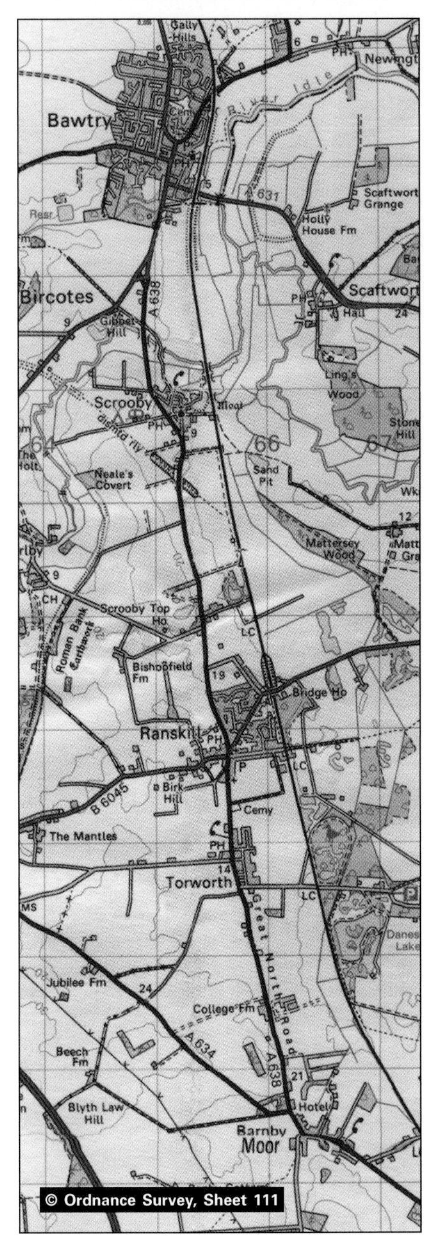

© Ordnance Survey, Sheet 111

We move on up the A638 and for a while it becomes a lonely stretch, skirting the villages of Torworth, Ranskill and Scrooby, before arriving at Bawtry. A farm on the left known as Scrooby Top House was originally a coaching site built by Thomas Fisher to compete with the Clark organisation in Barnby Moor.

This is Ranskill back in the days when the Great North Road ran through the village. Now a bypass of motorway standard for Doncaster has relegated it to the A638. My comparison photograph was taken outside the Blue Bell pub which is large enough to have been a coach stop.

Scrooby has one claim to fame. The one-time Master of the Queen's Post, William Brewster, who lived in Scrooby Manor, was a member of the Separatists, a group who were at odds with the recognised forms of Christian worship in the late 16th century. Eventually obliged to leave the country, Brewster and some of his family left on the Mayflower from Plymouth making him one of the original Pilgrim Fathers to the New World.

Moving on again we enter Bawtry with its wide High Street, unchanged for many a year, but, more importantly, we enter the county of Yorkshire which lays claim to almost a quarter of the entire Great North Road between London and Edinburgh. The first house in Bawtry has the address: 'No.1 Yorkshire'.

Today, Bawtry high street is a triple multiplex. The A614 and the A638 meet just short of town and run through it as one. On top of that, the A631 arrives from the west and shares a couple of hundred yards of the high street just before turning off east for Gainsborough. It was this meeting of the ways that gave Bawtry the opportunity to become (like Retford) a busy post town. In fact the A631/A638 course is built on the old Roman alignment from Lincoln to Doncaster. Although it expanded, the coming of the railways stopped it in its tracks and now the once-fashionable buildings remain as a timestamp of the early 19th century.

Our two roads split up again at the northern end of the high street at a fork, with the A614 heading north-east to Thorne and Goole and the A638 — our Great North Road — heading north. In 1900 there were no houses north of this fork.

High Street, Bawtry — then and now.

This is the Hare and Tortoise pub at Rossington Bridge, the view looking south down the Great North Road. This is believed to be at least part of a coaching inn that once stood on this spot although it was marked as a farm on some older maps.

The road from here to Doncaster was described by Tom Bradley: *'There is probably no finer stretch throughout the length or breadth of England than the nine miles that lie between Bawtry and Doncaster'.*

Apparently the road was wide and smooth and well kept. Nowadays the distance from Bawtry to the outskirts of Doncaster is barely five miles. Just before Doncaster we come to Rossington Bridge where there was a tollgate, marked on an 1854 map as 'Rossington Bridge Chain Bar', and yet another coaching inn, the Rossington Bridge Inn. Most of this site now lies on Rossington Bridge Farm but there is still a pub on the road called the Hare and Tortoise. I believe this to be at least part of the original inn.

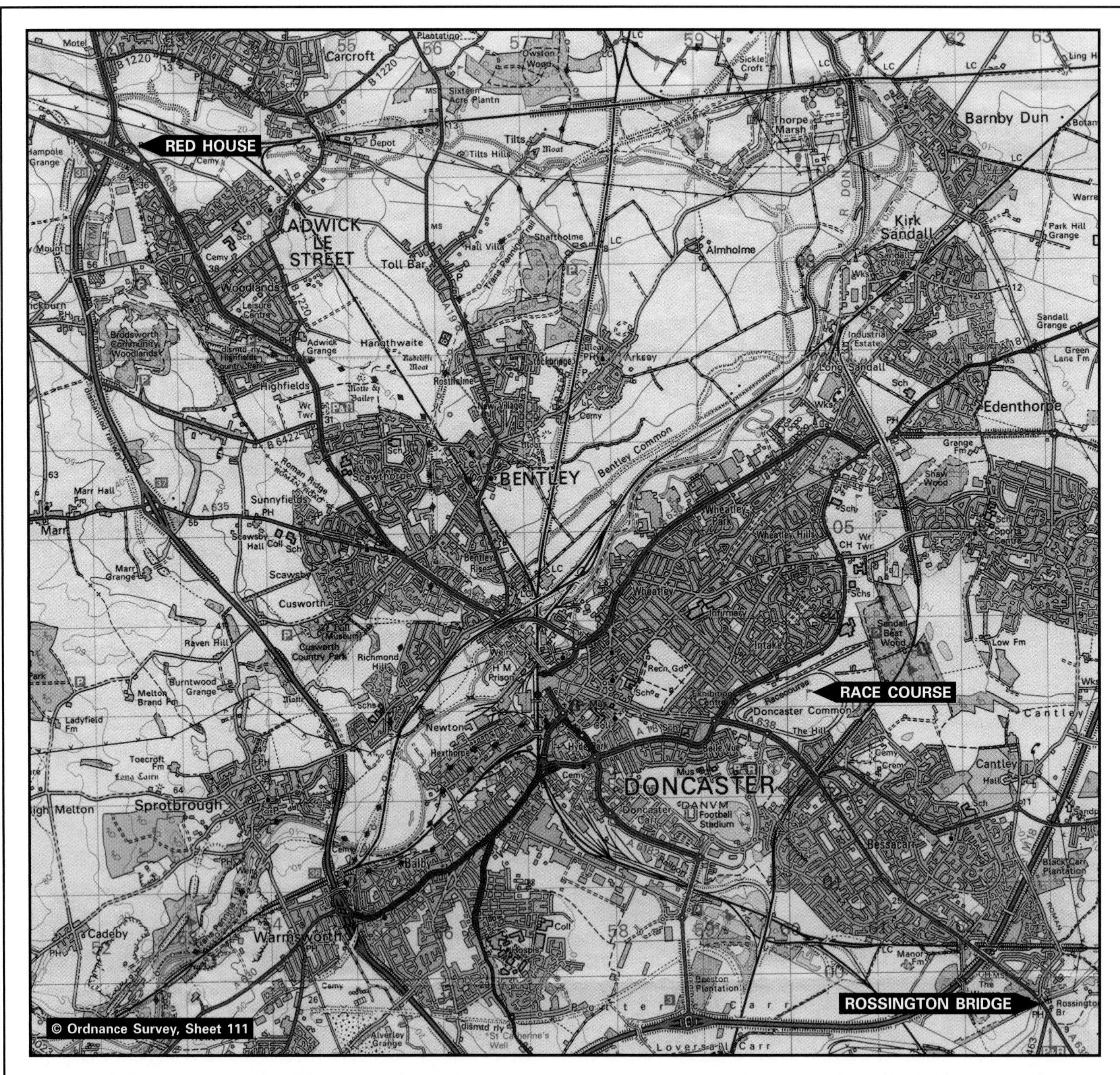
RED HOUSE
RACE COURSE
ROSSINGTON BRIDGE
© Ordnance Survey, Sheet 111
Carcroft
Barnby Dun
Thorpe Marsh
ADWICK LE STREET
Toll Bar
Almholme
Kirk Sandall
Woodlands
Highfields
Arksey
Long Sandall
Edenthorpe
BENTLEY
Bentley Common
Scawthorpe
Sunnyfields
Marr
Scawsby
Cusworth
Wheatley
Intake
Cusworth Country Park
Richmond Hill
H M Prison
Doncaster Common
Cantley
Newton
Hexthorpe
DONCASTER
Sprotbrough
Balby
Bessacarr
Cadeby
Warmsworth

This is South Parade, the northbound continuation of Bawtry Road which runs into Doncaster. The monument is Hall Cross, which was built by Doncaster Corporation in 1793 to replace an earlier cross which once stood on the site.

built and serviced. For a while the North Road took a back seat.

Hall Gate becomes the High Street and then we leave to the north on Frenchgate. There used to be a large level crossing here at the southern end of both the railway bridge and the road bridge over the southern branch of the river but this was clearly not ideal so a new road bridge was built in around 1910 which spanned both the river and the railway. The road then ran up what is now Marshgate and across the second branch of the river via Mill Bridge. The road, at this point built on a causeway because the area was a flood plain, then forked, about where the railway crosses the roundabout that exists there today.

This was a major parting of the ways. In earlier coaching times, much of the traffic from the south didn't go much further than York so it was at this point in Doncaster that the route began. It ran up the present day A19 via Selby to York and then on to Thirsk where it then took the A168 to Northallerton and A167 to Darlington. We, however, take the left fork and head out on the current A638 Great North Road.

Although the old fork no longer exists — it is a large roundabout today — the choice of A638 or A19 is still available. However

Crossing the bridge and heading onwards we very soon come into a built up area although in Charles Harper's day it was a 'long gentle rise, bordered by coppices of hazels and silver birches, [which] leads past Cantley to Tophall'. However there is no longer any trace of either village as the whole area has been swallowed up by suburbia. I believe Tophall village lay about where the Tesco Express/Esso garage currently stands on Bawtry road. Of Cantley there is no trace although there is a Cantley Bridge north of Tophall where the road crosses a railway. I have to assume that this is Harper's *'bridge over the railway cutting, Doncaster is seen with its great chimney-stalks and puffing locomotives down below, three miles away'*.

Going down the hill we pass Doncaster racecourse on the right and head for the centre of town on Bennetthorpe, South Parade and Hall Gate. Even in 1904 there were few houses south of South Parade but Doncaster was lucky. It was already an important place thanks to the transport of coal via the waterways, once the railways arrived it became a great terminus and then a centre where much of the rolling stock and locomotives were

Amazingly quieter than in former days as the through traffic has now been diverted around the much-changed road system in the town.

Doncaster High Street. Like many other city centre shopping areas in Britain, part has now been pedestrianised.

while the A19 is still a single carriageway road, the A638 is dualled all the way out of Doncaster clearly denoting which is the more important road. Unfortunately this is negated by the fact that a large retail park has been built just north of this junction and its traffic light controlled access roads make a mockery of free-flowing through traffic. It is probably no faster through there today than it was a hundred years ago!

We carry on along York Road. Most of Doncaster lies on the right bank of the Don, but by the 1950s it was getting very built up on the northern side too, and now it is like that all the way from the river to Adwick-le-Street. The suffix is an indication of a Roman road and indeed there is one running to the west of us in a similar direction, believed to be an alternative route between Lincoln and York avoiding crossing the Humber. It is known as Roman Ridge and as such stays near us for quite a long way although not always directly on our route. Interestingly, the original village of Adwick is to the east of the Great North Road and not actually on the Roman alignment.

This was the bridge which was built to avoid the dreadful level crossing that once blocked one end of the original river bridge.

Looking south into pedestrianised French Gate which is the north end of the High Street.

This is the junction of High Street and Frenchgate looking south. Behind me is the shopping centre which unfortunately does not have any upper windows so I was not able to take an exact comparison. It's a lot quieter, but only because this was a Sunday afternoon! Back in 1955, 24,000 vehicles poured through this street every 24 hours. Policemen had to work continuously to keep the traffic from coming to a standstill and race meetings and football crowds added to the confusion. Recalling the jams of former days, one old-time lorry driver told me that 'a long time ago there was a roundabout at Dishforth where one turned right on the A168 for Thirsk and, if you can recall going through Grantham and Stamford, then you will have gone through Newark as well. At the speed Pickfords went through, cluttering the place up, you could have walked through faster'!

This is another engraving from the coaching era. It shows the Red House Inn named for its red brick. It is still there although just a farmhouse now. The road here is actually part of the large Red House motorway junction which provides the southbound off-slip from the A1. It is rather appropriate that it has been named after the inn.

One of David Gregg's shots from the 1960s. As the Great North Road left Doncaster it was just a normal road and you can see the chimneys of the Red House above the hedge. However, the sign indicates that times are about to change. David comments that he likes to think that the person responsible for the wording had heard the song by Duane Eddy: *Forty Miles of Bad Road*. Although this stretch of road is still in existence, you can no longer head north this way.

Eventually we leave the built up area and find ourselves at a motorway junction. This is where the dual carriageway catches up with us again after we last saw it at Markham Moor although here it has been upgraded to a motorway. The Doncaster bypass was one of the stretches that was built to motorway standard back in the 1960s.

The dual carriageway coming up from Markham Moor runs into the Doncaster bypass near Blyth where for many years there was a roundabout. This roundabout was also removed in the 2009 upgrades but we can't leave here without mentioning the Blue Star or Hilltop transport cafe. Coming from the south it lay on the left-hand side but a concrete hardstanding over the safety barrier was all that remained after it was demolished in the 1970s. This part was a slip-road for northbound traffic as the main building was on the embankment above. Southbound traffic had to leave at the roundabout and use the front entrance on Blythe road.

The other end of the Doncaster bypass ends at the junction we have just arrived at called Red House. It was so named after an old coaching inn, built of red brick, which stood on the left side of the road as you came out of Doncaster. Right outside the Red House, the road forked with the right fork heading north as the Great North Road and the left-hand turning heading to Wakefield. Parts of the old road still exists as slip-roads of the motorway junction, but to follow its course past the Red House, you would have to turn round on the A1 and go south, leaving it at this junction. As you then proceed up the slip-road, the original Great North Road lies behind the hedge on your left. However, we join it right outside the old inn as if we'd come from Wakefield in olden times.

This is actually the original carriageway for the northbound Great North Road. If you start at the point of David's photo on the previous page and head toward the inn, you pass the Red House and would have curved north around the bend here. The original course ran slightly inside the curve of the current sliproad, rejoining it right opposite the Red House. I took this photograph directly across from the Red House looking in a north-westerly direction.

Red House to Boroughbridge

The next section is particularly interesting to me. Most of it I have known all my life as it constituted my many journeys between the Midlands and Yorkshire. Also it has been extensively upgraded mostly to motorway status in 2006-09 so I was able to watch it and note what happened to all the old parts of the road. Junctions are changed, roads are diverted or even destroyed and landscaped.

From Red House we set out north with the old road under the southbound carriageway. Not far north of the Red House junction is a Texaco garage with a Little Chef restaurant behind it. This used to be the Haven Truckstop at one time. We have a fairly straight course for the first couple of miles but then on the right there is what appears to be a large lay-by, some 500 yards in length, with a building and a couple of cottages at one end. This is all that remains of Robin Hood's Well, a small hamlet on a kink in the road that has now been ironed out. This was a busy coaching stop at one time with the New Inn on the east side and the Robin Hood opposite. The solitary building that remains is the sole remnant of the New Inn, now an office. Everything else is gone.

Top: **The engraving from an old book about coaching in Yorkshire shows the hamlet of Robin Hood's Well with the New Inn on the left and the Robin Hood on the right. Nowadays, this is a large ox-bow layby on the southbound side of the dual carriageway on the right (one can only access it from the south).**

Left: **My comparison was taken looking south with the New Inn still standing on the left now used as an office building.** *Right:* **This stone arch apparently marked the cap to the well although it was moved from its original position when the road was dualled. So now it is just an ornament.**

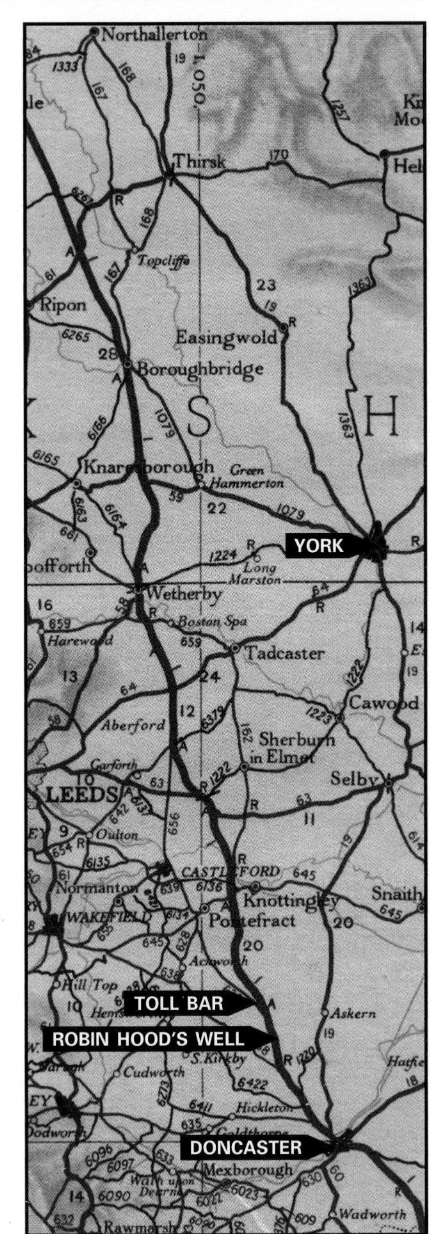

Barnsdale Toll Bar stood where the road to Pontefract and Leeds branched off.

The next place of interest is Barnsdale Bar. As the name suggests, there was a toll-gate a half-mile further south where a couple of roads branched off to the industry of the West Riding (the A639 and A6021). The junction has been altered slightly to accommodate a GSJ, but the site of the toll-bar is still quite clear: it was in the angle created by the A1 and A639.

The junction of the A1 and A639 has been altered to accommodate the dual carriageway but the toll bar stood here on the right. I have used a 1932 Ministry of Transport map here for a change to give a little flavour of the old days.

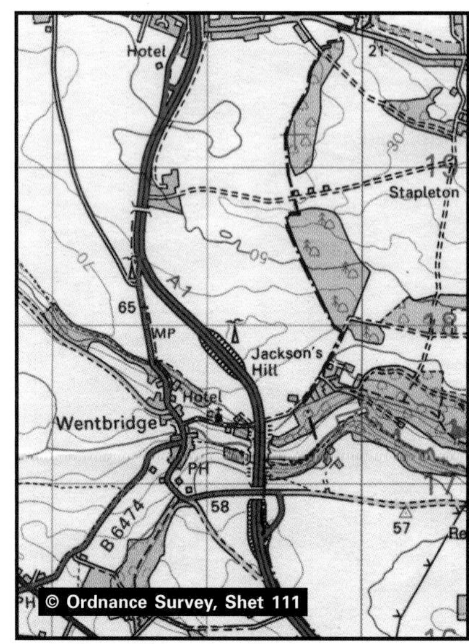

At Wentbridge, this is the view looking down into the village from the Blue Bell pub on the right. The river bridge is just out of sight round the bend at the bottom of the hill.

Moving on with our road mainly under the southbound carriageway, we come to another famously dangerous place to early travellers: Wentbridge. The River Went crosses our path in a steep gorge and the road running north swept down into it. Nowadays there is a modern viaduct but the old road leaves the dual carriageway and drops down a steady slope into the village. Note the Blue Bell pub on the right-hand side. This was a coaching inn and, apparently, also the haunt of many a bad lad as it lost its licence more than once.

We cross the river on an old stone bridge and go round a bend to be faced with a much more daunting climb. And this, believe it or not, is the easier one! It lies in a cutting that was dug around 1830 to ease the journey as the one on the original road was even steeper. You can still walk up it as it remains a public footpath, slightly to the east of the current road. There are tales of coach passengers being made to walk up the hill to give the horses more of a chance, and of other drivers who whipped up the horses on the way down to get speed up for the ascent, giving timid passengers quite a scare.

When the dual carriageway was built in the early 1960s, it was routed over a new viaduct half a mile to the east of the village, rejoined by the road out of Wentbridge.

We move on to Darrington. In between the two you will see on the right-hand side one of the few old-style transport cafes still in operation, the Waywest Cafe, at one time just called the A1 Cafe.

The Great North Road skirted Darrington village fractionally to the east where there was a crossroads which I believe to have been almost directly under the current A1 bridge. What was the northern arm is now the current slip-road used by southbound traffic. The little roundabout at the top is where Back Lane and Harcroft Lane met on the Great North Road.

Above left: **This is the view of the crossroads on the Great North Road at Darrington. On the left we have some cottages and on the right a couple of inns. The view is east with the road running left to right in the engraving, north being at left.** *Above right:* **The crossroads is long gone as well as the buildings. However, I can pretty much pinpoint it as directly under the dual carriageway bridge. The slip road on the right is called 'Old Great North Road' but actually it has moved slightly. Out of sight up the slip road, part of the original carriageway remains as access to some houses. It ran about a road's width further into the photograph and it would have emerged at the crossroads through the stone bridge pier. The northern arm of the crossroads is visible immediately past the bridge where the car stands.** *Below left:* **This is Waywest Cafe — one of the few original transport cafes on the whole road that is still in operation. It used to be called the A1 Cafe and also the Wayside Cafe. It looks to have been extended at both the front and the back since this picture was taken.** *Below right:* **Although it looks derelict in fact the café is still open in the extension just visible at the front.**

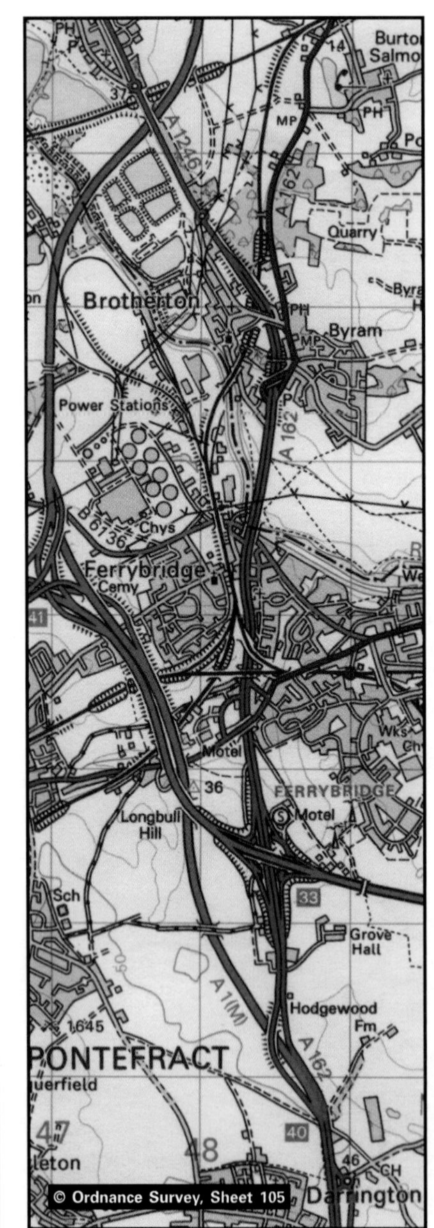

As we approach Ferrybridge the massive cooling towers of the power station dominate the landscape but on November 1, 1965 three of the towers blew down in a storm. The rest were all structurally damaged, caused, it is believed, by a tunneling wind effect.

Ferrybridge is one of those places with a wide open road at its centre. This is part of it looking west toward the bridge. The area is now vastly changed, dominated by the flyovers constructed during the transition from trunk road to motorway, but the three buildings on the right are still there as is the bridge.

The next 12 miles have seen huge changes in recent years. Just past Darrington today the motorist takes a swing to the left onto a motorway to travel parallel with the M62 for a short distance making this section the widest in number of lanes (although separated) in the UK. Then the motorway heads north to the west of Ferrybridge power station and we don't meet it again until we reach Bramham Crossroads.

To continue on our route we need to take the first slip-road where the motorway starts which brings us back onto the 1960's dual carriageway, now designated the A162. This is where we have the classic view of Ferrybridge power station. Almost immediately, we cross

This shot appears to show the dual carriageway being built. However it's a little confusing. I think that the cars are heading north on what eventually became the southbound carriageway. The original Great North Road is in fact the road hard up against the houses on the left which appears to go off into the distance. That finally became the southbound carriageway cutting off the small part in front of the houses which remains for access. The northbound carriageway hasn't been built yet. This is why my comparison appears to be at the wrong angle. In fact it's pretty well spot on.

over a large junction which was the A1/M62 junction until a couple of years ago. The Great North Road was the southbound carriageway that leads back south to Darrington. We pass Ferrybridge services which stand on the site of Ferrybridge Bone Manure Works!

Moving north we cross over the A645 Pontefract road and pass under a railway bridge. As we appear out from under the bridge there has been a small shift. Our Great North Road now lies the other side of the right-hand hedge, running parallel to the dual carriageway. To inspect it we need to go into Ferrybridge to locate this stretch. Although it is a no through road, it still has the name — Doncaster Road — and it is a dead end right up against the railway bridge approach. Our road leaves the path of the dual carriageway directly opposite the current slips for the A645 and runs along the front of three or four red brick houses to point straight at the railway bridge approach from the south side.

Returning to the other side of the bridge, our Great North Road is in a sorry state: another no through road ending with derelict industry. We pass under another railway bridge and come to a fork. It took me a while to decide which was our old road because this area has changed so drastically with the modern dual carriageway being driven clear through the area. However comparison of old and new maps indicates that the left fork is a later addition and we need to take the right-hand one. This leads into the Ferrybridge square where the post houses were. Ferrybridge then, as now, is on the crossroads of busy north-south and east-west routes, and was an important crossing of the River Aire. However it suffered badly when the coaching trade ended and much of its centre was demolished to build the dual carriageway. The ramps for the current bridge actually cross above the square.

The original road took a sharp turn west at the north end of the square to run along the river to where the old stone bridge stands. Built in 1805 on the site of an earlier structure, there is a fine extant toll-house at one end. It is pedestrianised now and well worth a visit although the whole area is dominated by the power station. The bridge crosses the river at an angle before the road turns sharp north again. The modern flyover sits high above it and I wonder how many folk even know it's there.

This is a view of the first power station. How it dominates the old bridge. However when I came to take the comparison, it was nowhere to be seen. Part of the building in the photo does in fact survive, but it is hidden behind the trees. The rest is gone and instead the flyover dominates.

***Left:* This is the old toll house for the bridge. *Right:* This is where the old road dodges away from the dual carriageway. It was blocked off by a railway embankment built later and is now a dead end.**

Incidentally, a chance discovery that an old lane running south from the bridge was called the Old Great North Road made me re-check my facts. This road seems to be the left fork mentioned earlier which does not show in 1907. It does however in 1938 so I have to assume that it was built to take through traffic away from the town centre. Only a couple of stubs remain as the dual carriageway runs straight across it.

'Welshphil' from Trucknet remembers Ferrybridge well:

'From 1947-50 we lived in the schoolhouse at Ferrybridge. The school buildings are still there now as small industrial units on the left-hand side as you drive north after the services slip. The road used the old bridge and there were many accidents involving southbound traffic overshooting the corner.'

A view of the road from the old bridge. You can clearly see that it has been raised above the surrounding mire.

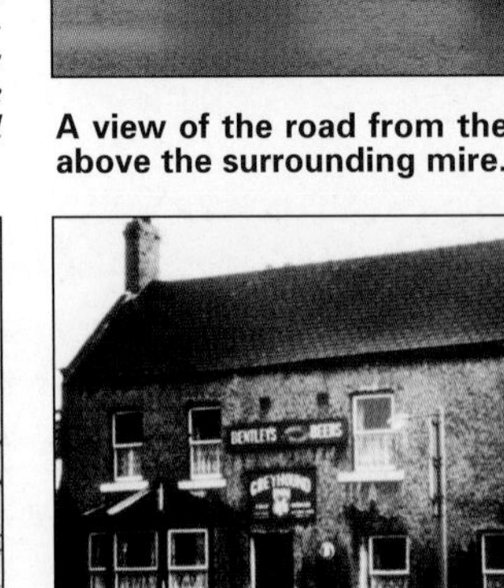

The Greyhound was a large coaching inn at the southern end of the High Street . . . going . . . going . . . gone!

In Brotherton, we have now turned left at the Fox. Its noticeable that the current pub appears to be a different building but I remember the Fox being there as far back as the 1970s so if it has been rebuilt it must have been before then.

The old and new roads recombine on the north bank of the Aire, a marshy area and so the road is built on arches much like the area north of Newark. At the north end of this stretch there is a road leading into Brotherton village, but we carry on a bit further to the junction for Tadcaster and take the slip-road which crosses over the dual carriageway. Where we meet the southbound slip on the other side is the continuation of our road. Nowadays this is the A162 and the old dual carriageway carries on under the designation A1246.

Just up and round the corner our Great North Road turns left across the front of the Fox pub (another Indian restaurant today), skirting Brotherton village as an unclassified road called the Old Great North Road. On our right here, there was yet another well-known transport cafe called Normans although I have reason to believe that this was also known as Ferrybridge Cafe although it was in Brotherton! We then rejoin the dual carriageway a mile north of the village at a roundabout.

This is a little further round the bend visible in the previous photo — the Great North Road has turned north again.

A roundabout on a dual carriageway? It will quickly be noticed that the road is not a dual carriageway anymore but now a fairly quiet S2 road still with the designation A1246. This is what happens when a road is downgraded. We are now on what was the northbound lane of the A1. The southbound carriageway lay to your right where the grassy verge is now but it is almost impossible to work out which side was the original. And then we come to Fairburn.

I remember the A1 at Fairburn well — a dual carriageway that drove straight through the centre of a fairly small village, cutting the place clean in two. As I recall, the two halves of the village were separated by a footbridge. In 1908 all of Fairburn was on the left of the road and the same appears to have been the case in 1953. So when the dual carriageway was built, it was positioned just to the east of the old road, leaving that for local use. The part of the village built on the other side would appear to have been developed later. The removal of that dual carriageway must have been such a relief to the inhabitants. As far as the new A1246 goes, it actually changes sides as it passes north through the village. From the southern roundabout we are on the old northbound side but it changes over and by the time we get to the middle of the village we are on the old southbound carriageway. Our Great North Road however still lurks between the modern road and the village and it leaves through a small children's playground at the north end of the village to rejoin the ex-dual carriageway.

As we continue, the verge on the left of the road is a long mound. This stretches for a mile, except for field gateways, and is the rubble heap from the northbound lane of the dual carriageway. We are on the old southbound carriageway which I also believe to have been the course of the Great North Road. They simply piled everything up and covered it with earth. I have a cat's-eye souvenir I took from that heap — a cat's-eye I probably drove over more than once!

Fairburn was cut clean in two in the 1950s by the building of the dual carriageway although I'm not convinced there was much of the village on one side until later. This photo shows Fairburn today. I am standing looking north on what was the central reservation of the A1. The old northbound carriageway is the new road (A1246) to my left and the southbound is under the grass to my right. However, note that this position changes about half way up where the new road for some reason dodges to the old southbound carriageway and it is the northbound lane that has been grassed over. Our original Great North Road ran just the other side of the trees on the left and is visible in the middle distance where the cars are parked.

Charles Harper writing in 1900 wrote that 'Leaving Doncaster, to the left goes the Ferrybridge, Wetherby, and Boroughbridge route to the North; to the right that by way of Selby and York. Both fall into one again at Northallerton; both claim to be the true Great North Road'. (See map page 111.) However, Charles's impression of Selby was not great: 'From this point of view Selby is distinctly disappointing. The glorious Abbey, now the parish church, is all, and more than, one expects, and the superlatively cobblestoned, Market-place, painful to walk in, is picturesque to look at; but the rest is an effect of meanness. Mean old houses of no great age; mean new ones; mean and threadbare waterside industries; second-hand clothes-shops; coal-grit, muddy waters and foreshores of the slimy Ouse, shabby rope-walks, and dirty alley's: these are Selby.' *Right:* So although we continue our journey on the western A1, in memory of Charles's visit in 1900, here is his sketch of Selby with my comparison over a hundred years later.

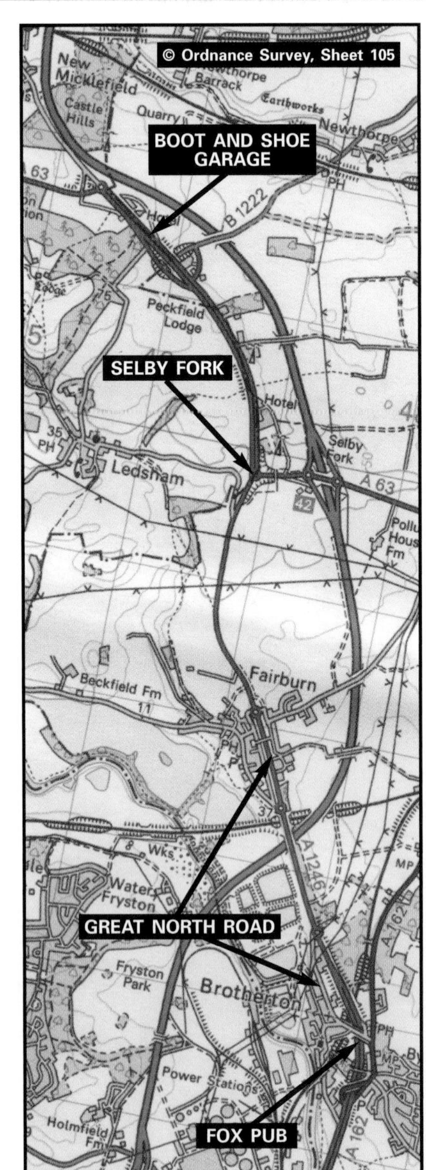

A63

SELBY FORK HOTEL

Up until 2005 the road at Selby Fork passed to the west of the motel of that name but an extensive upgrade led to a new motorway being cut through to the east, leaving a double roundabout on the A63 to Selby.

We then reach Selby Fork, known for the hotel of the same name which is of fairly recent origin. The old junction was triangular. The road approaching from Selby (now the A63) turned right and ran up behind the hotel and joined the Great North Road a couple of hundred yards north of the hotel. A small road cut across to Ledsham to make the triangle.

This all changed around the mid-1950s. A large roundabout was excavated where the small road joined the Great North Road and a dual carriageway was built which went over the top of it via a bridge at each side. The roundabout was served by north and southbound slip-roads and a new road, redesignated the A63, cut off the lane that ran up behind the hotel which still exists as an exit slip from the hotel and a garage which once stood there. And then 50 years later they pulled it all down again!

The present motorway runs half a mile to the east and so the bridges were removed, the roundabout was downsized and moved slightly, and the roads realigned. If you didn't know what you were looking at, you'd be hard pushed to see it as it was. Three of the four old slip-roads are still there in various guises, but the mighty A1 that soared across Selby Fork is gone. While this work was being carried out, I walked along the deserted and damaged dual carriageway and stood looking at the empty space where the bridge had once been — a bridge that I had crossed so many times. Although it was only a road I remember being strangely saddened; it was almost like the loss of an old friend.

For the moment, the road is still dualled for a short way to the north, having become part of the A63. There was an A1/A63 multiplex here but now the A1 bit is gone, it's simply the A63 for a mile. At the next roundabout, by the old Boot and Shoe inn, the A63 turns off again for Leeds. The Boot and Shoe wasn't a coaching inn, but it did cater for travellers and there was enough room round the back to park a number of lorries. It also had a late lease of life as an overnight stop for lorry drivers but, having been bypassed, it had seen better days and was almost derelict when it closed.

The Boot and Shoe pub was the landmark folk used to know where to turn off for Leeds as the A63 runs west from here. It had a huge parking area at the back and was used as a transport stop. You could get a meal and park overnight. I certainly used it at least once. The bushes at the far right of the photo are where the slip road to the A63 once was.

This was the Boot and Shoe garage long disused. It sits on the southbound side opposite the pub. Traffic crossed the A1 on a flyover and joined by a slip road. For some reason, the mile between the two has been left dualled although it ends at a simple roundabout at each end.

North of the roundabout we are finally back on the undisputed Great North Road. The dual carriageway here took a slight curve to the east to bypass Micklefield village and so we are once again on the original route. As we head into the village, the new motorway curves in to join us from the east. It runs almost alongside us for a short way leaving a flat area in between. When they built the motorway here they didn't put it directly on top of the dual carriageway, but sited it alongside. Once finished, the old dual carriageway was then torn up and grassed over which has left the corridor of flat ground between Micklefield and the motorway.

Our road makes its way through New Micklefield and then Micklefield, mining villages which string along the road for a mile and a half. They are more or less joined together now, but even a hundred years ago there was nothing built up between the railway bridge in New Micklefield and the Blands Arms in Micklefield.

On leaving the village we need to be alert as motorway construction has again made our route a bit difficult to follow as the extension of the M1 past Leeds to Bramham Crossroads has ploughed straight across our route. Fortunately we can get things in order with respect to the Roman Ridge alignment which just happens to be arriving over our left shoulder as the A685 from Castleford and Pontefract. We last saw it disappearing at Barnsdale Bar. Roman Ridge is in almost a dead straight line crossing the B1217 at Hook Moor where it becomes our Great North Road and heads into Aberford. So we can follow it backwards to Micklefield.

Currently the road out of Micklefield meets Roman Ridge just across the new M1 but previously it ran in an almost straight line and met Roman Ridge just where it crosses the B1217. Most of this stretch is now under the A1(M) slip-road but if you go to the crossroads of Roman Ridge and the B1217, stop and look back south off to your left is a road-shaped hole in the wood!

We carry on north along the original road to Aberford. This is a large village, well kept with stone houses and a coaching inn which still exists as a pub, The Swan. The road is very quiet now with the through traffic using the nearby motorway. As we pass by there is a road on the right that leads off to Towton which was the location of the bloodiest battle on English soil back in 1461. In the fields between Aberford and Towton, the battle of Towton Moor was fought where 30,000 Yorkists caught up with 50,000 Lancastrians and, in a blinding snowstorm, pushed them into a river and destroyed them, effectively ending the Wars of the Roses for some years.

Once a busy highway, now a quiet backwater. Here we are at Aberford standing on the main street outside the church. The bay window belongs to the Swan Hotel, the town's coaching inn. The bridge down the road crosses the Cock Beck, a tributary of the Wharfe.

The ford can still be seen alongside the bridge which has stood at Aberford at least since 1800. We are looking south back up towards the Swan — the white building in the trees. My mam is enjoying the September sunlight in 2012.

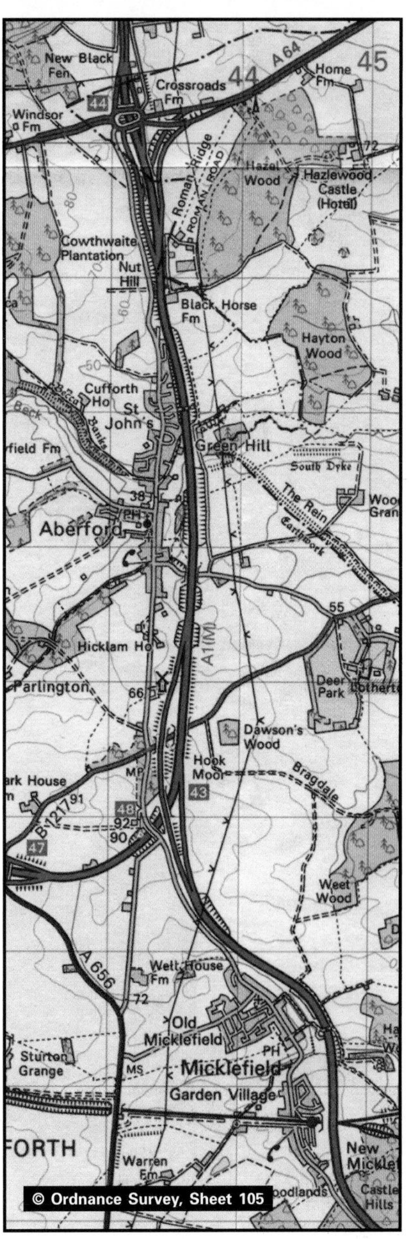

As we leave Aberford the motorway is again in our way. At the point where the present road curves to the left, there is a piece of road going straight on. This small stretch has a gate on it but if we could go through we would find ourselves up against the motorway. Going round by the current road, we go under the motorway to find the continuation on the other side, right by Black Horse Farm. Following it we pass a small industrial yard which I remember being a petrol station on the old dual carriageway. Here we can go no further as this whole area is now a large motorway interchange, named for historical reasons after the long gone Bramham Crossroads. Writing in 1901, Charles Harper said that *'the road two miles out of Aberford reaches that home of howling winds, that most uncomfortable and undesirable place, Bramham Moor. Here, where the Bramham Moor Inn stands at the crossing of the Leeds and York road, a considerable traffic enlivened the way until eighty years ago. Since that time the broad roadways in either direction have been empty.'*

Actually the whole area between Micklefield and Bramham Crossroads (called Hook Moor) has been thoroughly altered as first the M1 was extended to meet the A1 just south of Bramham Crossroads and then the A1 was upgraded to motorway. This means there are odd segments of road orphaned all over the place. This is one of them. It's a part of the Great North Road that was trapped between a slip road for the A1(M) and the realigned local road just south of Aberford. So it has been torn up and grassed over but you can still see the road shaped hole in the trees.

Bramham Crossroads is where the A1 crossed the road from Leeds to York. It is now a fairly major motorway junction but at one time it really was just a crossroads. Looking north with Crossroads Farm on the right. Note the rather prominent bay window.

Imagine my surprise to find that two arms of the crossroads are in fact still there. Just about! The north and the eastern arms are still visible down a small lane off Spen Common Lane. The bay window is still there too. Immediately behind me is one of the slip roads for the motorway junction.

Bramham Crossroads has been upgraded more than once, to a roundabout and then to a GSJ and eventually sidelined by the motorway junction that passes by to the west. So imagine my surprise when I discovered that two branches of the original crossroads still exist, as does the old inn that stood on the corner. Although Harper calls it the Bramham Moor Inn, the oldest map I can find (1849) calls it the White Hart and by 1900 it had become Crossroads Farm, the name by which it is known today. To find it we need to take Spen Common Lane off the motorway roundabout. Almost straightaway there is a small right turn that takes us down by the farm. This is the old northern arm of the original crossroads complete with a few kerbstones. It's a dead end, but climbing the fence at the end shows us that the slip-road from the motorway junction was almost certainly the eastern arm of the crossroads, and you can just get far enough back to get a comparison photograph. Looking north from here we can see that Spen Common Lane now takes up the course of the Great North Road

In later years the junction was upgraded to a roundabout. The bay window is still there on the far left of the photo.

This is the same place today. The modern A64 is dualled and goes by on an embankment behind me.

This is now Paradise Lane between Bramham Crossroads and Bramham Village. At one time this was the southbound carriageway.

There are yet more changes between here and Wetherby. It has been upgraded some three times in relatively recent years. We follow Spen Common Lane north to Bramham village although a comparison of field boundaries leads me to suspect that in fact our original Great North Road is under the motorway, at least from Paradise Farm to Bowcliffe Farm. However we are back on track when we arrive at the fork of Paradise Way and Bowcliffe Road in Bramham. Our original course turned left at Bowcliffe Farm and, after ducking briefly under the motorway again, joins us at the fork from the south and goes through the village via Bowcliffe Road, Front Street and Wetherby Road. But when the dual carriageway was built, it bypassed the village slightly to the west on the course of what is now Milnthorpe Road. When this area was upgraded again in the 1990s into a three-lane stretch from Bramham Crossroads to Wetherby, it was built next to the existing dual carriageway, not on it. This remaining part of the old southbound carriageway was left for access to places west of the motorway. Charles from Trucknet lived in Bramham:

'I think we moved there in 1953 when I was five. The A1 was a single carriageway going through the village. Our house was close to it and in our pre-telly days we would spend hours sitting on the garden wall watching all the traffic follow a lorry grinding its way up the little hill coming out of the village. I actually lived in a house at Bowcliffe Hall which was owned by Blackburn, the aircraft builder, then sold to Hargreaves, the coal firm. The Bramham bypass went in between us and the village which meant a quick sprint across the dual carriageway which kept us fit.'

At the top end of the lane, we reach Bowcliffe Farm. Here, a fork in the road led to Aberford on the right while the Great

North Road turned sharply round the farmhouse and up to Bowcliffe Hall.

We carry on for another mile or two with our Great North Road still extant as a local road off to the east of the motorway as far as the A659 junction. The original course of the road here ran through the east side of the current roundabout which explains why there is a building on the roundabout. This was the South Lodge at the entrance to the Wetherby Grange estate. It stood on the east side of the crossroads and was one of three. One no longer exists, but the other is still to be seen on the roundabout as we arrive in Wetherby.

Between here and Wetherby, the road took a large curve to the west which was straightened out somewhat when the dual carriageway was built, but the curve was later incorporated into a new stretch of road designated the A168 to carry non-motorway traffic when the A1 was upgraded. We will meet the A168 again.

So to re-cap, between Bramham Crossroads and Wetherby we currently have a three-lane motorway finished in 2005. This motorway was upgraded from an original 1991/2 upgrade built next to the 1960s dual carriageway, destroying the northbound carriageway of that road. Our Great North Road ran more or less where the southbound carriageway of that dual carriageway was and in some stretches still is. Phew!

At least in Wetherby there is no doubt about the course of our old road. The roundabout that stands at the south end of Wetherby today was a feature of the 1960s dual carriageway that turned hard right here off the old route, crossed over the river and created a new bypass around Wetherby. Parts of this road still exist, jammed in between the motorway and the town, still designated the A168. We however go straight on into town. Even in the 1960s there wasn't much more than a farm and a couple of cottages on the south side of the River Wharfe, but Micklethwaite Farm no longer exists and there is a housing estate on that site.

Wetherby was the first major coaching stop north of Ferrybridge and had a number of post houses and inns as well as a market. Crossing the river on a fine stone bridge, we are immediately in the High Street. On our left is the Angel, which was the main coaching inn in the town, and had a large stable behind it. Just north of here there was a kink in the road which was ironed out in the 1920s with the demolition of some buildings. Our road becomes North Street and heads out of the town centre. Known presently as the A661, it loses that status where the A661 turns right for York.

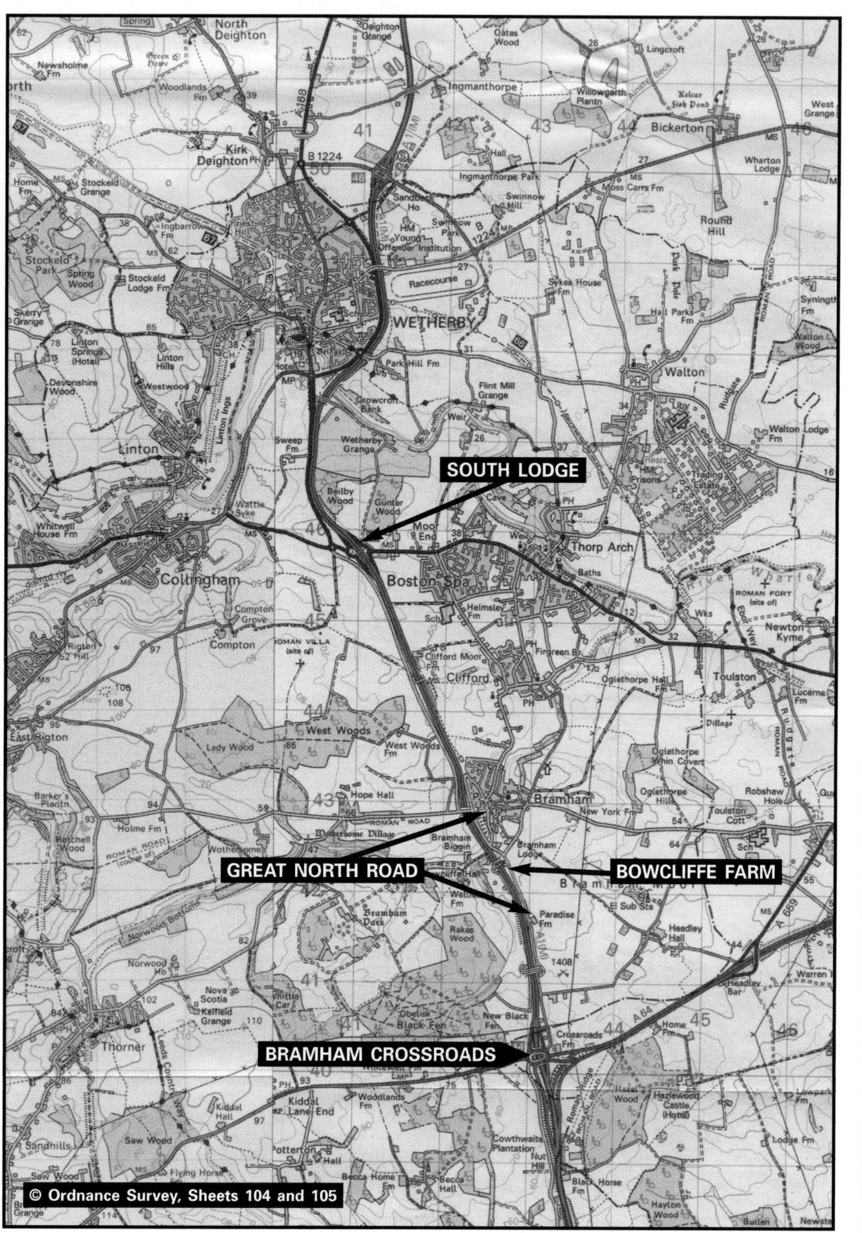

Road improvements never stop: this is the A1/A659 junction just south of Wetherby under construction in 1963 and today.

The Great North Road approaching the town from the south with very little change since the A1 was diverted.

From rural scene to suburbia — this is Deighton Road at Wetherby looking south.

This was the Midway service station between Wetherby and Walshford. I suspect it's called Midway because it is only a hundred yards or so from the site of the Old Fox Inn generally regarded as the half-way point of the Great North Road. When the northbound carriageway was removed, it survived but was just hedged off. The tarmac is still there and the hedge is where the central reservation was. In the comparison my back is up against the hedge with my trusty Suzuki Bandit standing in for the lorry on the forecourt.

Our road is now the B6164 and even in the 1950s there was very little in the way of building past the York road junction. As we leave Wetherby, the Great North Road passed what is alternatively called Deighton Gates or Deighton Bar indicating a toll-house. This stood at or near the entrance to Deighton Gates Primary School. Just north of here, the road forks with the left fork heading for the village of Kirk Deighton but we keep right.

The old picture shows cottages facing onto the Great North Road at Walshford. They now look slightly odd and I had to identify them from the roofline. This is because the current building no longer faces onto the old Great North Road so this is in fact the rear of the Bridge Inn which faces onto the A1 dual carriageway which in turn has been replaced by the A1(M) motorway and been de-dualled.

Here we meet the A168 coming from the south of Wetherby. In the 1960s, this was a dual carriageway although now reduced to one lane. It follows our route pretty much as it did before it became a dual carriageway with the old southbound side still extant and the northbound covered over although parts of it still exist as farm tracks. We continue until we reach Walshford where we meet the new motorway again. There was an old pub on this stretch called The Fox but I never remember seeing it other than derelict and it is completely gone now. Nevertheless it was a most important building as Charles Harper called it the half way point of the Great North Road. In other words 200 miles from both London and Edinburgh!

At Walshford the road crossed the river on a bridge on a slightly different alignment to the current one and ran through the village street. When the dual carriageway was built it bypassed the village just to the east but a roundabout gives access to the village street, now a dead end at both ends, but once the Great North Road. Just north of Walshford the road turned due north again, lying alongside and just east of the new motorway.

This same situation continues for some ten miles as the old road has been covered by the dual carriageway, which in turn has been partially covered by the modern motorway, leaving the old southbound carriageway remaining as the A168 for the use of non-motorway traffic which would once have shared the A1. We do not get our Great North Road back until we approach Boroughbridge. Although its course can be plotted as mostly under the A168.

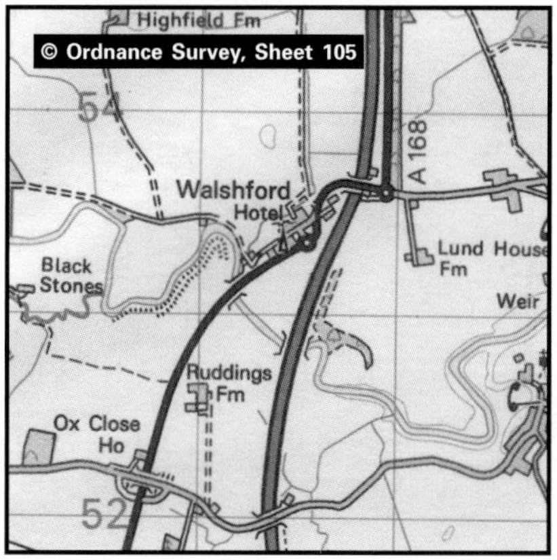

This is the southern end of Walshford village. Like so many others now a dead end.

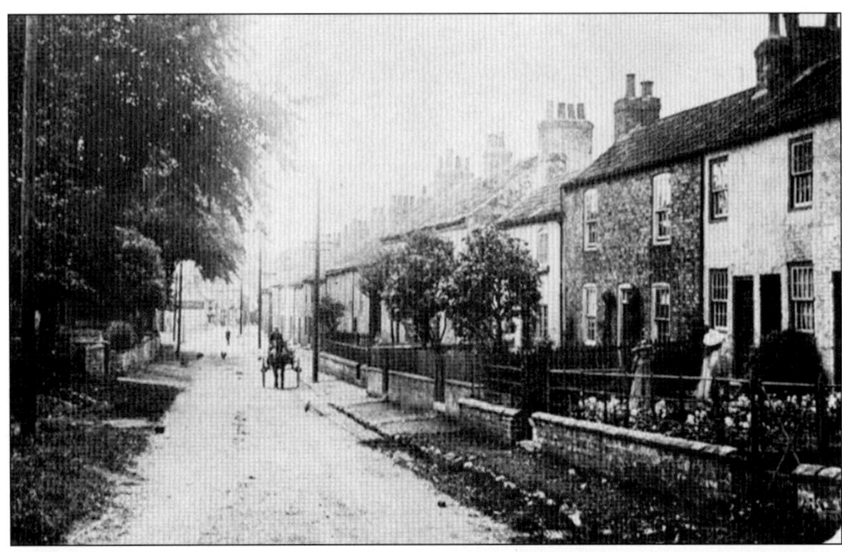

At Boroughbridge, the Great North Road forked with both branches heading for coaching inns and rejoining at the far end of the village centre. This is the right fork.

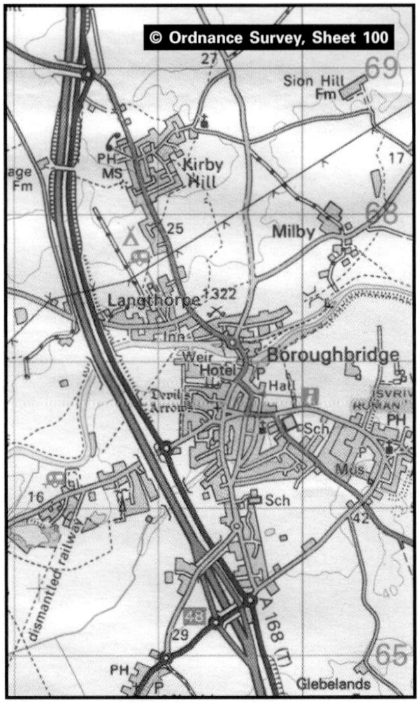

© Ordnance Survey, Sheet 100
Sion Hill Fm
Kirby Hill
PH
MS
Milby
Langthorpe
Inn
Weir
Hotel
Boroughbridge
Hall
Devil's Arrows
Sch
Mus
dismantled railway
A 168 (T)
PH
Glebelands

Boroughbridge to Scotch Corner

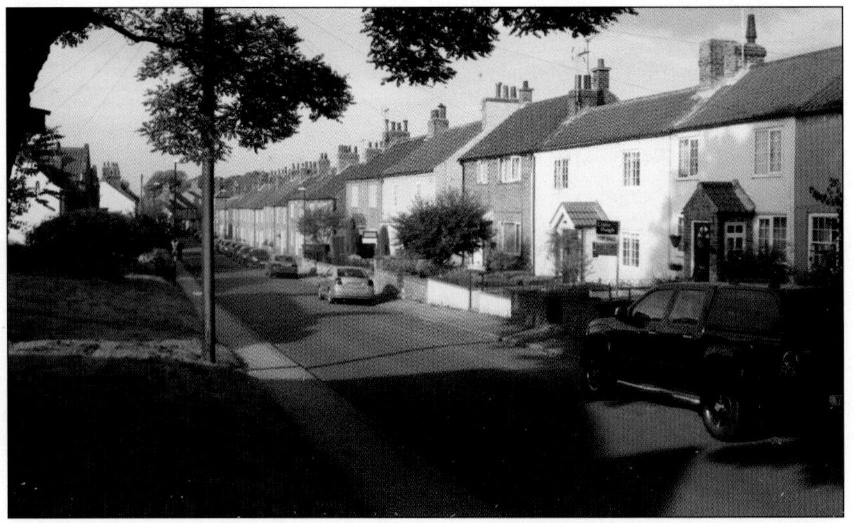

Boroughbridge. Known to the Romans as Isurium and the Saxons as Aldborough (Old Town), in fact Isurium/Aldborough is a village separated from Boroughbridge by half a mile or so. It is believed that a relocation of the River Ure crossing sometime around the time of the Norman Conquest may have instigated the new town which became the 'New Borough at the Brigg' (Bridge) to differentiate it from the Old Borough.

We approach it from Walshford up the current A168 and come into town via a roundabout. However, in earlier times, instead we would have arrived at a fork in the road which is still there but now some way into town where New Row splits off from Horsefair. New Row leads into the centre of town joining the road from York and becoming the High Street. Our road however is the left fork that runs to the west of the High Street, meeting it at its northern end. This does not appear to be a case of the centre being bypassed as both roads appear as far back as 1854.

The two branches of the road meet and rejoin each other outside the Crown Hotel which is still open for business.

From the Crown we cross over the river, the bridge being less humped after it was rebuilt following an accident.

Boroughbridge was another important staging post in the coaching era and had many inns including The Crown which apparently had stabling for 100 horses. Just north of where the two roads join up again is the bridge over the river. Built by John Carr in the late 1700s, it lasted until 1944. Mr Whitfield takes up the story:

'During WWII, when American equipment and troops were pouring down the A66 and then down the A1, the centre span of the bridge at Boroughbridge collapsed when a tank on its transporter was crossing. The whole lot went into the river. A pal and I cycled down to Boroughbridge to see it after school on our bikes from Darlington. A Bailey bridge was quickly built downstream to keep the traffic moving.'

I wonder if Mr Whitfield means after school at the weekend as a round trip from Darlington to Boroughbridge is about 50 miles! The span was repaired but with less of a hump than previously which is noticeable in old photographs.

Once over the River Ure, our road bends to the left past the Grantham Hotel where in 1930 the traffic appears to be being directed by an RAC man. In 2012 my mam was a handy stand in for the patrolman.

The Great North Road passing Dishforth aerodrome . . . in 1942 and 2012.

Heading north from the bridge we leave Boroughbridge on Leeming Lane and skirt the village of Kirkby Hill after which the present road curves to the left to meet a roundabout. Leeming Lane is another name that will stay with us for some distance. From Boroughbridge we are on a Roman alignment known as Dere Street that ran from York to the north. It is clearly visible on a map as a straight Roman road and can be followed for a long way.

The main road here has been upgraded twice; once from our old road to a dual carriageway and then to motorway standard in the 1990s. The problem with the second upgrade was that to preserve rights of way for non-motorway and local traffic — farm access for instance — side roads had to be built to join up places cut off by the motorway. This necessitated all sorts of re-landscaping and very often our old road has been lost. Having said that, to our right as the road bends is a large lay-by, a remnant of the original Great North Road.

The small road that runs up the side of the motorway is numbered the A168 and squeezes in between RAF Dishforth and the motorway. After the aerodrome it becomes part of a large junction where a spur splits off the A1(M) and becomes a dualled A168 and takes traffic off to Thirsk and Teesside. There used to be a roundabout there as Archie Paice remembers:

'Dishforth on the way south from Scotch Corner, had a gate right in front of you as you approached the roundabout: it was the gatehouse to RAF Dishforth. If I recall correctly, you went off three parts round the roundabout — there was a road off immediately left to Catterick, then the Gatehouse, then the A1.'

So does 'Night Shift Bri':

'I think it was the mid-eighties when Dishforth roundabout was done away with. I went on containers in '84 and remember leaving Felixstowe at the crack of dawn so we could get through the road-works at Dishforth and miss the tailbacks which were horrendous, then up to the Quernhow for breakfast. There was also another roundabout north of Dishforth with a BP filling station on the northbound side right on the roundabout.'

I mentioned in the introduction that I was going to divert from the original 1922 Ministry of Transport designation of the A1 in one area. Well here we are as between Boroughbridge and Darlington there are two possible routes. One is the current A1 alignment and the other going from Dishforth to Topcliffe and then by way of the current A167 via Northallerton to Darlington.

Although Leeming Lane had been recognised as the main route to the north for centuries, the Northallerton route had been favoured by horse-drawn traffic which required shorter stretches between towns and, when the fledgling Ministry of Transport created its road classifications in 1922, it apparently based them on the old coaching routes. So the route via Northallerton was designated as the A1 and the Leeming Lane route became the A66 all the way through to Boroughbridge (and then on to York). However, the Northallerton route was not as amenable to motorised traffic and there were soon many complaints. Added to reports from local highway engineers, by mid-1924 the designation A1 was switched to the Leeming Lane route while the other road was demoted to the A167. There is no doubt that the A167 was a coaching route and I know there is a school of thought that would have it as the Great North Road. One commentator states that the absence of Darlington on milestones on Leeming Lane shows that Darlington was not a recognised destination on that route.

In fact the name Great North Road seems to disappear altogether between Boroughbridge and Darlington, but our route is persistently called Leeming Lane and it appears then important enough to be given a name of its own which is not the case with the A167. Checking some 19th century maps would indicate that this was the case then too.

Bradley writing in 1859 states that some coaches went north *'by way of Topcliffe, Thirsk, Northallerton and Yarm'* (no mention of Croft) but by no means all. He also states that a man called *'Mr Ferguson, who was a man of very gentlemanly manners, was one of the best-known men on the Great North Road'*. Mr Ferguson was the owner of the George in Catterick (an earlier name for the Bridge Inn).

I suspect that either route is viable. At the widest point they are barely six miles apart and we could in fact call them two branches of the GNR! My choice for this narrative is Leeming Lane purely because that is the route that was (eventually) designated A1.

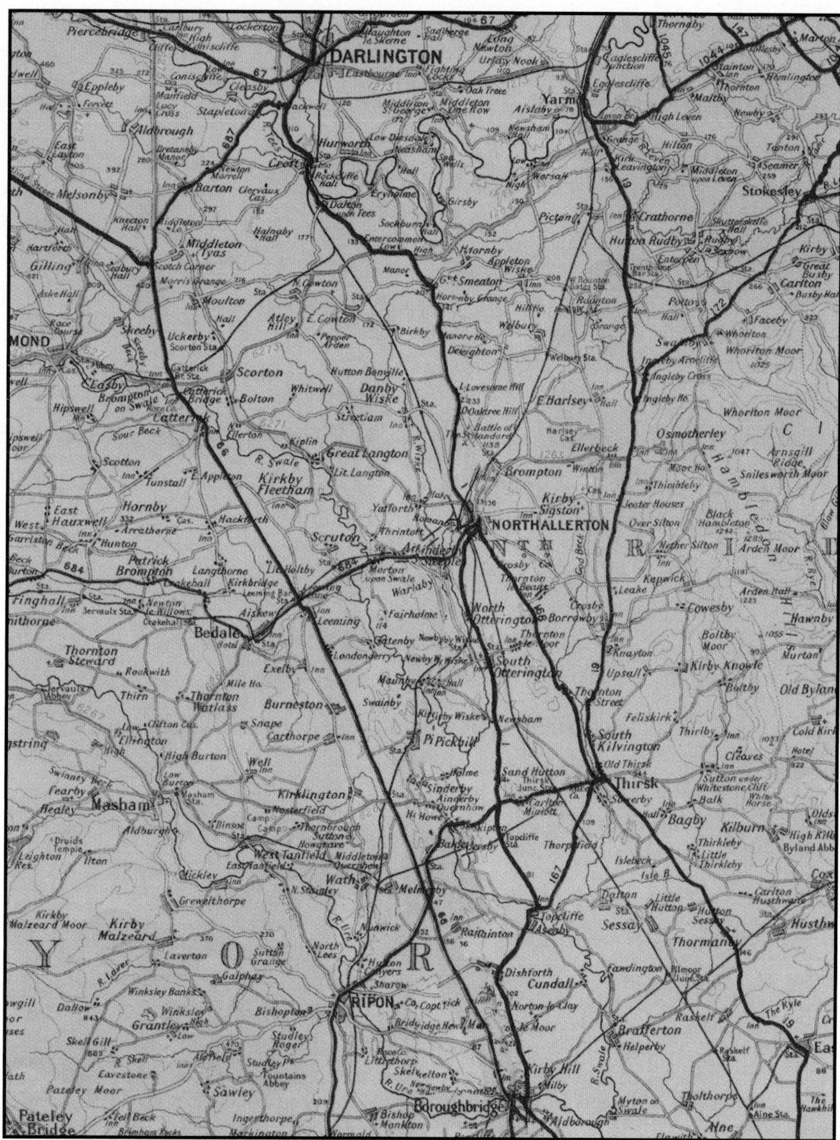

To further add to the controversy over the route between Boroughbridge and Darlington, this early motoring map labels the A1 as the road through Northallerton. And look, if you really want to get your kicks, we have our very own Route 66!

Dere Street is a Roman road that runs from York up to Scotland. Between Boroughbridge and just beyond Scotch Corner it is our Great North Road and is called Leeming Lane. There aren't any large places on that stretch, but there have been odd spots to stop up and down its length. However in 2009-2012, the A1 dual carriageway was upgraded to motorway standard between Dishforth and Leeming. The motorway was built immediately to the east of the dual carriageway and afterwards one carriageway of the old road was removed. This spelt doom for anything that was on the old southbound carriageway. The Rainton services are on the northbound side just past the A168 turn for Teesside. The area in the foreground on the side of the road is also believed to once be the site of a transport cafe called The Ponderosa.

Boarded up and deserted. I wonder how long it will be before it is hidden and forgotten.

This is the Quernhow Cafe which was named after the nearby village of Ainderby Quernhow. Up until a couple of years ago this road was the northbound cariageway of the A1. Now it is just a two-way side road and the cafe is about the only one left open on this stretch.

Immediately north of Dishforth were two well-known cafes, one on either side of the road. The one where Rainton services now stand was the Ponderosa, and opposite was the Windmill. Then we pass the Quernhow Cafe on the left, another haunt of lorry drivers for many a long year and still in business.

Having said that it has fared better than this garage which was almost directly opposite. This photo was snapped by Brian Hodson passing on his way south and the garage has already been boarded up and shut off ready to be demolished.

Believe it or not this is the same spot. When I said they built the motorway just to the east of the old road I really meant *just* to the east! The grass hump is on the southbound carriageway of the old road and the garage is under the motorway.

This bridge was on the Great North Road but when the road was dualled it was left as access to a farm (New Inn Farm!) I was expecting to find it gone but fortunately the motorway just misses it by about 30 yards. There is a small monument at the far end which is a commemoration stone for the building of the Dishforth-Leeming motorway. There are three roads here: the remains of the dualled A1; the new A1(M), and a small piece of Great North Road in between!

The villages of Londonderry, Leeming and Leeming Bar are on a large ox-bow stretch and the dual carriageway dodges round it. Entry and exit are by a couple of junctions off the A1(M). Although they have been altered recently during the motorway upgrade (which currently ends at Leeming Bar) the Great North Road running through the villages is unchanged. There is a large RAF airfield next to the road and in times gone by they actually stopped traffic to allow aircraft to take off or land. Apparently there were a couple of airmen stationed on permanent road duty.

For ten miles our road sits directly under the northbound carriageway of the dual carriageway but this will not be the case for much longer. As one of the last stretches of non-motorway A1 in the area, the road between Dishforth and Leeming was subjected to an upgrade to motorway status in 2012, leaving only the few miles between Leeming Bar and Scotch Corner as it was. I don't believe that any major deviations from our path are taking place, but there will be more disruption to the route of our old road.

Just after we pass the turn-off for Gatenby and RAF Leeming, the observant traveller may notice what looks like a small grass-covered slip-road that leads up to a gate in the embankment on the southbound side. That is what Leeming Lane used to look like! It is the Great North Road coming south from Leeming at the point where it was bypassed by the dual carriageway. To reach the other side of the gate we have to take the next exit and cross over the A1. At the T-junction, turn right for Londonderry and follow the road right through the village to the end.

Standing outside the Poplars, you can look over the gate and see how the dual carriageway runs straight at you before deviating at that point to form the bypass. Turning round, you will see a well-preserved section of the Great North Road stretching away north in the same straight line we have been on for

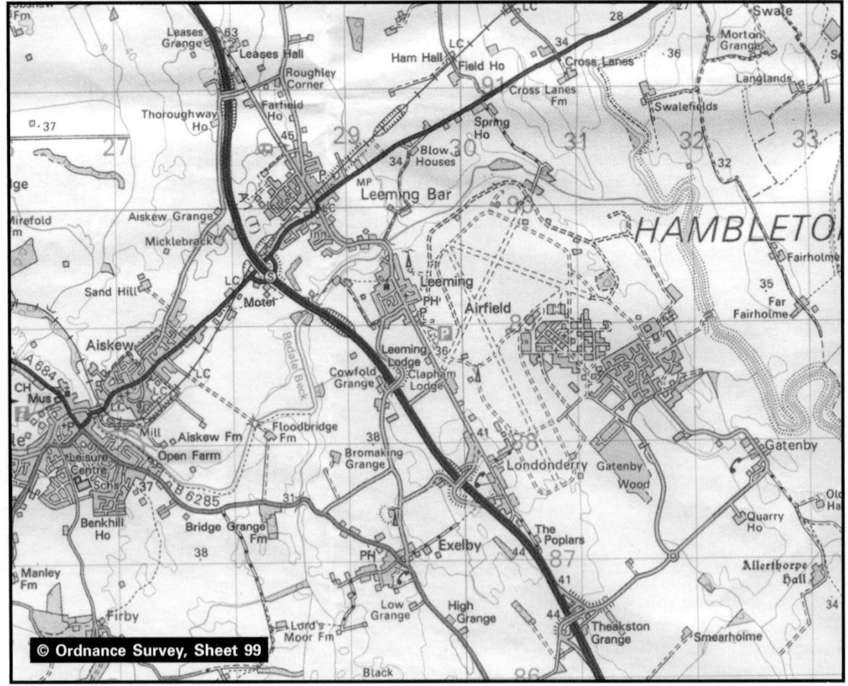

Garage owner Jack Farmer explains: 'Petrol was first marketed in three grades, usually known as Nos. 1, 2 and 3. No. 1 was the best grade; No. 2 called taxibus spirit was somewhat inferior and No. 3 was produced for commercial vehicles. No. 2 was dropped soon after World War 1 but Nos. 1 and 3 carried on and would be roughly equivalent to the 4-star and 2-star petrols. In the mid-20s, petrol pumps began to appear. Each had an glass globe which was lit up at night and we had some wonderful shapes. In the early 1930s, Tetra-ethyl-lead was introduced to combat 'pre-ignition knocking' or 'pinking' as it was called. Anglo American Oil introduced it first, and made a great show of depicting Pratts Ethyl as a pump made to look like a young lady. Then they went one better and put a pump in their adverts made to look like a young man called Tommy Prattkins. This was a fatal mistake for the lads soon did a bit of re-arranging which I will leave to your imagination! Soon after the name 'Pratts' was withdrawn and 'Esso' substituted.'

This is the garage on Leases Road in Leeming Bar. The building has changed but the pump platform is still in the same place. Note in the old photo how many different petrol brands they are selling.

the last ten miles, past Londonderry transport cafe, once known as Lawsons, still in business after many years. On our right is RAF Leeming built in the 1930s and still the home of fighter training squadrons, their Hawk jets being familiar all over North Yorkshire skies. There is a small observation area just on the right of the road where you can sit and watch the jets take off and land.

We pass through the villages of Leeming and Leeming Bar (yet another indication of a toll-bar) travelling in a large S-curve between the two to cross Bedale Beck. In Leeming Bar just across the junction with the A684, we can see one of the dreaded Great North Road level crossings. It is still in situ as the line here is part of a preserved railway.

Neither village seems to have changed very much with the exception of an industrial estate just off the old road at Leeming Bar. The road having straightened out after the beck is once more on the Roman alignment and you can follow it all the way out of Leeming Bar to arrive at a gated dead end, the other side of which is the dual carriageway again. To reach it we have to backtrack into Leeming Bar and take the A684 to the A1 and turn north. Once we have passed the gate we are back on course with the old road under the southbound carriageway.

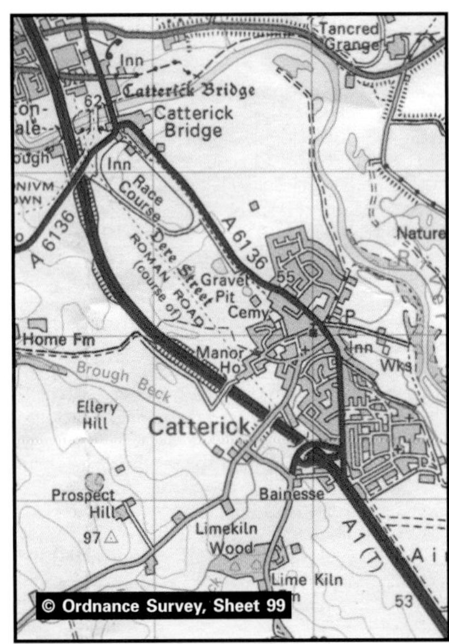

At Catterick, the Bridge House Inn has a history going back to coaching days. Note that the course of the old Roman road runs close to the racecourse.

Surprisingly, the road deviates from the Roman path on arrival at Catterick. It turns off it and runs a couple of hundred yards to the east past the RAF station and into the village as the A6136 where it is still called Leeming Lane. This area has a very long military tradition. A Roman camp was located here astride Dere Street (which was about where the racecourse is now) and the town that grew up around it was called Cataractonium. It then became a Saxon town and later the Normans built a castle near where Brough Beck meets the River Swale.

The airfield, which is now part of the larger Catterick Garrison, has been there since 1914 as a training station for the Royal Flying Corps. With the formation of the Royal Air Force in April 1918, the station became RAF Catterick and is one of the oldest military airfields in the world.

Catterick itself was a very small village even 60 years ago and the road did not in fact enter the village until it had crossed Brough Beck where Beckside is now. We pass through and carry on north on the A6136 past the racecourse to reach Catterick Bridge, named after the crossing over the Swale. Right by the bridge is the old coaching house, the Catterick Bridge Hotel.

Just north of here we come to the crossroads with the road from Brompton to Scorton. On the north-west corner once stood the Railway Hotel. It is long gone but it served people coming here via Catterick Bridge railway station that stood on the left-hand side a little further to the north, opposite where the skip waste site is today. Here there was yet another level crossing. Catterick Bridge railway station was on a branch line to Richmond, and just after the station another line branched off to serve Catterick Camp. Established in 1914 as the 'Aldershot of the North', it is now known as Catterick Garrison and is claimed to be the largest army camp in Europe with a population of some 25,000.

Neither of these rail lines exist today but the camp branch line ran alongside the main road from Catterick Bridge to the camp. 'Bumper' recalls that *'there were four cafes in Catterick. Tyne House was on the right going south, then the Tudor House with the Bungalow just before the railway crossing, and Joe's in the village.'*

September 2012. The only thing going up the A1 at the moment is the River Swale! Taken looking north from the A6136 bridge.

Joseph Appleyard's sketch (www.josephappleyard.co.uk) of Scotch Corner . . . how it may have looked a hundred years ago.

North of the level crossing our road rejoins the Roman alignment just past the large industrial estate on the left and then merges with the dual carriageway shortly thereafter. Travelling a short stretch of about two and a half miles, with our original road under the northbound carriageway, brings us to Scotch Corner.

This famous junction was no more than a crossroads right up to the 1930s when it was upgraded to a roundabout. The adjacent hotel, to this day called the Scotch Corner Hotel, was built on the site of an earlier inn called the Three Tuns. It is called Scotch Corner because this is where traffic for western Scotland, Glasgow, and parts to the north branch off. In summer travellers would go by way of Teesdale and Alston and Brampton to Gretna but in winter they would use the A66/M6 route familiar to us today. Even so the old A74 cannot have been much fun in a coach at the best of times!

The Three Tuns Inn changed its name to the Scotch Corner Hotel before it was demolished around 1938.

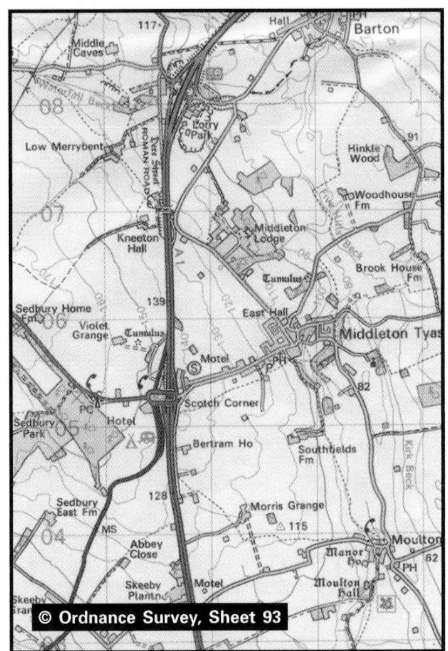

© Ordnance Survey, Sheet 93

This was the hotel which replaced the Three Tuns — the crossroads still being an A-grade roundabout whereas now it is an elongated overpass.

It should be noted that this was also a junction back in Roman times and both the A1 and A66 are on Roman roads at this spot. However for some reason the Roman alignments do not quite join up. The A66 takes a curve off the Roman route about a mile before Scotch Corner and dips slightly to the south. Had it not, the original crossroads would have been a couple of hundred yards further north.

When the crossroads were upgraded to a roundabout, the approach roads were straightened out as well, leaving an ox-bow stretch alongside the current northbound slip-road which is now the access to Violet Grange Farm. The area was upgraded again to a GSJ when the road was dualled and the whole alignment was shifted slightly to the east with an elongated roundabout replacing the old one.

Half a mile past Scotch Corner we arrive at the beginning of another stretch of motorway, the A1(M) Darlington bypass. This was opened in 1965 and, together with various stretches added over the next few years, continues as a motorway all the way to the outskirts of Gateshead, a distance of some 35 miles.

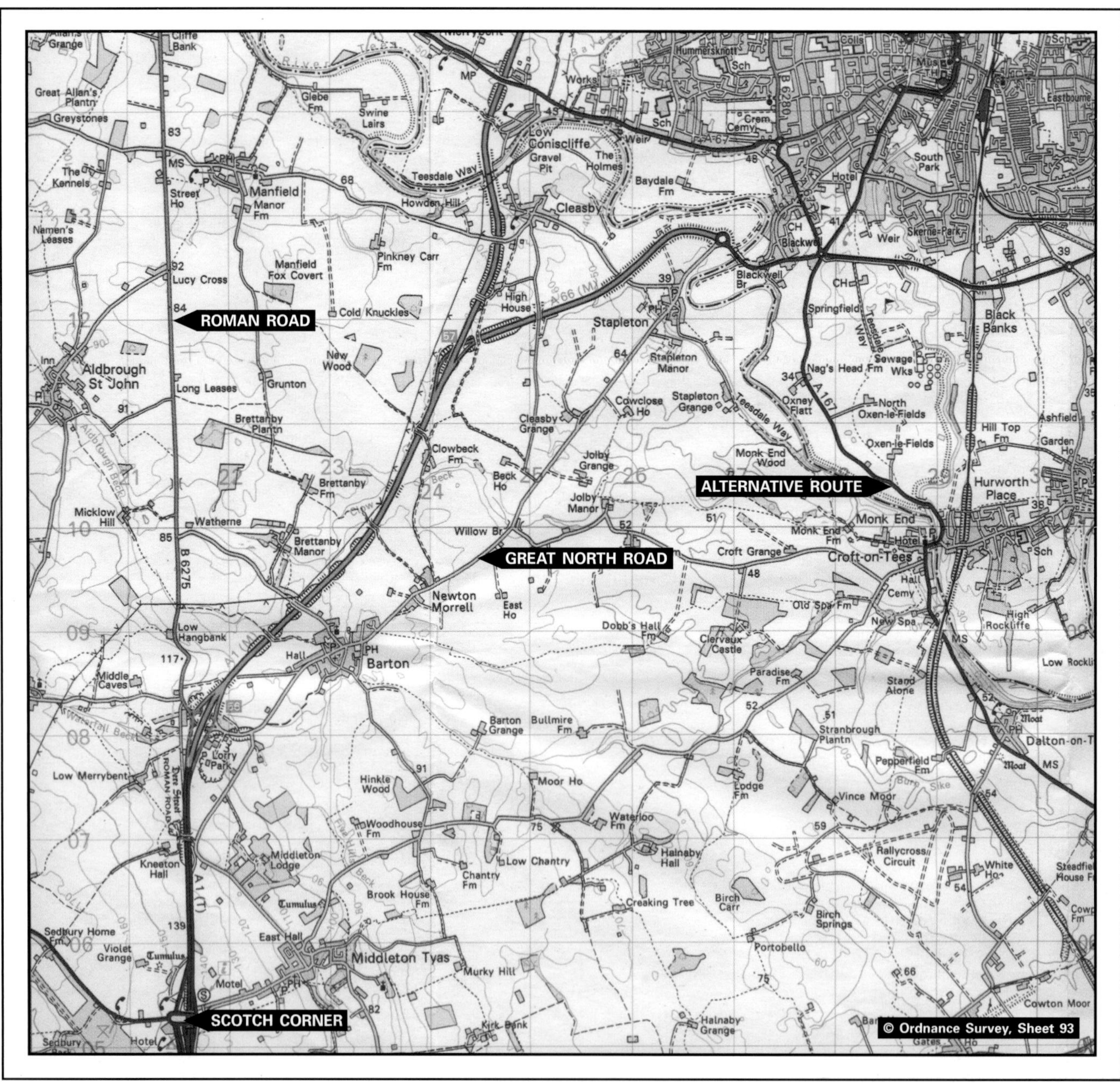
ROMAN ROAD
GREAT NORTH ROAD
ALTERNATIVE ROUTE
SCOTCH CORNER
© Ordnance Survey, Sheet 93
Manfield
Cleasby
Low Coniscliffe
Stapleton
Aldbrough St John
Barton
Newton Morrell
Croft-on-Tees
Hurworth Place
Middleton Tyas
Blackwell
Dalton-on-T

The Cleveland Bridge company of Darlington was a successful engineering company responsible among other things for Middlesborough transporter bridge. The wealthy owner was one of the first men in Darlington to own a motor car. But when you have the first car, where do you get it serviced? He set up a small garage as the Cleveland Car Company located in this mock-Tudor building on Grange road

Scotch Corner to Seaton Burn

Checking the map, one can see a lane approaching the dual carriageway from the east which then makes a sharp turn away from it without actually joining it. This used to be where the Great North Road made a curve to the right, away from the Roman alignment which now carries on north, heading for Darlington as the B6275. There is a corresponding ox-bow lay-by on the southbound side of the dual carriageway that helps to pinpoint the exact spot where the roads diverged — just where the lay-by exits onto the southbound A1. Our road follows the lay-by to its mid-point and then goes through the hedge to become Kneeton Lane.

To reach it we have to leave the motorway at the first exit and cross over the top where we rejoin the Great North Road as it heads for Barton and Stapleton. On the right between the two villages is the interestingly-named Murder Hill which is shown by that name on maps as far back as the early 1900s. There is a small ox-bow stretch on the right where a new bridge over the beck has been built.

After passing through Stapleton where there has also been a small realignment, the road takes a sharp turn to the south-east to cross the River Tees on Blackwell bridge. Today there is a roundabout here linking up a motorway spur, the A66(M) with Darlington, but in earlier times this was simply a sharp bend. Half a mile after the bridge, we meet the A167 arriving from its alternative route through Northallerton. Today, this takes place at a large five-way roundabout where the A66 and A167 cross with a spur of the A67.

The building was eventually demolished in 1974. Darlington's road system is also vastly changed with the town centre's old roads pedestrianised and through traffic being routed around on a small inner ring road. Grange Road is cut by part of the ring road here and is a handy parking area.

Only a few doors up from the Cleveland building was the Duplex Motor Garage an early supplier of motorcycles and pushbikes.

We head into Darlington on the A167, now travelling on the Great North Road. Unlike other towns, it hasn't expanded much along the approach, probably due to the grounds of Blackwell Grange and Skerne Park lying on both sides of the road. The built-up area begins today in the vicinity of Blackwell Lane.

The buildings are still there on the left as we go north although there are more cars parked outside compared to when it was a garage!

A few doors up again but looking back south. The Imperial Hotel on the corner of Grange Road, Coniscliffe Road and Blackwellgate looking south. The Great North Road is the left fork and the garages will be on the right.

Darlington, like Doncaster, fared well after the coaching era, becoming the cradle of the railway industry. There is of course some irony in that as it was here that the world's first railway journey took place. George Stephenson's Rocket, which was basically a stationary mill engine on some wheels, transited the Stockton and Darlington railway in 1825. In later years there were three separate railway works in the town which had a bustling Victorian centre.

Our road runs straight through via Grange Road, Blackwellgate, and into the market place as High Row. The old coaching inns were superseded at the time of the railway prosperity and are no longer to be seen. And today it has all changed again as the old road is pedestrianised in places.

We leave the market square and travel up Northgate and on via High Northgate and North Road. In 1857, you would have been leaving town by the time you had gone under the railway on High Northgate although by the 1940s the town was much larger due to the influx of workers for the railway works.

At the side of Northgate stood the Bulmer Stone. Mentioned by Charles

Left: **The Great North Road inclined to the right at the hotel and entered Blackwellgate, the start of the town centre shopping area. The hotel is behind the photographer. Bainbridge Barkers was a large department store that was open from 1899 to 1961.** *Right:* **Pedestrianised Blackwellgate in 2012 — the glory is faded and so has the paintwork.**

The top end of High Row becomes Northgate and then North Road. We are looking north up North Road.

This comparison was somewhat difficult to take because most of the buildings in the foreground have been demolished and the inner ring-road comes through here. There is a very busy roundabout in that space now and to avoid that I had to take the picture further forward. I am probably about where the truck, behind the bus going to Doncaster, is heading north in the original photo. The building with the turret on the left is an old college now used by Darlington Borough Council and it is behind the railings at the base of this building that you will find the Bulmer Stone. 'Our' road now follows the A167.

Harper, this was apparently a large rock that stood at the side of the road outside a row of cottages. It had been there forever and it was believed to be glacial debris. It is still there although behind the railings of the old college which is now used by Darlington Borough Council.

Moving on north we go up Harrowgate Hill a journey described by Harper: *'Harrowgate Hill conducts out of Darlington and leads on to Coatham Mundeville, a tiny hamlet on the crest of a hill, with an 18th century house, a row of cottages and an inn, making together an imposing figure on the sky line although when reached they are commonplace enough. The village of Aycliffe lies beyond.'*

The name Harrowgate Hill appears to pertain to a suburb of the town rather than the road itself, with the old village of Harrowgate having been swallowed up by suburbia. It was around the area where the White Horse pub is today.

Our road becomes Beaumont Hill just past here and it is a long and steady climb which must have been hard work for coach horses. You cannot see Coatham Mundeville until you are right on top of it because of the hill, but when you get there, there is a house, a row of cottages, and an inn (the Foresters Arms) on the right-hand side of the road.

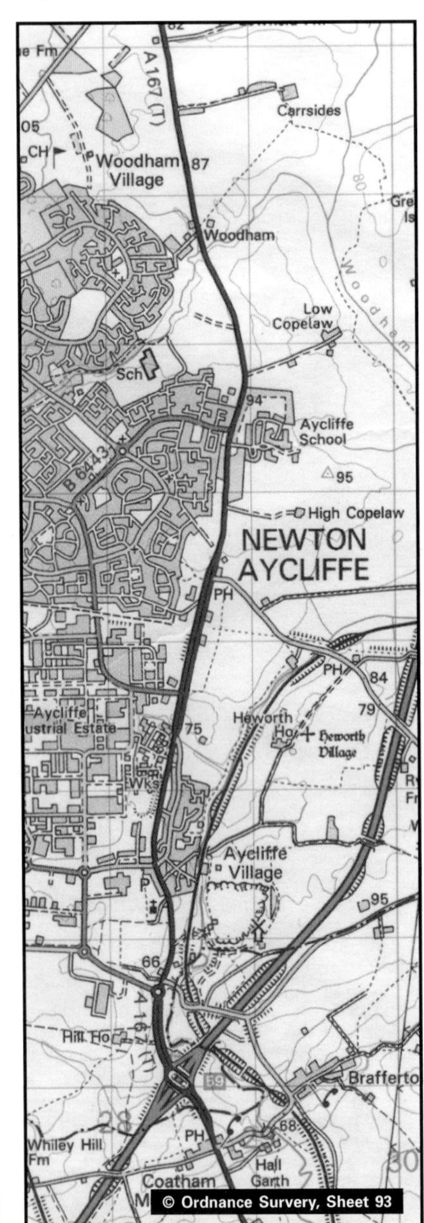

For anyone looking for Newton Aycliffe, this isn't the place. That whole town is a new town and it didn't exist when our road was numbered. It did however go through the tiny village of Aycliffe after which Newton Aycliffe was named. Coming from Darlington, this is the first view of Aycliffe you would have had. The road curved to the right just past the North Briton pub which is on the right just out of sight.

The road now goes straight on at the North Briton. You can see that the houses that stood across the end of the road have been demolished as have two or three of the cottages on the left.

At the far end of town the road bends back to the north.

We soon meet the motorway coming round from the south side of Darlington and heading north. We cross above it via a roundabout junction, although on a slightly different alignment, and there are still a couple of stubs of Great North Road in the trees either side of the junction. Harper's Aycliffe began about where the North Briton pub now stands and our road went around a right-hand bend to become what is now called West Terrace. Then, as the road turns north and becomes North Terrace, one would have already left the village but today things are very different.

The first thing we come across after crossing the motorway is another roundabout that leads off to the huge Newton Aycliffe Industrial Estate which dominates the left-hand side of the road for the next mile or so. As we come to West Terrace we find it has become a minor right turn and a new stretch bypassing the village squeezes between the village and the industrial estate rejoining the road out of the village (as Durham Road) a little further up. On our left, however, the industrial zone stretches on and on and eventually gives way to more housing and a built-up area that would have Harper scratching his head. The lonely moor has become a town.

At the far end of town the road bends back to the north.

So what happened here then? During the war, the site west of Aycliffe village was selected as a munitions factory and large grass-covered bunkers were built. After hostilities were over, the site was chosen for building Newton Aycliffe, a new town of some 30,000 folk, that stretches between the original villages of Aycliffe and Woodham, both on our original road although the new town was built just off it. Between the two villages were two post-houses, the Travellers Rest and the Gretna Green Wedding Inn, but today only the Gretna survives as a Premier Inn motel.

The next place of any note is Rushyford where the A689 east-west route crosses the Great North Road. Here is another large post-house right by the bridge over the river. Once called the Wheatsheaf, it is now the Eden Arms, but in between it must have been another casualty of the loss of the coaching trade to the railways as Harper tells us that 'the old house still stands and faces down the road, but has long ceased to be an inn and remodelled in recent taste, it is now a private residence.' Times change and change back it seems!

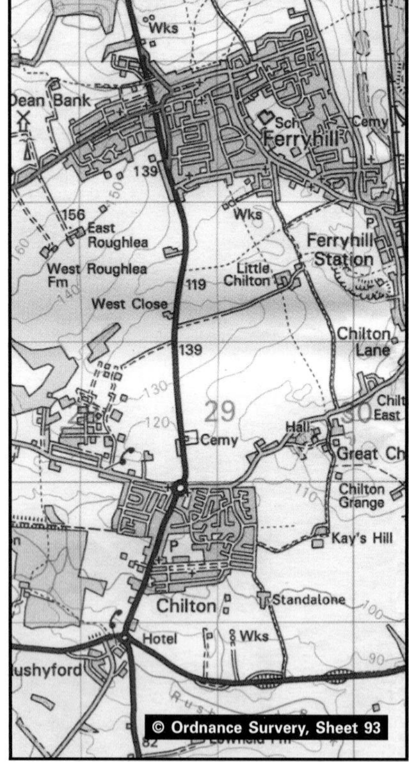

North of Rushyford, our route ran through Chilton which, although bypassed now, was a small blip on the road serving yet another of County Durham's coal mines, the industry having been active in the area for a very long time.

At Chilton, this garage lay on the left-hand side as you entered the village.

With the heavy traffic that once used this stretch of the Great North Road now a distant memory, the garage, too, has long since gone.

Ferryhill, the next town, originally stretched along a long village green, down the line of the current North Street and Market Street right at the top of a hill which is in fact one of the highest points on the Great North Road. To use the original route to the top of the hill, we need to turn-off the current A167 onto Darlington Road. Needless to say coach traffic struggled up here, and in the early 19th century there was an attempt to reduce the steep climb by digging a cutting into the side of the hill, quite close to the old road which is still in use today, On the north side of Ferryhill, the road has been elevated slightly to ease the ascent into the cutting athough whether this was done at the same time is not clear. It was Harper who gave the clue as he includes this engraving in his book, *The Great North Road,* looking south towards Ferryhill. He says that the unfinished embankment would have been a road coming from the cutting to ease the descent, but that the works were abandoned due to the advent of the railways. I suspect that Harper's illustration was made off to the left of our road on the original alignment and is looking back at the embankment that the road is on today. In other words the cutting was built, an embankment was planned to join up with it but cancelled, but then in later years when motor traffic appeared, the job was finished. The old alignment is almost totally gone without trace. In more recent times, the cutting was bridged to allow access to parts of Ferryhill built on the west side of the road.

Another town that grew up because of coal was Ferryhill. Up until the start of the industrial revolution, it was an agricultural hamlet but it grew rapidly in the 19th and 20th centuries. It sat on a steep ridge and the road went up and over the ridge. In later years a cutting was dug to ease the passage of through traffic. It was decided that for through traffic a lower alignment was required and so a cutting — nick-named 'The Cut' — was begun. The job was left half finished when the railways took the road traffic (and when Charles Harper sketched there in 1900) but it was finished off in the 1920s with the rise of road transport. The original route ran slightly to the west of the current one and further down the hill which is why the engraving appears to be drawn from a lower elevation down the present road, i.e. to the left of the cyclists on the next page.

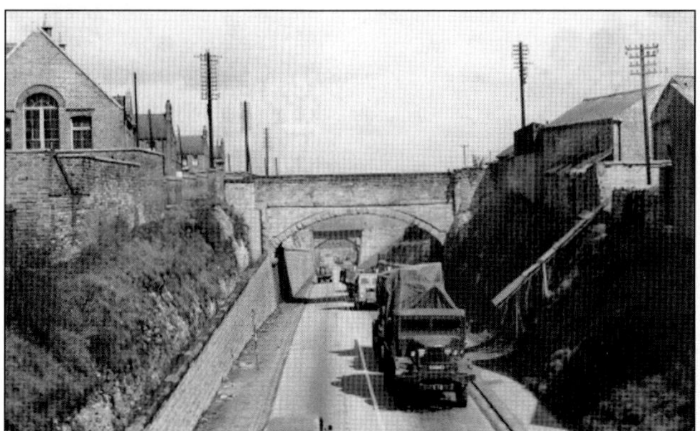

This is looking from a footbridge that crosses 'The Cut'. The building on the left is Ferryhill Primary School.

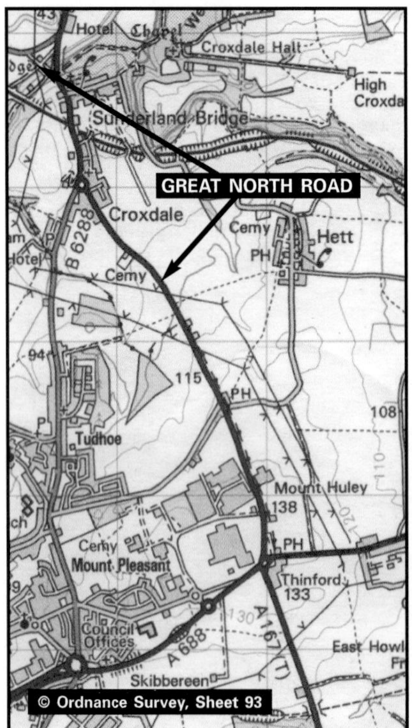

A couple of hundred yards beyhond 'The Cut', these cyclists are pedalling their way north to the next village: Thinford.

Once we have passed Red Hall Farm, we are back on the original alignment for a while with the exception of a small realignment at Thinford to accommodate the new roundabout. This has left a couple of small orphaned stretches of Great North Road, one in front of the Thinford Inn, and the other running down behind a BP petrol station which has been partly built on. North of here there is more industry on our left, which is part of the growing towns of Spennymoor and Tudhoe, but as yet they haven't reached the road so we pass on to Croxdale and Sunderland Bridge.

This rather poor photo was taken at Thinford looking south back toward Ferryhill and the chimney is believed to be the colliery so dating the picture to pre-1960. The comparison is taken in the correct place as the road was moved slightly to accommodate a new roundabout. We are looking south at the crossroads. You can follow the southern arm by the white stones, the corner being where that line meets the current kerb line. The little garage was about where the McDonald's is now, and you can just see the current road far right. There was generally a queue here because of the roadworks on the roundabout.

With the exception of a roundabout, Croxdale has not changed much in a hundred years although fifty years before that there was nothing here at all except our road. A little further on is the village of Sunderland Bridge which spreads along a right turning off the Great North Road. Just past this right turn you will notice a road leading off to the left behind the safety barriers. This is yet another small section of the original road that crosses the River Wear on an old bridge.

To explore we need to go on, over the 'new' bridge (built around 1930) to reach the junction where the B6300 turns off to the left. Take this turning and a couple of hundred yards further down there is another left turn which leads to the old and rather attractive stone bridge. There was a fatal coach crash here in 1822. We then come up against the safety barrier mentioned earlier. Turning round we can then follow the old course northwards, noting the drive to the house on the right immediately at the end of the bridge. Partly fenced off now, this was the original fork in the road. And our Great North Road forms part of the drive and joins the present-day road through the trees near the present B6300 junction. Currently a private residence, this house was the Bridge Inn although it is not noted as an inn on any map later than 1923. When the new bridge and approach was built, this section was cut off, Great North Road traffic simply going straight on. Then the B6300 was later diverted to its current junction and the old bridge was no longer used.

Just north of Croxdale, the Great North Road went down a steep little hill and over a narrow bridge crossing the River Wear to then take a sharp right turn. It was ironed out with a new piece of road but the old bridge is still there. Here is where the new road splits from the old. Immediately over the bridge the road turned right past the front of the Bridge Inn, now a private house. I wonder if the owners know their drive was once the Great North Road!

Moving north from here, we come to a short section of dual carriageway where some kinks have been ironed out leaving an ox-bow on the left between Herwood House and the drive to Burn Hall. The road then runs on unchanged, apart from being dualled, until we reach the Cock O' the North junction just south of Durham.

Here the A167 proceeds north, bypassing Durham just to the west, and at one time this route was given the designation A1. Known as Elvet Moor, and then Darlington Road, we come to the junction with the A690. Nowadays you cross straight over but in earlier times, northbound traffic had to turn right and then left up St John's Road which was the north road as recently as 1960. As we head north from this junction over Crossgate Moor, we pass the site of the Battle of Neville's Cross which was fought here in October 1346.

This battle is well documented as it was fought under the gaze of the monks of Durham Minster and was yet another example of misguided Scottish belief in France as an ally. At this time, England and France were in the middle of the 100 Years War and the French who were losing tried to get Scotland to invade England to take off some of the pressure. David II of Scotland was told by Philip VI of France that northern England was a 'defenceless void', so the Scots invaded with some 12,000 men. They bypassed Carlisle and headed for Durham where they camped and tried to arrange a payment of 'protection money' from the City of Durham. However their intelligence was wrong. England did have an army in the north, around 7,000 Cumbrians, Northumbrians and Yorkshiremen led by the Archbishop of York. Two thousand of these were separate from the army but the other 5,000 caught up with the Scots who arrayed themselves in a defensive line at Neville's Cross. (The 'Celtic Charge' as portrayed in the movie *Braveheart* simply did not happen.) Although outnumbered two to one, the English tactics were far superior and the Scots were dealt a very heavy blow. They lost a number of leaders including David II himself who was captured and held in English hands for 11 years.

The road crosses the battlefield as Newcastle Road and heads uphill until it arrives at the roundabout where the A691 joins from Durham city. The Great North Road ran through the city but it is not difficult to see why the western route (the A1) was preferred. The approach to Weardale is steep on both sides, and after passing through the market place, the crossing has to be repeated to leave the city. The city centre roads are very narrow but as they are the original route it is worth just following them through, although I would guess that any traffic that didn't have to stop in Durham would take the easier route.

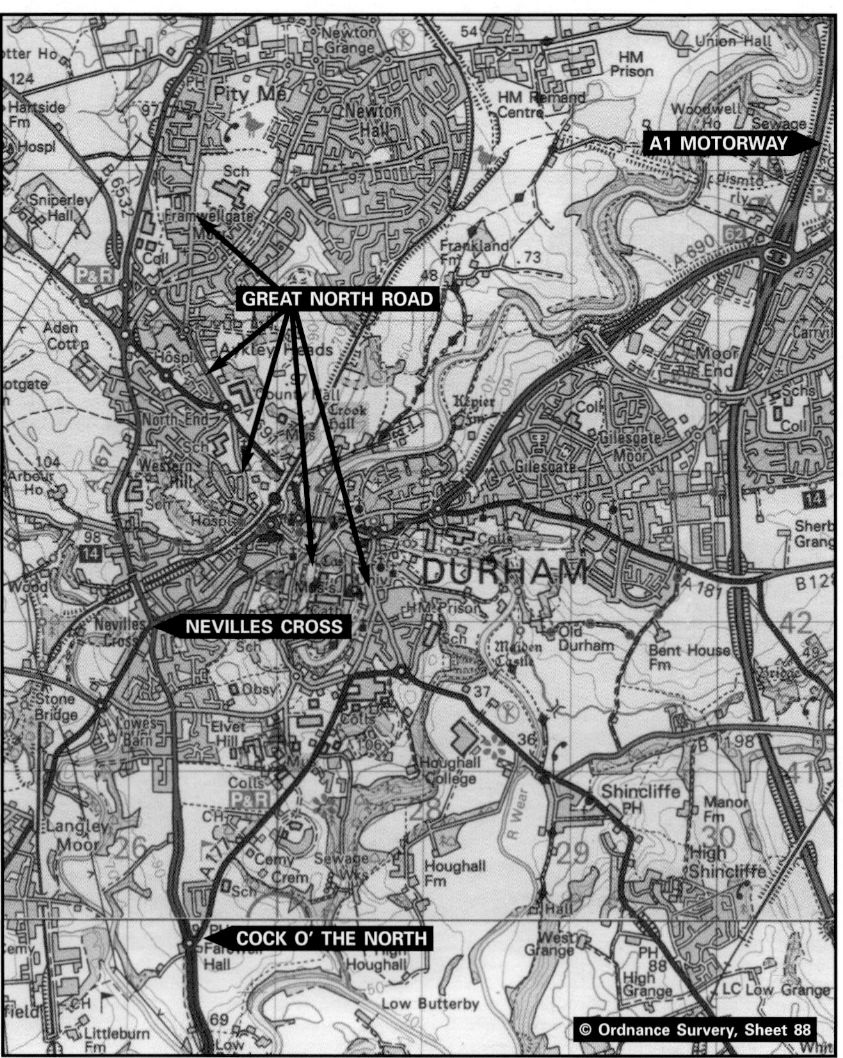

At Durham, the Great North Road takes two routes: the first bypassing the city (now numbered the A167), and the other road going right through the centre (the A177). Now of course the official A1 is the motorway to the east.

We have already seen the Great North Road cross one battlefield at Barnet (see page 31) now here is another on the western suburbs of Durham. In 1346, the French used the Scots to try to divert Edward III's attention from France. It didn't work, and a northern army crushed them at Nevilles Cross. The Scots nobility was decimated and their King taken prisoner.

To re-trace the Great North Road, we need to go all the way back to the Cock O' the North roundabout and take the right fork which is numbered A177. Durham city is on a promontory created by a loop of the River Wear which encloses it on three sides: west, south and east. Our road runs up the eastern side via South Road, Church Street and New Elvet and then turns sharp left at the junction with Old Elvet to cross the river via Elvet Bridge. It ran up the hill to the market place then down the other side to cross the river yet again via Framwellgate Bridge where it became North Road and left the city.

This route is driveable but it is very tight in places and has restrictions. Through traffic has a new route with two new bridges and passes by a little north of the centre. These routes all join up near the Durham city council building at Dryburn, the main road having a new alignment as the A691 joins up with the A167 western route coming up from Neville's Cross. The Great North Road steers a slightly more eastern course as the B6532 through the old villages of Framwellgate and the quaint Pity Me, rejoining the A167 at the northern end of Pity Me. It is believed that this is a Roman alignment.

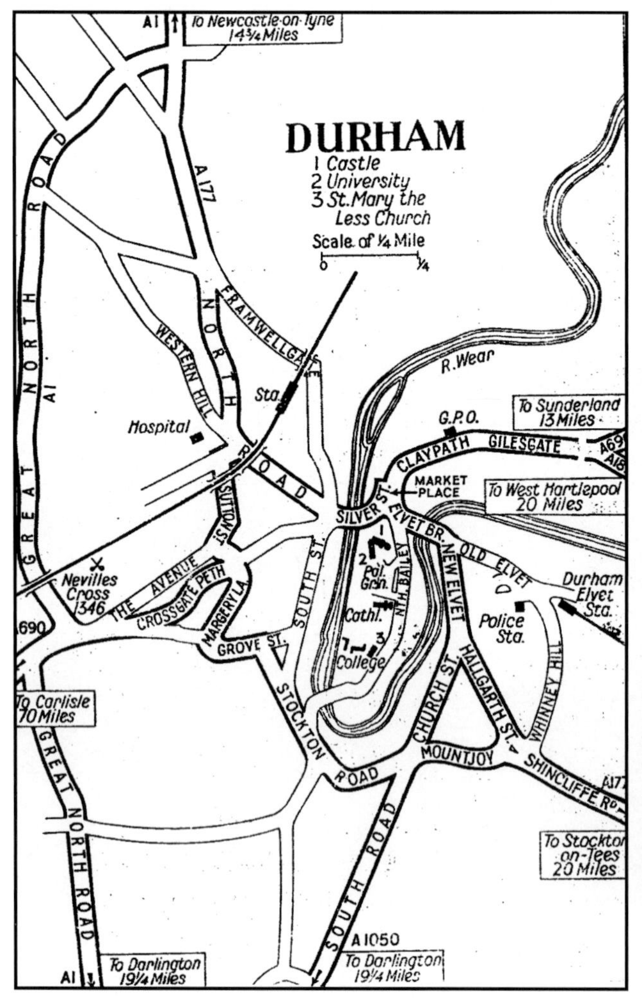

We arrive in town at the top of New Elvet — the plan coming from the RAC handbook of 1938-39.

Most of the old housing has gone apart from a few buildings at the bottom where New Elvet and Old Elvet meet up.

This view looks in the opposite direction to the photograph on the opposite page looking up towards the market place.

The pedestrianised area starts at the point where the road turns hard left and crosses Elvet Bridge.

Left: **The photographer who took this picture was standing at the end of Framwellgate Bridge, looking at the point where the road curves away north up North Road.** *Right:* **My comparison shows where the pedestrian area ends.**

Once again the modern road here is dualled, but it is fairly clear that the southbound carriageway is the addition and the northbound is the original, with the exception of a lay-by on the right, just above Plawsworth, where a curve has been ironed out.

At Chester-le-Street there is evidence of a very early bypass. When we get to the Durham road roundabout, the A167 diverts to the east but our road heads up Durham road straight through the town on the Roman alignment.

Chester is another place that has grown significantly. The village as it was, started about where Ropery Lane is on the right and the workhouse lay opposite where the hospital is now. The road then crossed a beck that joins the River Wear just to the east. The bridge is gone, the beck has been covered over and runs in a culvert below the bus station. The bridge was near the Horners pub.

Going back to the A167, it skirts around Chester between the town and the river past the Riverside Cricket Ground, home of Durham County Cricket Club. We started our journey close to Thomas Lord's first ground and now pass the most recently designated Test cricket ground! The A167 bounces off the A1(M), which is still lurking off to our right-hand side, at a junction and comes back as the A693 although not for very long. Where we meet the road coming through town, the A693 disappears to the west and once again we are running north on the A167.

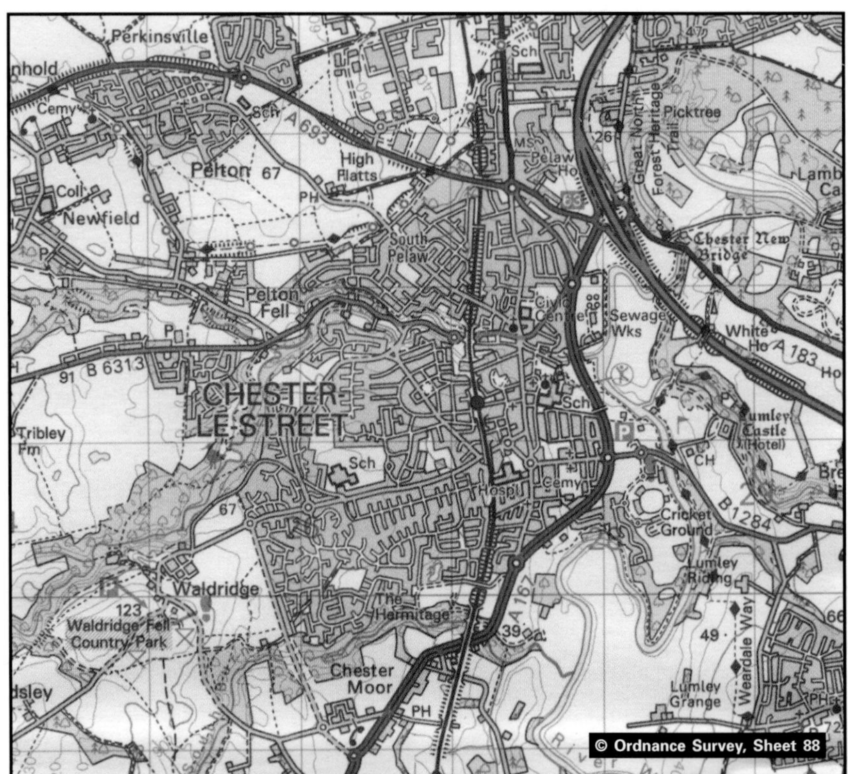

Chester le Street was bypassed quite early so the front street has not changed much. Later it was bypassed again by the A1(M).

This was the Chester Rest House, a service station and garage lying on the road between Chester and Birtley. It is marked on maps as late as the 1950s but by 1960 it had been transformed into a public house.

Junction 63 of the new A1(M) takes shape at Chester le Street; these are views from 1967 and today.

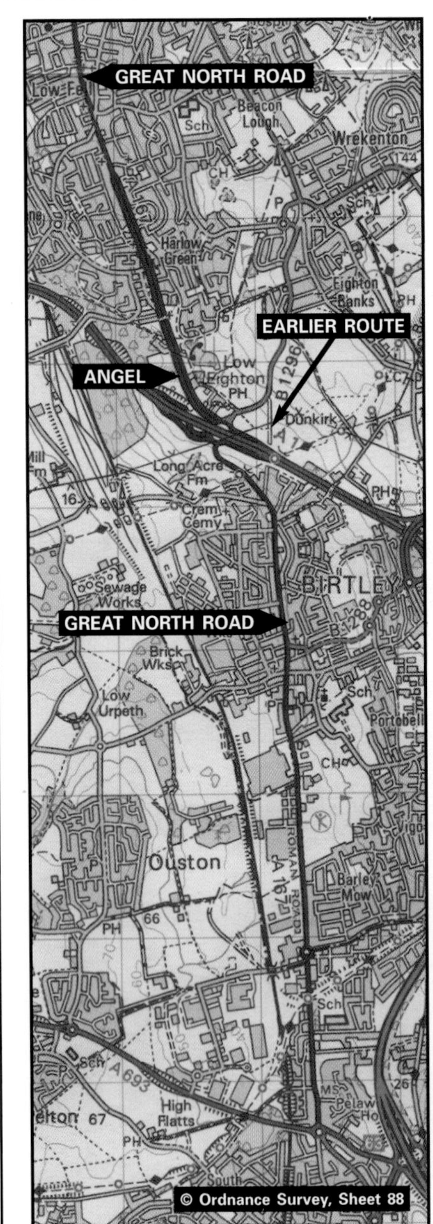

Birtley High Street — the Great North Road since Roman times.

Today the road through Chester does not appear to be particularly tight or congested, and the eastern bypass has in fact been there since the early 1920s as possibly the bridge over the beck was a bottleneck. A 1921 map clearly shows it rejoining the Great North Road via what is now Park Road North before the arterial bypass was built in around 1950. The arterial road in question is now part of the A1(M).

From here on, we are pretty much in suburbia all the way to Gateshead. We skirt the outskirts of Washington new town although it does not quite straddle the road. On our road, Birtley was just a speck, the Three Tuns inn was half a mile north of the village in 1921, and the Coach and Horses was even further away from anywhere. The road bends just after this pub and today is part of a large junction with the current A1. Looking over

to the right, just before the roundabout, you may notice another small orphaned spur of Great North Road. On the other side, passing the Angel of the North, we stay on the original alignment all the way through to Chowdene and Low Fell. In 1923, the left turn at Chowdene Bank denoted the start of the first houses since we left Birtley.

We continue into Gateshead on Durham Road until we get to the Gateshead flyover which is the beginning of an area which has been heavily modernised in more recent times. So we must start doing detective work again. Going back to the Coach and Horses north of Birtley, there is a right turn just past it called Long Bank. It's a dead end, but only because it has been cut off by the modern A1. In fact on the other side, Long Bank continues up a steep climb becoming the B1296 through Wrekenton and eventually becomes the Old Durham Road. This route would appear to be the continuation of the Roman alignment from Chester and was the one used in medieval times. However, due to its steepness, the route that was turnpiked was the easier one through Low Fell which thus became the Great North Road and subsequently the A1.

These days Long Bank is a right turn off the main road. It is quite probable that it was the original north road dating right back to mediaeval times but now it terminates up against the A1(M).

When we get to the A1(M) roundabout between Birtley and Low Fell we can take the B1296 for Wrekenton. A little way from the roundabout, this piece of abandoned road appears on the right behind a gate. It is in fact the continuation of Long Bank in Birtley. It becomes Old Durham Road and eventually Gateshead Hight Street.

This is the Old Durham Road at Low Fell between Wrekenton and High Fell looking south.

Durham Road in Low Fell in 1939 looking northwards towards Gateshead and a tram stop. The pub on the left was called the New Cannon Inn but is now Ye Olde Cannon — that aged quickly!

It was clearly easy to stand around in the road in the 1930s but almost impossible these days to do it long enough to compose and take a photograph. The trams disappeared in 1951.

Back at the A1(M) roundabout, we take the A167 to stay on our Great North Road. Looking south towards the roundabout, I don't think Telford saw this one coming. 'Rusty Rita' or the 'Geordie Flasher' are the nicknames for the Angel of the North. Most of us raised an eyebrow when she first appeared but we've got used to her and now it's a well-regarded landmark.

As Durham Road approaches Gateshead it becomes High West Street and then West Street and starts to slope downwards towards the steep banks of the Tyne. West Street runs parallel to and about 200 yards west of the High Street which is the continuation of the Old Durham Road.

In Gateshead, these two roads, the Durham Road and the Old Durham Road don't quite join up. Originally they ran parallel to one another and formed the centre of the town as West Street and High Street respectively (it is the older route which has become the High Street). The Great North Road as West Street arrives near the river by Gateshead station and then cuts across via Hill Street to merge with the High Street and become Church Street which in turn became Bridge Street and crossed the Tyne via the swing bridge. This bridge, built in 1876, stands upon the site of earlier Tyne crossings including a many arched stone bridge reminiscent of others we have met on our journey. It was only removed when river traffic on the Tyne increased.

There is some evidence that in later years traffic may have used the alternative High Level Bridge over the Tyne. This is a railway bridge built in 1849 which also carried road traffic. Traffic would certainly have had to use it between 1868 and 1876 when the old bridge was replaced with the Swing Bridge. Traffic using the High Level Bridge could take a slightly different route through central Newcastle. However, whether it was actually officially called the Great North Road is not known. The High Level Bridge was unpopular because of steep tolls so, apart from the 1868-76 period, I suspect many will have used the traditional route. There is also some evidence that the High Level Bridge route was

Due to the fact that the whole area has so changed, even I had difficulty in matching this location. Eventually, with the assistance of PCs Soulsby and Copeland of Northumbria Constabulary, I found it but there is nothing left of the first picture except the railings on the wall in the bottom left-hand corner. Everything else has utterly disappeared. The top of the Tyne bridge, which can just be seen in the far distance, gives us an idea of just how steep the banks are.

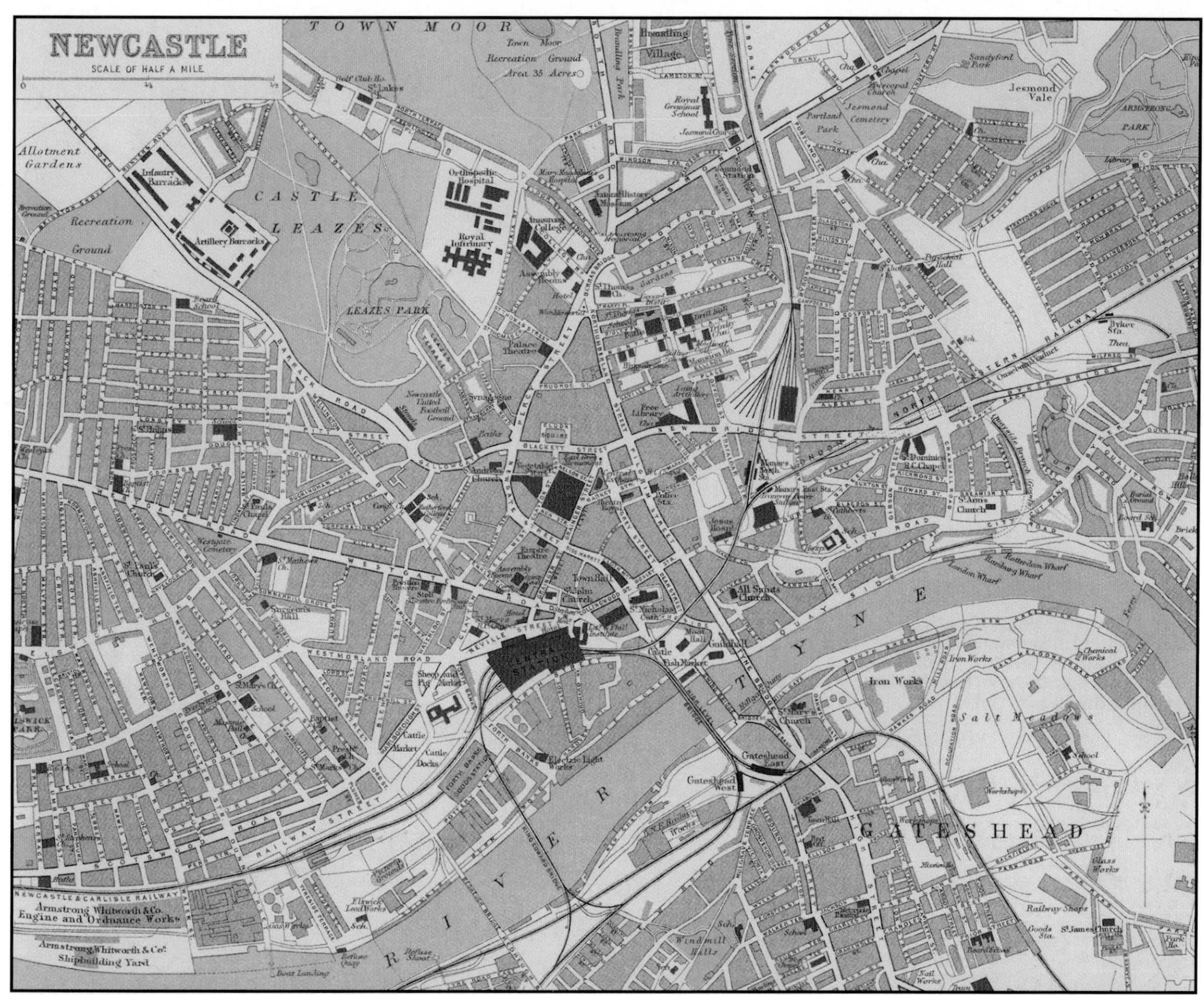

Newcastle, famous for its shipbuilding, lies on the left bank of the Tyne. Before the war it was the location of one of Britain's extensive coalfields, and one of the chief ports for coal exports, the phrase 'To carry coals to Newcastle' being a synonym for any superfluous action. As far as the Great North Road is concerned, the city's main claim to fame is that in 1829 Robert Stephenson built his 'Rocket' locomotive here in his factory on Forth Street, the development of which spelled the end of the coaching era, the last mail coach to Scotland departing on July 5, 1847. Later Robert designed a high level railway bridge in 1850 which now links Newcastle with Gateshead on the southern bank of the river. A roadway was hung below the railway with tolls in 1939 being a half-penny for cycles or motorcycles, while motor cars cost 4d.

This engraving shows both the High Level Bridge (opened 1849) and the original stone bridge (removed in 1868) so it has to have been produced between those two dates.

originally designated A1. This will not have lasted long as by 1928 the Tyne Bridge was opened and the road shifted back to the traditional Pilgrim Street/Northumberland Street route. It is possible that at the time of the road numbering in 1922, the plans for the Tyne Bridge were already known. So the A1 was signposted by the alternative route for the duration of the disruption caused by this.

The mighty Tyne Bridge we use today was opened in 1928 and the embankment for it starts where the two old roads meet at the top of Church Street. Nowadays the whole area is vastly altered and I doubt that a time-traveller from the early 20th century would find his way. Through traffic no longer comes this way as anything travelling up the modern A1(M) is diverted around Newcastle to the west. And even this has been changed as at one time the A1 was the road to the east through the Tyne Tunnel!

The old bridge was replaced with the Swing Bridge in 1876.

Again this is an area that has been totally changed. My photograph was taken at a slightly different angle otherwise I would have to stand with my back to a lot of traffic to get it exactly right. Also unfortunately the road works spoiled the view. You can still see the cathedral tower across the river. The approach to the Tyne Bridge was pushed through here between 1925 and 1928, obliterating the top of Church Street. Bottle Bank is still there and you can even drive down it now. The digger stands at the top of it which looks lower because of the bridge approach dominating the scene. The road on the left is the bottom of Hill Street with the remains of Church Street off to my right. Reflecting back on Charles Harper's visit in 1900, he writes that 'high overhead goes the High Level, and the smoke and rumble of its trains mingle with the clash of Newcastle's thousand anvils and the reek of her million chimneys, but there still stands against the skyline — most fittingly seen from the Gateshead bank at eventide — the coroneted steeple of St Nicholas and the great black form of the Norman keep'.

West Street forked, with the left turning being Wellington Street and the right Hill Street. The Great North Road took the right fork and dropped down to where Hill Street became Church Street which curves round by St Mary's church to Bridge Street and the Swing Bridge. Bottle Bank was a narrow lane which cut out Church Street and led directly down to Bridge Street but it was not suitable for motor traffic. In the photograph above we are looking at the top of Bottle Bank with Church Street to our right and Hill Street to our left. Now look at the roadsign: apart from noting the dangers of Bottle Bank, it states 'To Newcastle A184'. So what has happened to the A1? The eventual conclusion is that for some reason the alternative route via Wellington Street and the High Level Bridge was given the designation A1 in 1922 and this photograph is the only evidence that I have been able to find to support this. Note the ornate tower of Newcastle cathedral above Bottle Bank. Beyond is Newcastle United's football ground, St James's Park, home of the famous 'Toon Army'.

The banks of the Tyne are as steep on the Newcastle side as they are on the Gateshead side. I have included this shot of The Side, although not the Great North Road, to show what it was like once you had crossed the Swing Bridge.

The Great North Road actually ran to the right of The Side up Akenside and into the lower end of Pilgrim Street. Akenside still runs under the Tyne Bridge but the lower part of Pilgrim Street shown in the old photo is now lost underneath an office block.

In 1926, the old route across the mighty Tyne, lauded in both rhyme and song, was changed forever. This picture appears to have been taken at the opening of the new bridge which started at a high level on both sides and removed the necessity to wend your way down the river and back up again. Note that the bridge approaches are higher than a five-storey building.

This Wynn's heavy haulage outfit is crossing the Tyne from south to north. There are what look like shipbuilding cranes in the background on the south side.

It was the same on the other side of the Tyne. Traffic coming over the old bridge had to find its way to Pilgrim Street. Originally, vehicles would have turned right into Sandhill to cross the Lort Burn, apparently a steep-sided beck that ran into the Tyne. Then climb up the twisting Akenside Hill into Pilgrim Street. Eventually the Lort Burn was culverted and filled in to level the area out and the resulting byways became Dean Street and Grey Street which could also be used. Later the new Tyne bridge led traffic straight onto Pilgrim Street. From there, drivers would have headed north up Northumberland Street, Newcastle's main shopping venue, which today is pedestrianised and vehicle free.

The only thing visible there now is the seashell-like Sage — a purpose built music, art and theatre centre on the river bank in Gateshead.

This view is looking north up Pilgrim Street. The first building on the right is Newcastle police station.

Pilgrim Street runs straight into Northumberland Street, Newcastle's main thoroughfare and shopping street.

Today it is entirely pedestrianised but I was able to get this comparison thanks to the girls in a solicitor's office. Looking north.

Our road heads north out of the city as the B1318, along the eastern side of the Town Moor, a large area of common land. On the right was the village of Jesmond and ahead the village of Gosforth. It is interesting to note that although parts of the city further west didn't exist in the 1920s, this area was already somewhat built up. Just off to our left is a large sprawl of forbidding stone buildings which is now a hospital but in 1921 was the Newcastle Upon Tyne City Lunatic Asylum. Must have been a grim spot.

Northumberland Street emerged onto Barras Bridge and the Great North Road turned right away from the photographer. Once upon a time this was a roundabout but today it is a traffic light controlled junction. The new glass building is part of Newcastle University. The road coming from the left would be the one used if coming from the High Level Bridge.

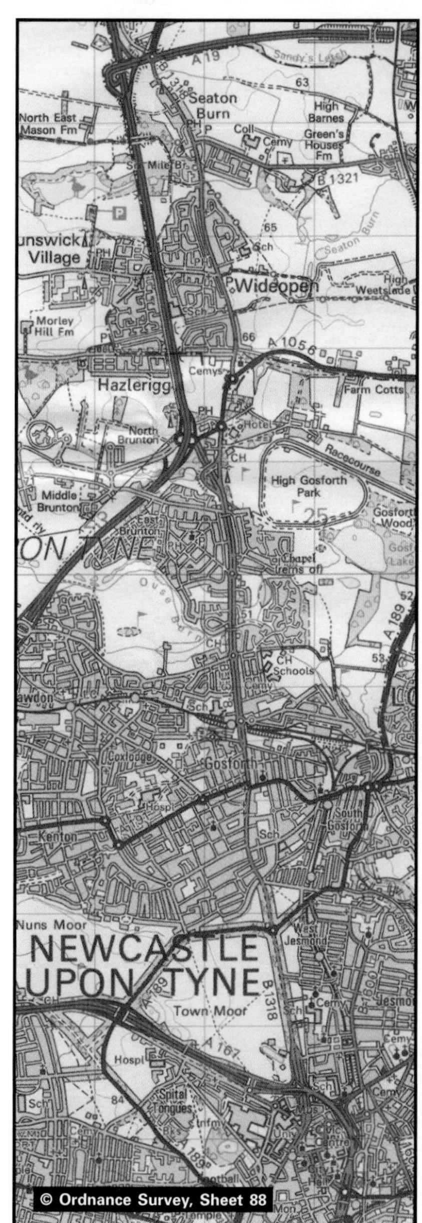

As the Great North Road exits the city it passes the Town Moor — an area of moorland which still exists to the west of the road.

If we were to retrace our route all the way back to Darlington, and stay on the motorway instead of going into the town, we would eventually reach the location where the motorway splits, near Birtley. The left-hand road is the current A1 which turns westwards past Team Valley and the Angel of the North. It then goes along the river to Blaydon where it turns north and crosses the Tyne before turning north-east to rejoin the north road near Gosforth.

The right fork, now numbered the A194(M), heads north-east to Jarrow and joins the A19 (the same A19 that left us in Doncaster) to pass through the Tyne Tunnel built in 1967. Once through the tunnel, the A19 curves back west around the top of Newcastle and joins the Great North Road just north of Seaton Burn. This route held the designation A1 between 1967 and the mid-1980s when the Gateshead bypass was extended over the Tyne and around to Gosforth (the left fork) when that route became the A1. Confusing isn't it!

The Royalty screened its last film on December 30, 1981.

On the far side of Town Moor we enter the suburb of Gosforth — once a town in its own right. This is the Great North Road masquerading as the High Street. The domed building just beyond the junction with Church Street was the local cinema.

We pass through on Gosforth High Street and then the road is once again named the Great North Road. As we cross the railway at the top of the High Street, in 1921 we would finally have left the city but today it is built up as far as Brunton Lane. The Three Mile Bridge inn stood here on its own. At North Gosforth today you can rejoin the A1 as it arrives from its journey around the west of Tyneside, but we stay on the B1318 for a short while longer. We have to take a slip-road and cross over the top of the A1 access road to stay on the B road, and southbound it follows the original course. We go on up to the village of Wideopen; then past the Travellers Rest inn and the two rows of terraces that stretch south from it. It is much larger today, even more so than the next village Seaton Burn, which in 1920 was the larger of the two. This village marks the last place on our procession through Durham, Gateshead and Newcastle.

The road north of Gosforth is an urban dual carriageway with trees up the middle and is bounded by a wall for much of its east side. However, the positioning of milestones would indicate that it is the west (northbound) side which is the original. So there should be trees between the photographer and the wall in the original. The only place which comes even close was this stretch just before the village of Wideopen which now has a roundabout on it, the break in the wall being the entrance to a hotel.

If you stand at the north end of the village of Seaton Burn, outside what is currently an electricity sub-station and look north, you will note that the existing road curves away from you to the right to meet the roundabout that stands there now. Our road used to run a tad to the left of that through the clump of trees, bypassing the roundabout and rejoining by the entrance to the Travel Lodge.

Outside the existing Holiday Inn, the road ran in a straight line to the junction with the lane to Brenkley outside Seven Mile House Farm, so called because it stood near the seven mile milestone out of Newcastle. The older route was removed when the dual carriageway was built and the road curves to cross on a bridge. A rare case of a kink being put in a road rather than having it removed!

Once back on track we head north again past the grounds of Blagdon Hall and we briefly merge with the dual carriageway to cross the River Blythe on Stannington Bridge but leave it again straight after to pass through Stannington village. The original bridge is still visible as the northbound carriageway uses it – there is an ornate brick parapet on the left and a modern metal one on the right.

Immediately over the bridge you may notice yet another of those fenced-off roads off to the left that looks as if it was once the continuation of the one you are on. That of course is because it was. This was the original route into Stannington which described a bit of an S-bend through the village. Sometime between 1940 and 1950 this was straightened out, but the new road still ran through the village so it was not a bypass. This newer part still exists as the slip-road off the dual carriageway and into Stannington. To explore the older route, turn left at the mini roundabout as you come into the village; it's marked as a dead end. At the same mini roundabout we go straight on, but the pre-1950 route took the right turn here, curved past the Ridley Arms pub and rejoined the road a couple of hundred yards further on at another mini roundabout.

As we leave Stannington, we cross from one side of the dual carriageway to the other. The old road has now been eradicated by the junction so we have to cross via a pair of roundabouts. The next small hamlet is known as Stannington Station as a railway station was in operation there until 1958. It is possibly better remembered than Stannington itself because there was also a fuel station and transport cafe there.

Seaton Burn to the Border

At one time Seaton Burn was barely a speck on the road — a few houses and a pub clustered around a colliery. Yet the pub, the Moor House, is still there in this view taken looking north.

Looking south down the original road from Stannington village to where it used to cross the River Blythe. Now cut off by the dual carriageway.

Victor, a Trucknet member, says:

'There was a talking mynah bird just through the door. Can't remember the name, but someone will remember the name of place and maybe bird.'

Someone does remember the bird — Chris Webb:

*'I remember that mynah bird at the Stannington cafe. There was a notice that said: "Do not swear at this bird" which of course was an invitation to do so. I'm sure it used to say "BRS drivers are b*****ds". We used to changeover at Stannington all-night garage on the right going north. We tried changing over in Morpeth town at night until one Scottish trunker was late and our driver fell asleep, waking up to being surrounded by market stalls being erected for the Bank Holiday.'*

And so does Kevmac:

'I don't remember the name of the mynah bird but boy could it swear!!' Clearly a very memorable bird!'

Moving on, we can no longer go north from Stannington Station as it is a dead end becoming the southbound off-slip from the dual carriageway. So we have to go back and rejoin the dual carriageway, but only briefly as we come straight off again on the current A197 into Morpeth.

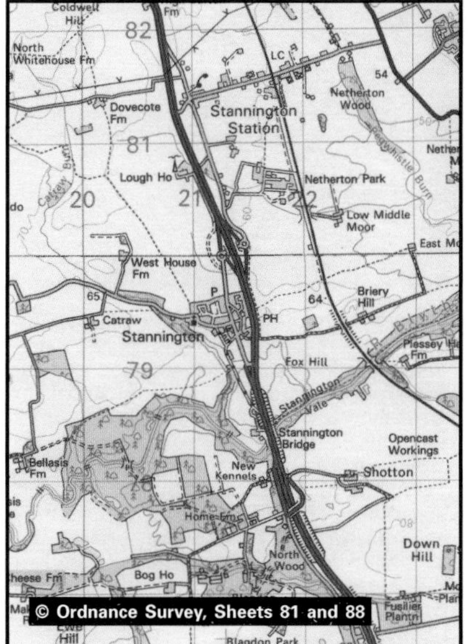

© Ordnance Survey, Sheets 81 and 88

The site of the Stannington Station transport cafe. Sadly no Mynah bird today!

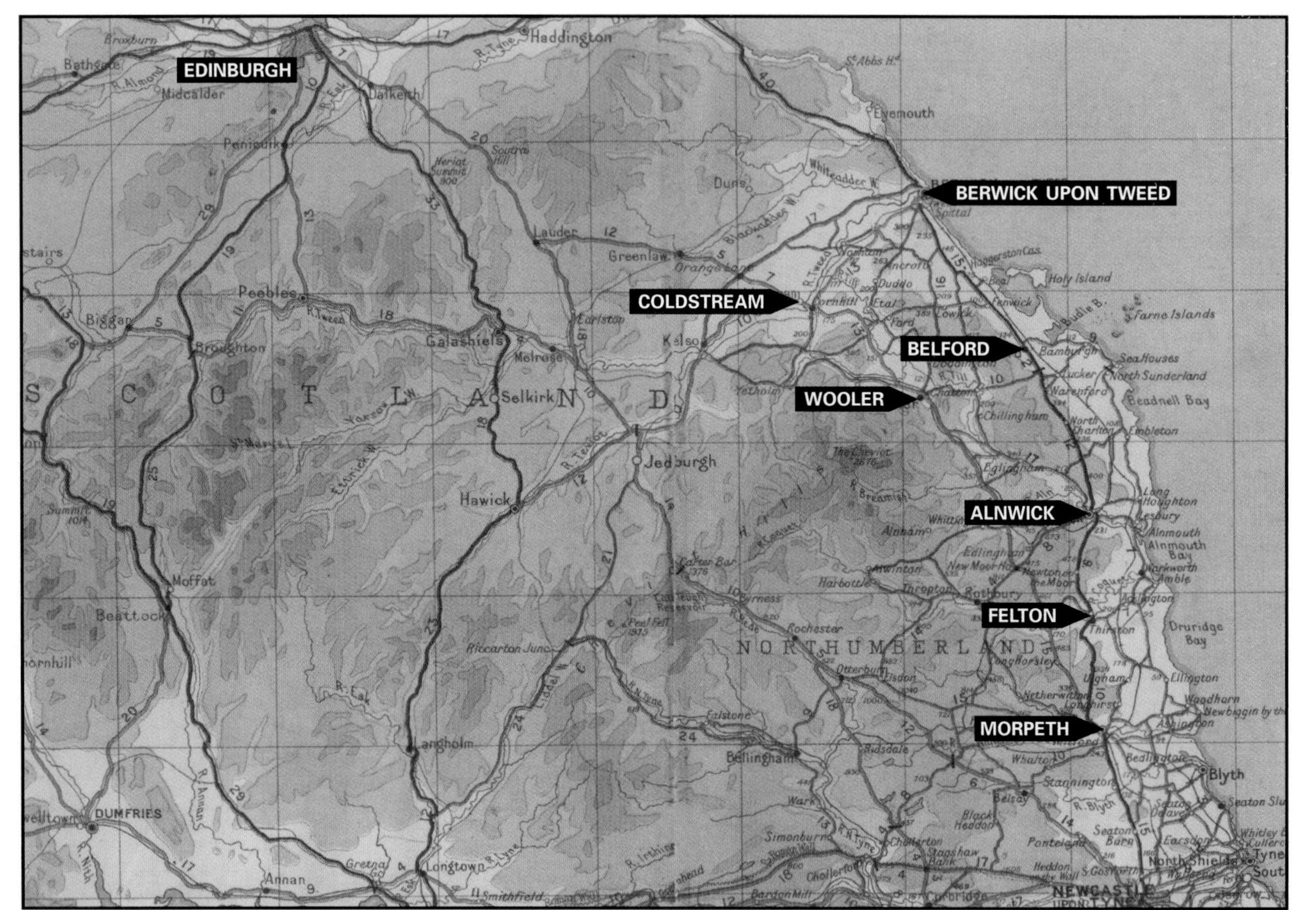

The Automobile Association has been serving motorists for over 100 years, this map being reproduced from an early member's handbook which explains how the organisation began. 'After the passing of the Motor Car Act in 1903, it was almost impossible to go anywhere in a motor car without receiving summonses for exceeding — sometimes by a mere fraction — the legal speed limit of twenty miles an hour. To meet the situation some motorists organised and maintained at their own expense a few cyclists on the London-Brighton road whose task it was to warn all passing motorists of "police traps". In August 1905, the work was put on a permanent basis and the Automobile Association came into existence with exactly ninety subscribers. The week-end cyclists on the Brighton road were the first A.A. patrols. To-day more than 20,000 miles of road in the British Isles are regularly patrolled by an army in distinctive khaki uniform. But whereas in very early days the warning of police traps was given to every motorist, service and the salute are now reserved for members only. The majority of the men are mounted on motor-cycles with yellow side-cars which contain full equipment to enable the riders to deal with the minor troubles which may still beset the motorist. Changing wheels, repairing tubes, clearing carburetters, tracing and remedying ignition faults, supplying oil and petrol in emergency, warning members about weather and road conditions ahead, giving local information concerning hotels, garages, camping and caravan sites, all these things are but part of the daily duties of every A.A. patrol. Only one day in the whole year — Christmas Day — is this cheerful and efficient service absent.'

Morpeth was bypassed in 1970 but our Great North Road originally went into town. Even in 1924 there was very little between the current A1 junction and Morpeth Castle. Downhill all the way, the road crosses the River Wansbeck on a stone bridge built in 1830 and then it turns sharp left to run all the way along Morpeth's Bridge Street until at the far end it turns north again as Newgate Street. Rising steadily all the way, we leave town as the A192 and rejoin the bypass coming around from the south. This is a common feature of the whole northern stretch of our road. Regular sharp descents to cross rivers and becks that are running down from the fells of the north Pennines and Cheviots, and then climbing back up again. Our wagon drivers remember them well.

Just north of where we rejoin the dual carriageway, the modern A697 forks away to our left for Wooler and Coldstream. Had things turned out differently, we could have been taking this fork as in the early 1800s Thomas Telford had been asked to survey the whole northern road with a view to upgrading it as he had already done with the London to Holyhead road. His chosen route was this

Arriving in Morpeth we cross the River Wansbeck and turn left into Bridge Street. Judging by the cars and dress, this photograph was taken around 1950 but the town has not changed at all.

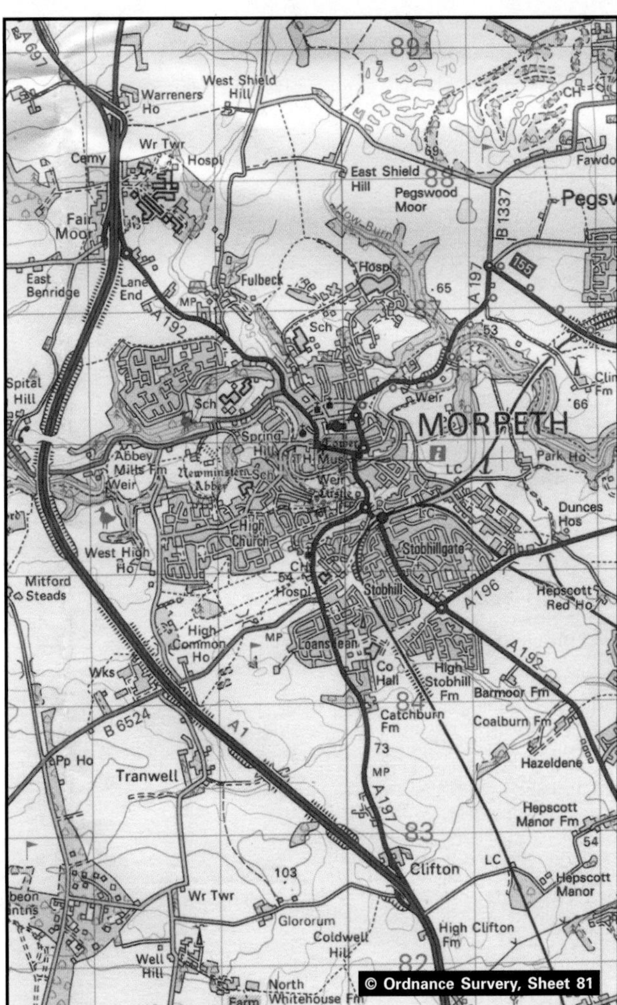

Market day in Morpeth in the early 20th century. The wagons are parked outside what looks like a stable building. This appears very much like the scene of a cattle market today except that the vehicles would be engine-powered.

A697 that joined the modern A68 and entered Edinburgh by way of Dalkeith. At the time this was not the favoured route, as that further east, although further in miles, had less in the way of steep inclines. Telford would have ironed these out as he did elsewhere, but this was another project that was dashed by the arrival of the railways. (Incidentally, if you are in no hurry, the A68 between Dalkeith and Corbridge is a stunningly beautiful drive and I heartily recommend it.)

One hundred years have passed and although the stable has gone, the other buildings remain.

At Felton, the Great North Road originally ran alongside the River Coquet and turned sharp left to cross the river on the old stone bridge. There was then a nasty dog-leg on the north side around the cottage which stood on the corner. ***Right:*** **Later, a new bridge was added which was wider and had the purpose of straightening out the difficult turn.**

And now at last we come to the Great North Road in its full majesty for once we have passed the A697 junction, the A1 shrinks to a single carriageway. Apart from town and village bypasses, this is the original course and, for the first time since we left London, the original un-dualled road actually has the designation A1. Nevertheless, even the single carriageway has odd ox-bow sections on both sides where curves have been straightened out and villages have been bypassed. Most noticeably on this first stretch is Causey Bridge where the old road dipped through the village centre and at Bockenfield.

Just north of here, at West Moor Farm, the road curved away on what is now the B6345 into Felton. Well-known by haulage drivers as a bottleneck because, as elsewhere, there was a steep drop to a river crossing and another steep climb out again, it was exacerbated by the fact that the road bends at a right angle to cross the Coquet River so they couldn't even get a run at the slope.

'Night Shift Bri': *'I remember going through Felton on the old A1. You couldn't get a run at the bank because of the sharp left-hand bend at the bottom.'* Archie Paice recalls the cafe in Felton out the front of Pendleton & Hares' yard: *'A good place that was to stop.'*

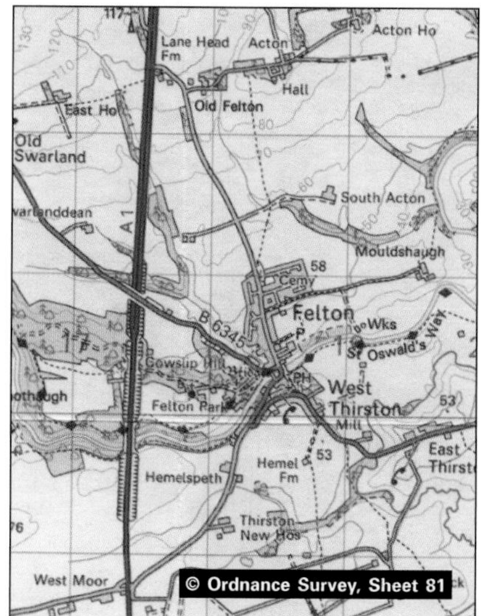

Trees and the new bridge make accurate comparisons impossible but this is a view at the southern end of both bridges. Rising away from the crossing is the slope mentioned in the text by our wagon drivers.

The whole section between Morpeth and Berwick was upgraded in bits and pieces between the mid-1960s and 1980s and then some of it was dualled at a later date, also in dribs and drabs, so it's not easy to say when any particular stretch was built or dualled. But it seems that Felton was bypassed in the early 1980s. When we arrive at the bypass coming out of Felton, we don't actually join it as the old road still exists. As the junctions here are not GSJs, we have to turn right, onto the dual carriageway and then turn left off it where it is signposted Swarland.

At one time this was just a curve in the road, but it has been cut in two by the current A1 which was realigned here to avoid Swarland and Newton-on-the-Moor. The old road crosses and re-crosses the new one a couple of times and they eventually combine just where West End from Shilbottle joins the A1. Incidentally, immediately south of this junction on the right, is a small stretch abandoned in a wood! The road sign for Shilbottle is regularly defaced by those who see the opportunity of some smut!

We stay with the modern dual carriageway for half a mile or so passing a small ox-bow stretch at Cawledge Bridge and then we come off at the A1068 where the Great North Road entered Alnwick. It followed South Road into Alnwick Street and goes past what looks like a railway station. This is because it *was* a railway station but nowadays it's something much more interesting. This is Barter Books one of the largest second-hand bookshops in Europe and well worth a visit. All I can say is that it's a good job they don't have room for artic parking because I would have spent far too long there over the years, and would have had to have been chased out by my boss many times!

Alnwick was another of those places, like Stamford, which was on the road as a coaching stop but later became a bottleneck to modern traffic. Narrow streets and the remnants of a town bar (gate in the town wall) were a real hassle to through traffic. At the point where Alnwick Street becomes Bondgate Without, we come up against Bondgate or Hotspur Tower. This is a remnant of the town walls, having one narrow arch that now restricts traffic to one way at a time, and nothing higher than a van would fit under it. Passing through it, our road becomes Bondgate Within but freight traffic had to turn left before the bar and go around

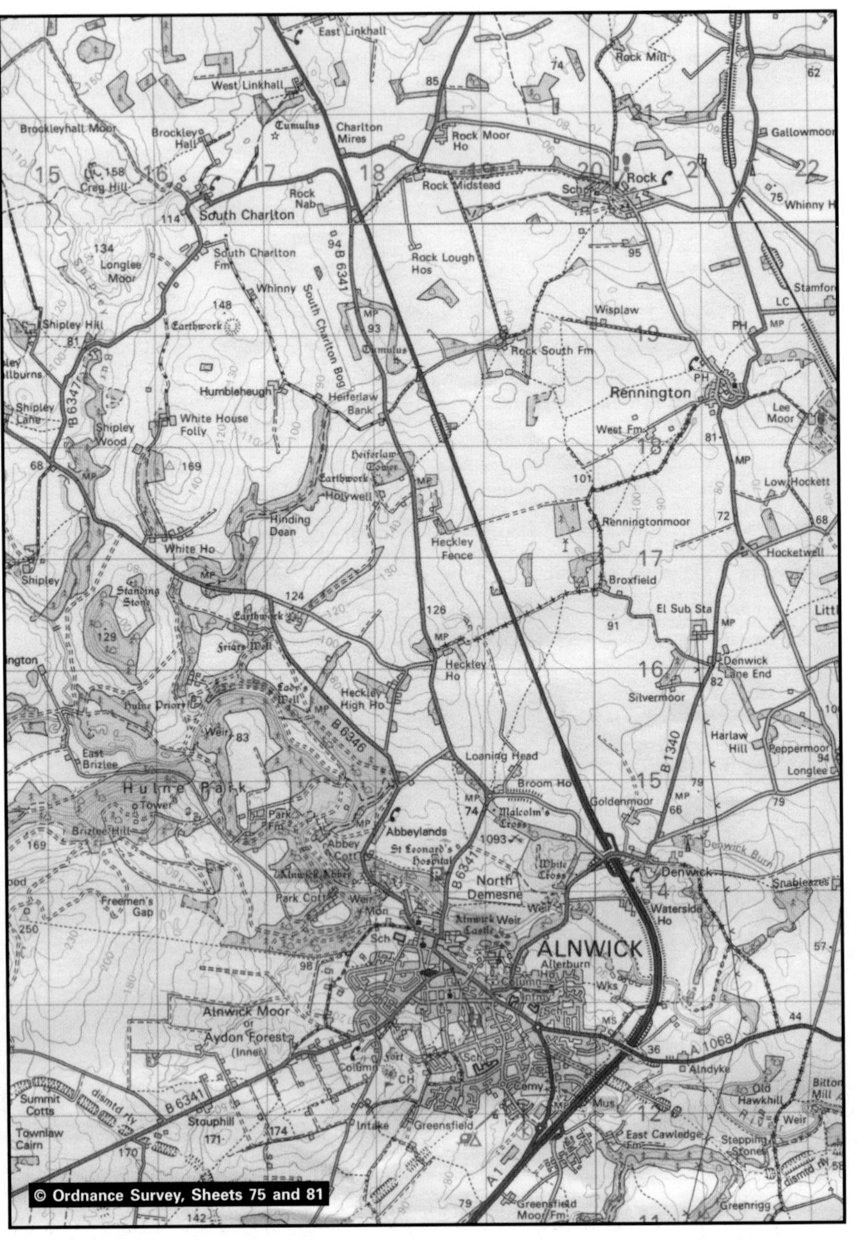

© Ordnance Survey, Sheets 75 and 81

In this picture, it appears that Alnwick is gearing up for a visit from Edward VII. This is Bondgate — also the Great North Road.

the houses to rejoin us at the other end of Bondgate Within where it becomes Narrowgate. Called Narrowgate for very good reasons, it runs around the side of Alnwick castle and then as The Peth steeply downhill to the river. Trucknet's freight drivers remember it well. 'Bumper' recalls *'them towers in Alnwick were a pain. There was two routes you could use, the main one was where you turned left at the tower, and followed it through the town. You will remember Narrowgate, then The Peth. Must have been about six or seven lorries a year went back down The Peth — I think the lions were more often in the river than on the bridge! Unless we were delivering or loading in Alnwick we would use the Denwick route, a bit longer but better than getting stuck in Narrowgate.'*

The Peth leads onto the Lion Bridge that crosses the River Aln. The stone lions on the parapets are the emblems of the Dukes of Northumberland. Turner painted a view of the Lion Bridge and Alnwick castle which can be seen in the Art Gallery of South Australia in Adelaide.

Once over the bridge the Great North Road runs north again as the B6341, rejoining the current A1 again at Charlton Mires, and once again we are on one of the remaining single carriageway sections. There are oxbow stretches at Shipperton Bridge and also Brownieside where there was another well used transport cafe. This later became a Little Chef but is currently closed and derelict at the north end of Brownieside village. It stands on an orphaned stretch of Great North Road that can be followed on foot into the undergrowth for a couple of hundred yards.

Taken further up the street, judging by the cars it's the 1960s. The Lion garage is now the local Co-op.

Yet another couple of hundred yards back from the previous photo, still looking back south, we have the aptly named Narrowgate. Vehicles that couldn't get through the Bondgate rejoined us here on the right. This must have been a total nightmare for the drivers of large vehicles . . .

. . . especially as the southbound ones had just made the climb up The Peth from the river. This shot is looking north from the end of Narrowgate outside the castle gateway. If there was any kind of queue for Narrowgate, it could strand heavy vehicles half way up the slope with disastrous results.

Looking back up The Peth from the river bridge. The lions were the symbol of the Dukes of Northumberland and, as our wagon drivers recall, were 'more often in the river than on the bridge' due to lorries not making it up The Peth. It may be telling that when I visited Alnwick in 2012 I discovered that there was only one lion left on the bridge.

The shadows lengthen at the end of a long day. For about five miles northbound out of Alnwick we stay on the old road (as the B6341) before rejoining the modern A1. It wanders through Northumberland in all its wonderful glory.

We return to the A1 where we proceed on the original alignment all the way to Warenford where three long curves have been ironed out, bypassing the village and leaving two other ox-bow lay-bys. At the Belford turn we leave the A1 again to follow the old road. On turning off the A1 we come to a sharp bend north where there is also a left turn. This is the original course. Turn left and follow it and after a few hundred yards we come up against the new A1 and we can go no further. This road is called South Road and was the Great North Road recently enough to have the remains of cat's eyes and white lines down it's middle but the verges have encroached enough to give it the appearance of a country lane. We turn round and pass quickly through the village noting only one old coaching house, the Blue Bell and then we start to climb up North Bank, a steep climb out of the village, again remembered by our wagon drivers.

Chris Webb has a tale:

'Belford brings back memories, I remember one of our Newbridge trunkers going up there and he missed a gear in a Scania 81. The trailer load locks came adrift, a couple of belts snapped, and about 15 cages of tinned meat smashed through the roller shutter, flattened the tail lift, and spewed out onto the A1.'

Twelve miles further north we reach Belford.

This is the main street in Belford — now the present-day A1 bypasses the town.

'Bumper' remembers it too:

'Belford bank was the same as The Peth at Alnwick and Felton. The steepest part was about three-quarters of the way up. Got stuck behind one of S. C. Cooks old Scammells one day. His second man was sitting on the near-side front wing. As soon as they hit the steepest bit, he pressed the cold start and you couldn't see or breathe for black smoke. Seemingly this was a regular thing for them. At least we could skip gears on the banks but the Scammell had to go down through the box — their left leg and arm must have been a blur! Tested your skill of gear change and driving in them days.'

And Archie Paice reminds us how dangerous things were at one time:

'Do you remember that big hill down through Belford? A friend of mine was killed coming down there, he was on for S.A .Bell of Malton, and had been up Scotch delivering Wards Steel and was coming home empty.'

At the top of North Bank, we can see how close we are now to the sea. For much of the northern trek we have been slowly getting closer and closer to the East Coast and now it is clearly visible, as are the fortresses of Bamburgh and Lindisfarne castles. We rejoin the single carriageway A1 that runs for the

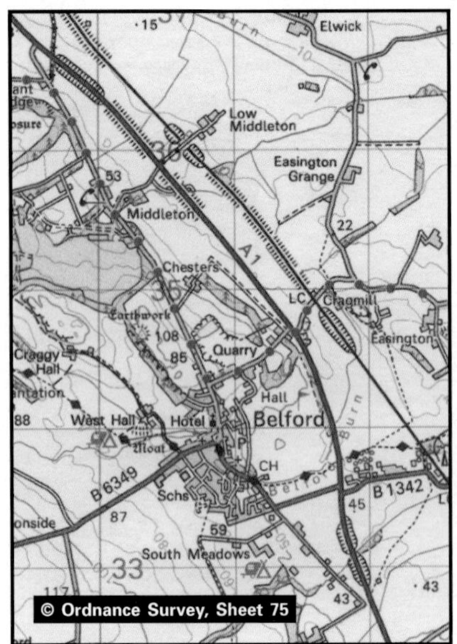

next six or seven miles directly on the old Great North Road, with the exception of a tiny ox-bow stretch at West Mains and one other small diversion.

On the right we reach Haggerston Castle caravan park. This was originally a castle but the estate has long been sold off. It does however have one claim to fame — or possibly infamy — depending on your view. A former owner of the estate developed a tree from two types of cypress that had cross-pollinated at another family estate. The resulting hybrid was called after him: the Leyland Cypress', probably better known as the Leylandii of many a neighbourly dispute!

As we approach Haggerston, in former times we would actually have taken a left turn by the entrance to the park and then turned right half a mile down the road. This dog-leg was ironed out in around 1970.

North of here we travel another few miles on the original route until we arrive at the junction for Scremerston. The modern road curves to the left here becoming the start of the Berwick bypass, leaving a little bit of orphaned road between it and the turning for Scremerston. We turn right down this road to continue on our journey. According to old maps, it used to be called Richardson's Stead although there was a mine here called the Scremerston mine. Whatever the reason for the name change, the village has hardly changed at all except that the mine has closed. We go through in the blink of an eye. At the far end the road curves off the old route slightly to meet another turning off the current A1, leaving a very small piece behind a house which remains as a footpath. On the other side of this junction we quickly get back on track and head straight for Berwick. On the right here there used to be a transport cafe and a bit further up the small cottage on the right called Scremerston Cottage used to be the Miners Arms pub.

Back in 1925 there was nothing on the road until one passed the spot where the roundabout for Billendene Terrace is now. On the left, just past it, was a large sawmill called the Tweed Sawmill. It has been replaced by Tweedbank Retail Park and on the right a large railway goods yard that served Tweed Dock.

Our road ran between each of these and under the railway bridge — which is still there — becoming Main Street on the other side. This dipped towards the riverbank to

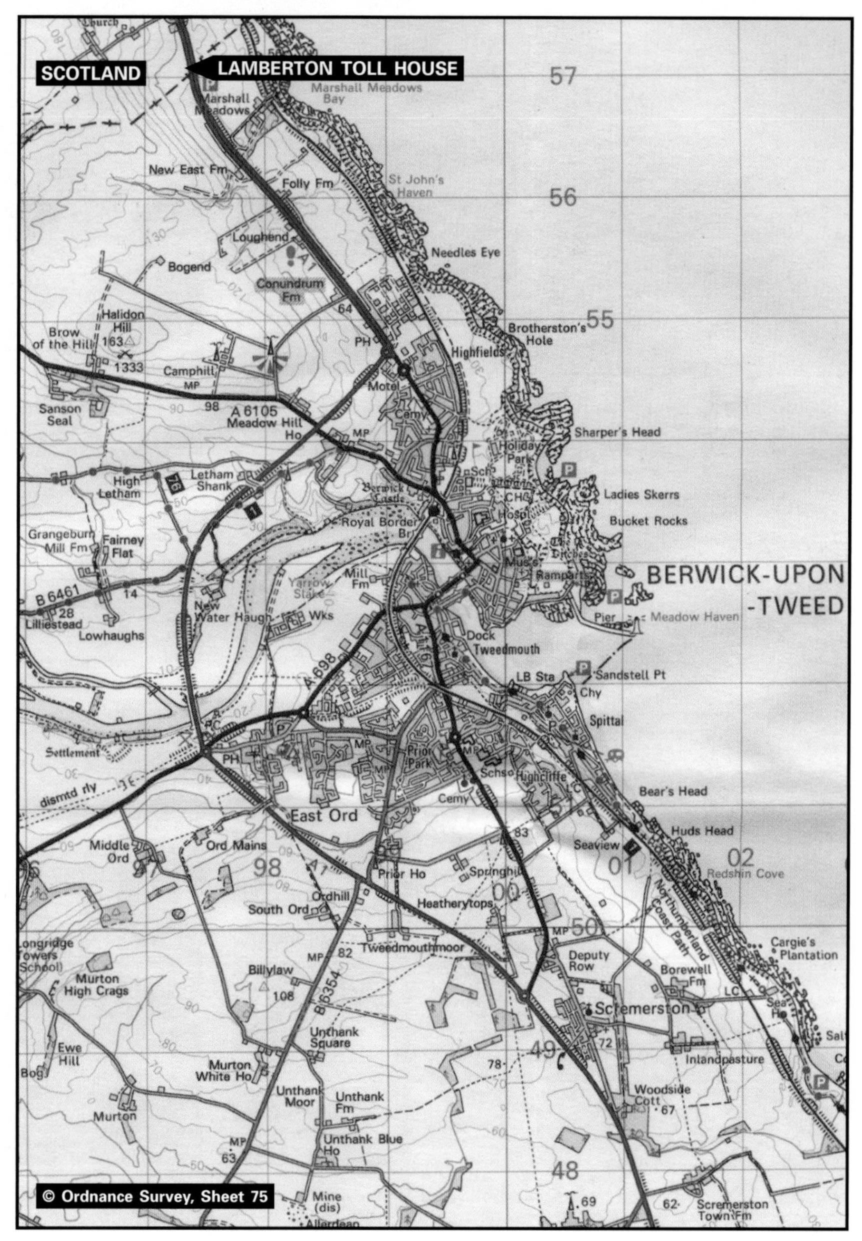

The old bridge over the Tweed was built in the early 17th century, apparently on the orders of James I who had to travel over a dilapidated old wooden bridge on his way to London for his Coronation. It is a 15-arch sandstone structure but quite narrow and today is only one way.

A view of both the old and new bridges — new being a relative term as the Royal Tweed Bridge was built back in the 1920s and served to carry the A1 across the Tweed until the 1980s. Now an even newer bridge takes the motorway across the river but further upstream.

turn hard right and cross the old stone Berwick Bridge, a 15-span bridge over the Tweed. This was built in the early 17th century, allegedly on the orders of James I who passed through Berwick on his way to become King of England and Scotland on the death of Elizabeth I. This bridge is very narrow and nowadays takes traffic in one direction only.

At the far end we go via Bridge Street and Hide Hill to turn left on Marygate, the market area of Berwick. In the 1920s a new bridge was built. Known as the Royal Tweed Bridge, it is a short distance upstream of the old one and at a higher elevation. The Great North Road was shifted with it, extending up Prince Edward Road to the new bridge, and joining Marygate a little further up on the far side. This avoided the very narrowest parts of Old Berwick but large vehicles still had to negotiate Scotgate and the old town wall bar.

Whichever way we cross over, Marygate soon becomes Castlegate and we pass over the same railway line we went under on the way into Berwick and there the road forks. The left turning goes to Chirnside while the Great North Road veers right and leaves

Shipbuilding took place in Berwick between 1950 and 1978 and the shipyard was on the quayside by the old bridge. This lorry with its nautical load is negotiating the left turn into Marygate. I would not like to try this today with a modern day artic.

town as the A1167. In 1925, the cemetery on North Road marked the outer limit of the town, but today it is built up all the way out to where we meet the current A1 bypass coming round from where it left us at Scremerston. The A1 is dualled again here and is a direct continuation of the road out of Berwick. It runs almost along the cliff-tops with views out over the North Sea.

About two miles on from the roundabout at Berwick there is a large lay-by on either side of the road; we have now reached the England-Scotland border.

On the site of this lay-by in previous times stood Lamberton toll-house which, for some reason, is not as well-known as the Blacksmith's Shop in Gretna although it performed the same function.

Charles Harper tells us that it had a sign which read: *'Ginger Beer sold here and marriages performed at reasonable terms'.*

The toll-house has gone but is believed to have still been standing, albeit in a derelict state, in the 1970s.

Welcome to Scotland! The old toll house stood right on the border next to the carriageway. The road here is now an ox-bow lay-by created by the dualling so we can pinpoint the location of the toll house exactly. The actual border between England and Scotland is now marked by cobbled stones set on either side of the road.

Scotland

On the site of this lay-by in previous times stood Lamberton toll house which for some reason is not as well known as the Blacksmith's Shop in Gretna although it performed the same function. Harper tells us that it had a sign that read '*Ginger Beer sold here and marriages performed at reasonable terms*'.

We have all heard of Gretna Green on the western route to Scotland via Carlisle but Lamberton was equally popular for eloping lovers seeking to get married. Under the Marriage Act of 1754, if the parent of a minor, i.e. under the age of 18, objected, they could prevent a marriage going ahead but this requirement did not apply in Scotland. There, all that was required to solemnise the marriage was a simple declaration by the couple — 'This is my husband' and 'This is my wife' witnessed by the toll-keeper. George Lamb, the 'parson' at Lamberton Toll, had been imprisoned for six months in 1807 for obtaining money on the false pretence of marrying people and is credited with marrying over 1,800 individuals between 1804 and 1816 when he died. However, after the Marriage (Scotland) Act of 1856 was passed, the contracting parties had to be resident in Scotland for 21 days. This is Charles Harper's sketch of the toll-house as it appeared in 1900.

This is the Flemington Inn at Burnmouth. It stood on the right-hand side of the road next to the Gull's Nest pub. It had the legend 'First Pub and Last Pub' emblazoned on each gable end.

Unfortunately, the inn burned down in 2006 and it could not be saved so the remains had to be demolished, but this is the spot where it once stood.

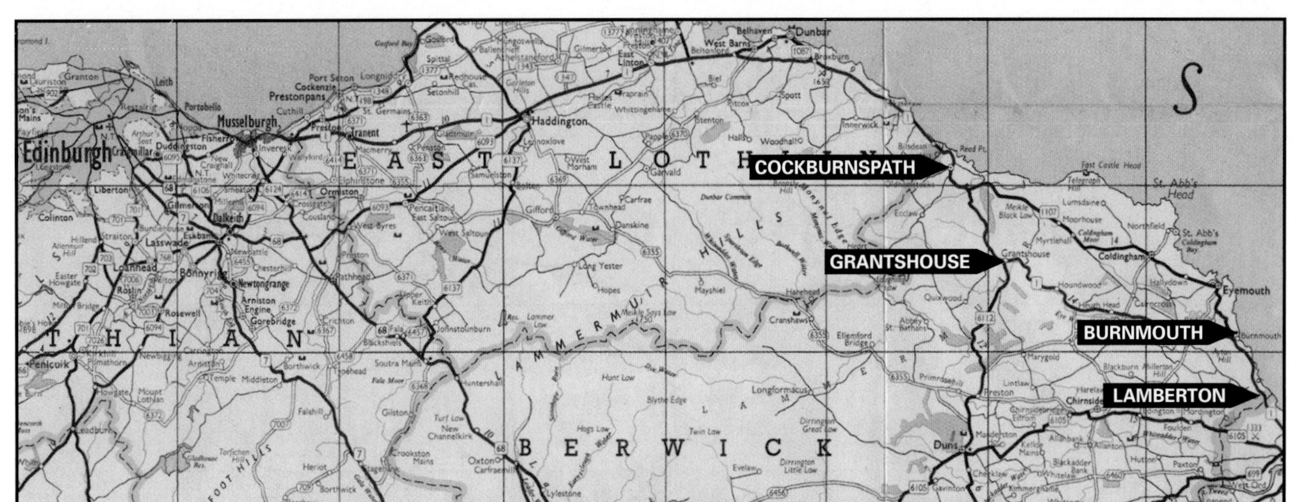

As we enter Scotland the Great North Road diverts from the modern road. We need to take the junction for Lamberton village and, although we don't enter the village, we follow this ox-bow stretch for about a mile before rejoining the current A1 which is no longer dualled having reverted back to S2 as it passed Lamberton.

We stay on the original route through to Burnmouth except for a short ox-bow section at Greystonelees. In Burnmouth there was a fork in the road. The left fork was our road and the other was an alternative route via Eyemouth and Coldingham rejoining the current road just south of Cockburnspath mostly as the A1107. There is some evidence that the latter route was an earlier north road and the section from Ayton to Cockburnspath was built in the early 19th century to supercede it. The Flemington Inn stood between the roads at the fork.

On the other side of Burnmouth we pass another ox-bow lay-by on the right and then, after passing under the railway bridge, we need to take the slip road signposted for Ayton and Chirnside to follow the Great North Road, leaving yet again the modern A1. This road took over from the old road through Eyemouth in around 1817 and runs through Ayton village turning right at what was a crossroads and becoming Ayton High Street. At the other side of the village we rejoin the current A1 again.

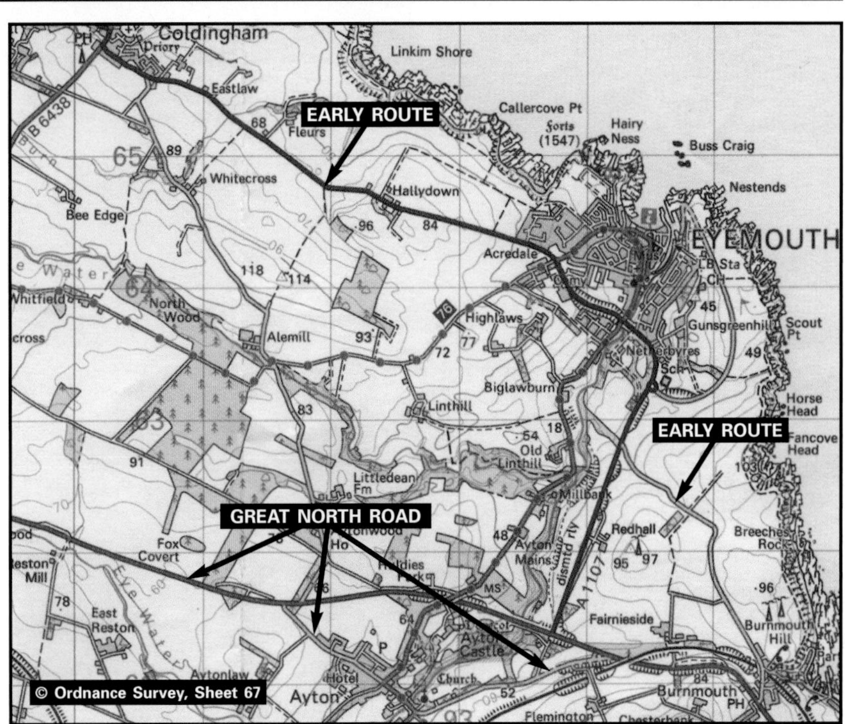

Between this point and Cockburnspath we are essentially on the original 1817 course although a number of curves have been ironed out and junctions altered as this stage has been dualled in recent years. However we are now passing through the Lammermuir hills and we are sharing the valley bottoms with the becks and the railway so not too much alteration can take place and numerous small ox-bow stretches lie to one side or the other, particularly at Houndwood and Renton.

At Grantshouse, old road, new road and railway run alongside each other like three lanes of one highway! There was still space to fit another transport café in though as the Trucknet lads will testify. 'Flip' remembers the Grantshouse café: *'Has anyone mentioned my favourite cafe, the name of which escapes me? It was between the road and railway just north of Grantshouse, unfortunately derelict now but they used to serve cracking grub in there.'*

'Bumper' too: *'I only knew it as Grantshouse cafe. It closed as a cafe in the early 70s, opened as a tourist and tartan shop for a while then went back to a cafe. The last time I went past it was been used by some plant/machine outfit.'*

The old transport cafe at Grantshouse, much-beloved of long-distance lorry drivers. Now it is derelict with boulders across the entrance to prevent overnight parking.

If you turn off the A1 for Penmanshiel and follow the lane round, you will come to a spot where the road turns right for Penmanshiel. In front of you a track leads straight ahead. Once upon a time this was the A1 and the Penmanshiel road was actually a right turn off it. I took this photograph looking straight down the track. At the end you reach this barrier with a railway line in front of it. This is where a railway tunnel collapsed killing two men which meant that the railway line had to be realigned slightly. This, in turn, required the road to be moved leaving this orphaned piece behind. The railway tunnel was intended to go through the hill on the right of the photo.

Moving north again we are still more or less on the original course although there is an interesting ox-bow stretch which we cannot drive fully because of railway alterations. Take the turning for Penmanshiel, marked as a dead end. After a hundred yards or so the lane turns right but you can also go straight on down a rough track which you can follow

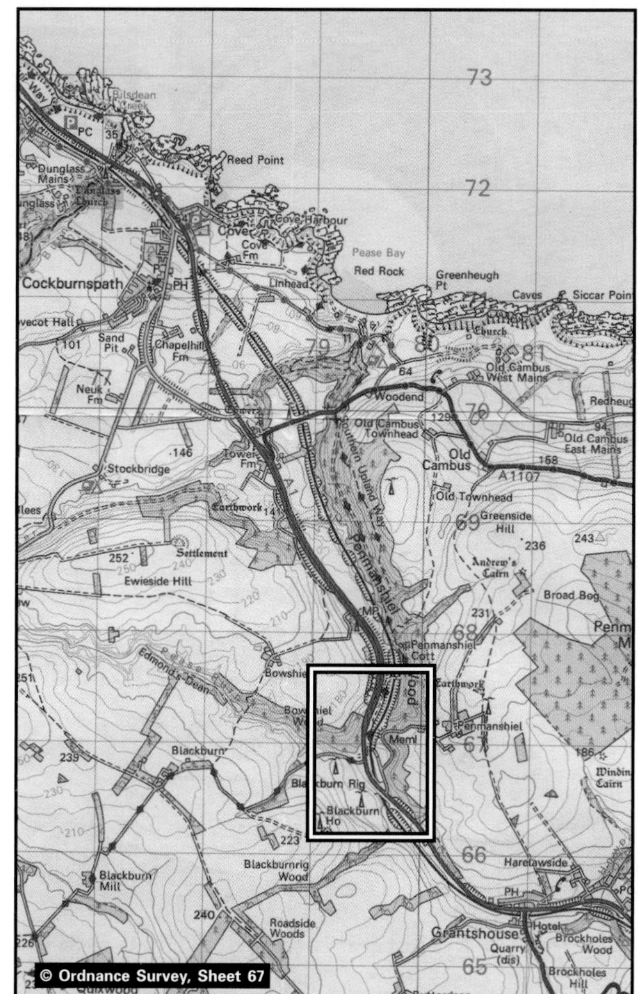

for a few hundred yards until you come up against a railway line by a rocky outcrop. This is because at one time the railway here was actually in a tunnel. In 1979 part of the tunnel collapsed during maintenance work and it was decided that the collapse was so bad it wasn't worth trying to dig out the rock fall so a cutting was made slightly to the west to reroute the railway which of course destroyed that section of our old road. It reappears on the other side of the railway line and runs between new road and railway for a few hundred yards before rejoining. Incidentally, the old railway tunnel is classed as a grave as the bodies of the two men killed under tons of rock were not recoverable and there is a monument to them above the tunnel site.

The extract from Google Earth shows the same area that is outlined on the Ordnance Survey map. You can see where the old road forks away from the new one and what was originally the side road to Penmanshiel. This crossed the railway and its continuation is visible in the trees just east of the new road.

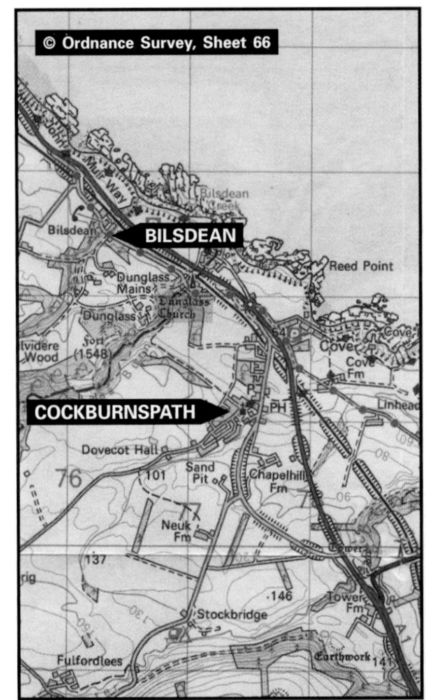

Above: **This is the Great North Road at the point where it crosses the present A1107 coming down from the cottages.** *Below:* **Looking across the main road, we can see where the Great North Road turned left and ran down to the burn.**

This map from 1899 shows the winding North Road crossing the burn at Tower Bridge, Cocksburnspath.

A little further on we come to a right turn signposted A1107 to Coldingham. This is the other end of the earlier route mentioned previously. We still need to take the right turn though to explore some Great North Road changes. Turn off the A1 but stop outside the cottage before going round the bend. You will note a track away to your right and you may note another lane running in front of the cottage and away to the left, almost parallel with the road we are on. Including the road we have just turned off, there are three incarnations of our Great North Road/A1 here, almost on top of one another. Let me explain.

If we consider a point on the existing main road, about 100 yards south of where we turned right as our starting point, this is where the earlier two routes diverge from the modern road. Sitting outside the cottages we can then see where those two diverged. The original Great North Road from this point appears as a driveway down to the cottages and then curves across along the front of the cottages running away across the field about 100 yards to our right. The later A1 opened in 1932 is the road we are on. If we now follow it down to the next bend and go around the corner we can see where the Great North Road comes down through the field from the cottages and actually crosses our path.

We can't drive it but, if we could, we'd turn left off the road here and follow the track which would curve first sharp left to cross the beck and then sharp right to climb up past the ruins of Cockburnspath Tower. It then turned north-west and crossed what is now a field to join up with the road coming from Cockburnspath village. This was a horrible dog-leg that was ironed out in the early 1930s by a road that started by the cottages and went in a shallow curve straight across the beck missing out all the dog-legs. The only part of this left is the first hundred yards or so of the A1107 from outside the cottages down to the bend. When this section was dualled in the 1990s the junction was altered again.

Staying on the current A1 which is dualled here, we come to the junction for Cockburnspath village and again we leave the A1 briefly to follow the Great North Road through the village.

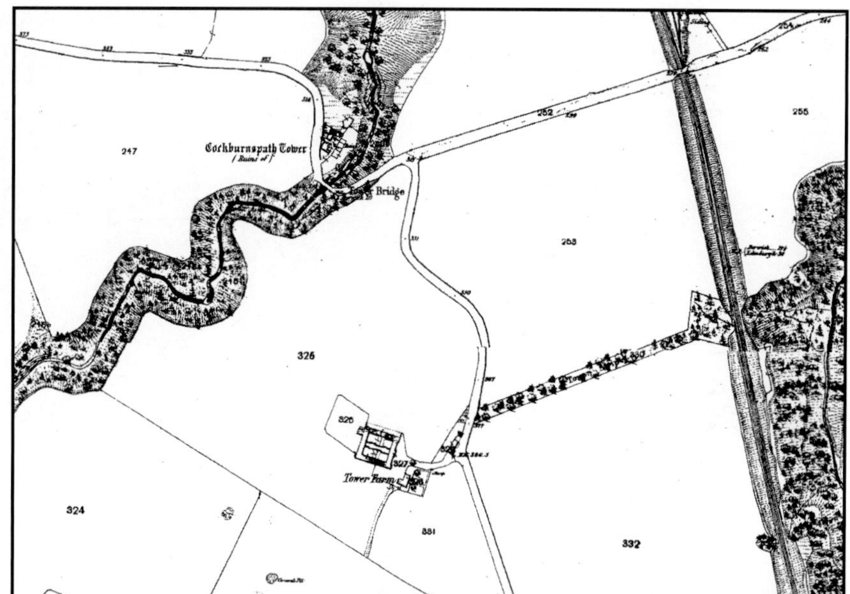

The A1 scything across the countryside is the 1990s one.

Left: **Wonky white lines? No, actually a wonky road. This small piece of tarmac was part of the original Great North Road here. When the 1932 alterations took place, this remnant was left as access to some houses and although the road curves off to the right, the remains of the white lines tell another story. The building in the distance is the Torness nuclear power station which the A1 passes quite close by.** *Right:* **Dunglass New Bridge, the Great North Road up until 1932.**

On the other side things become even more confusing as there would appear to have been three or possibly four realignments in a very short period. Today, as we leave Cockburnspath, we arrive at a roundabout with the current A1. The original road actually crossed straight over this area without any junction passing Castle Dyke cottages which are the white buildings just off the present roundabout. Passing the front of the cottages, the road then curved south-west crossing the current A1 and joining up with the unclassified road on the other side just before it goes under the railway bridge. It then crossed Dunglass Burn on a bridge called Dunglass New Bridge, ran up through Bilsdean and rejoined the present route.

However in 1932 a new alignment on the course of the present A1 had taken precedence, leaving the old one just before it went under the railway and crossing Dunglass Burn on a new bridge just to the north of the railway bridge. However, for some reason, when the new road that bypassed Cockburnspath was built and the roundabout was put in, the road was realigned slightly yet again and this bridge was not used and another one built almost next to it. This means that including the railway bridge, there are four bridges over the Dunglass Burn right next to each other!

And a few yards downstream there is a fifth. Note that earlier I said the original alignment went over Dunglass New Bridge. This implies that there is an older one somewhere, and sure enough there is. If we follow the lane past Castle Dyke cottages we come to a fork in the lane, both arms of which are just tracks. One of those tracks though leads to Dunglass Old Bridge. The oldest map I have seen (1854) shows both the old and new bridges so presumably this is an old alteration, but was Dunglass Old Bridge on the Great North Road at one time?

The 1932 and 1990s bridges. It is believed that the older one was not reused due to structural problems.

The various crossings of the Dunglass Burn just to the south of Bilsdean.

The Great North Road at Bilsdean — this stretch was bypassed in 1932 leaving it a quiet backwater.

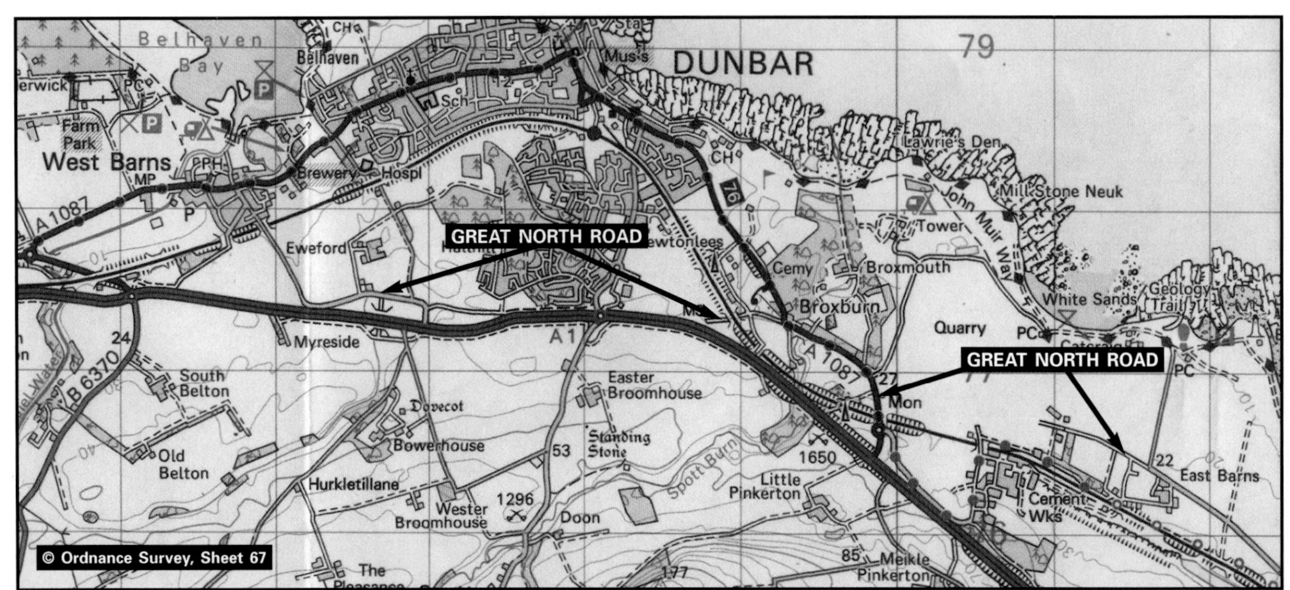

After the various routes recombine at Bilsdean we stay on the current route for a couple of miles then our Great North Road turns off again. Just past the entrance to Torness power station, we should take the lane on the right signposted for Skateraw and East Barns. This runs just north of the current A1 the other side of the railway line. However part of this route has been destroyed by quarrying and we cannot follow it for more than a couple of miles.

To get back on track we carry on along the current A1 to the first junction for Dunbar, the A1087. Taking it, a couple of hundred yards after crossing the railway there is a small lane on the right. This is where the Great North Road came through if we could have followed it through the quarry. We stay on the A1087 for a mile to the village of Broxburn where it curves sharp right for Dunbar. We take the road on the bend though, the left turn, which is the course of the Great North Road which didn't actually go into Dunbar. We cannot follow it very far as we come back to the current A1 which cuts it off so we have to retrace our steps and go back to the A1 and turn west as, for the last part of our trek, the road runs west towards Edinburgh.

This is the now-orphaned stretch between Broxburn village and the dualled A1.

Noting another small ox-bow stretch at Eweford, we come to a roundabout where the A1 is signposted as straight on and the right fork is indicated to the A199. We take the A199 and cross under the railway to Beltenford roundabout where the A1087 arrives from its run through Dunbar. When I first started using this part of the A1 regularly, the first roundabout wasn't there. The Great North Road was on its original alignment and is joined directly at the second roundabout. In the early 2000s, the entire route from here to Edinburgh had been dualled and our original road renumbered the A199. So we will follow the A199 leaving the dual carriageway behind.

From Beltenford, which was originally a simple fork in the road, we head west to East Linton. At one time we would have gone through the village via the B1377 and B1407 but in the 1930s the current bypass was built and we pass by to the south. Still on the original alignment we come to the A1 junction for Haddington which we must cross to stay on track.

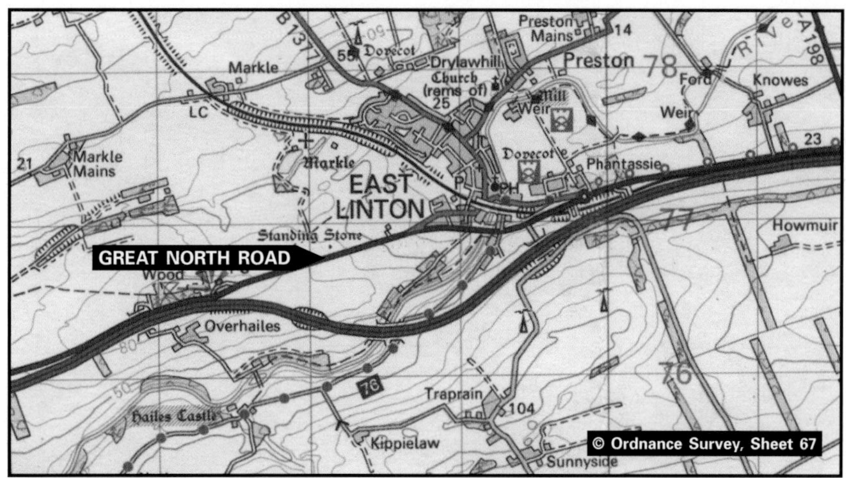

The Great North Road entered East Linton from the east via this bridge over the River Tyne although the town centre was bypassed to through traffic in 1928.

Charles Harper, writing in 1900: 'At East Linton we cross the Tyne, which, crawling through the meadows, plunges here in cascades under the road bridge, amid confused rocks. The railway crosses it too, close by, spans the road beyond; and the village huddles together at an angle of the way. A long ascent out of it commands wide views of agricultural Haddingstonshire, and of that surprising mountainous hill, Traprain Law, rising out of the plain to a height of over seven hundred feet.'

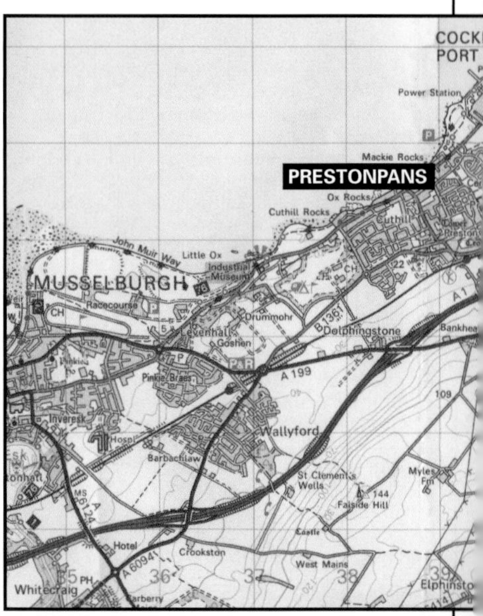

Now on the south side of the current A1 we follow the A199 skirting the north edge of Haddington. However this is a more recent path. At one time we would have had to pass through Haddington itself by way of Dunbar Road, Hardgate, Market Street, Court Road and West Road (the A6093 and B6471). This route was bypassed in the early 1930s.

Haddington is the county town of East Lothian (known as Haddingtonshire prior to 1921) and is a busy town which was a major stopping place for the Edinburgh coaches. It is the first town for a long way with the large market place-cum-High Street area typical of coaching stops, with the large George Hotel still incorporating a stabling area. Harper in particular is scathing about the state of the roads in Haddington and the area in general stating that although it was only 17 miles from here to Edinburgh, a coach would be lucky to do it in a day!

Haddington's market square was built up in the middle so that westbound traffic could use either the High Street or Market Street. Today this is a one-way system with westbound traffic using the High Street and eastbound using Market Street. Here we are looking west.

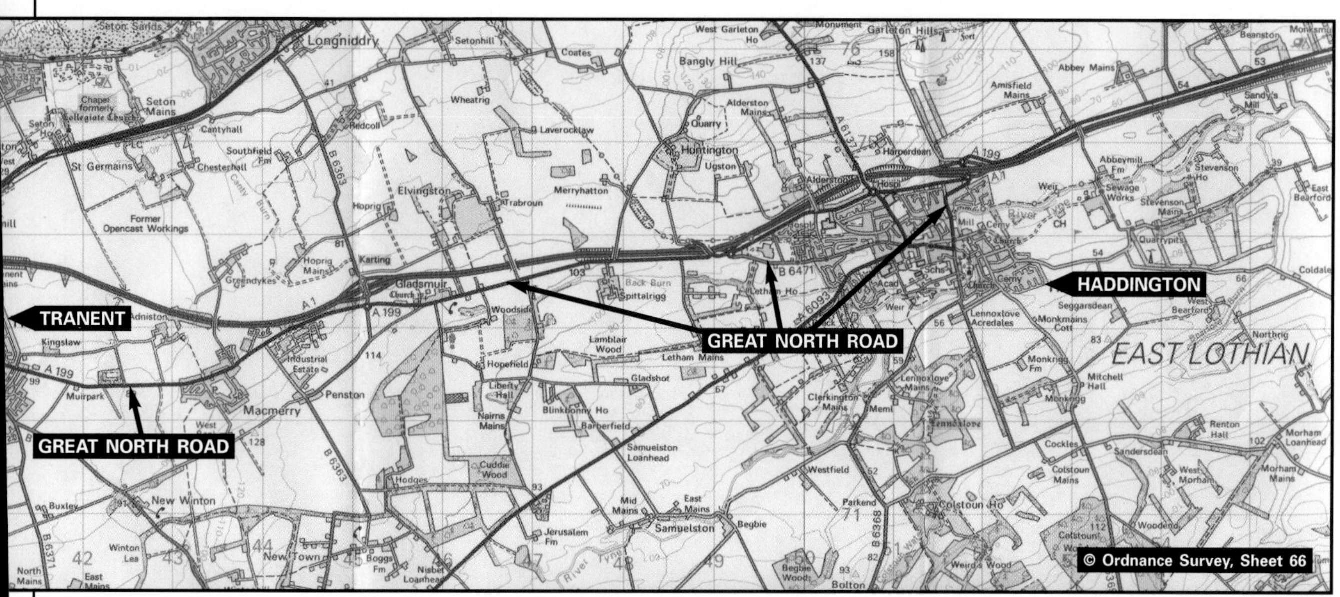

Our journey is now a little better and we carry on to where the B6471 rejoins the A199 and head on along the road which passes undisturbed through Gladsmuir, Macmerry and Tranent, the latter being somewhat larger than the other two villages and acting as a dormitory town for Edinburgh, although it was far smaller even 50 years ago.

Charles Harper: 'Here begins Haddington, and here end good roads for the space of a mile; and not until the burgh is left behind do they recommence. The traveller who might set out in quest of bad roads and vile paving would without difficulty discover the objects of his search at Haddington. He might conceivably find as bad elsewhere, but worse examples would be miraculous indeed. We have encountered many stretches of road, thus far, of a mediæval quality, but the long road to the North boasts nothing nearly so craggy as are the cobble-stoned thoroughfares of this "royal burgh". The entrance of the town from the south resembles, in its picturesque squalor, one of the decayed towns of Brittany.'

The Great North Road in Tranent High Street.

As Charles Harper reaches the end of his long cycle journey with this view of Edinburgh looking from Tranent, so do we.

Here we are looking across the modern A1. The Forth road and rail bridges in the far distance are 18 miles away.

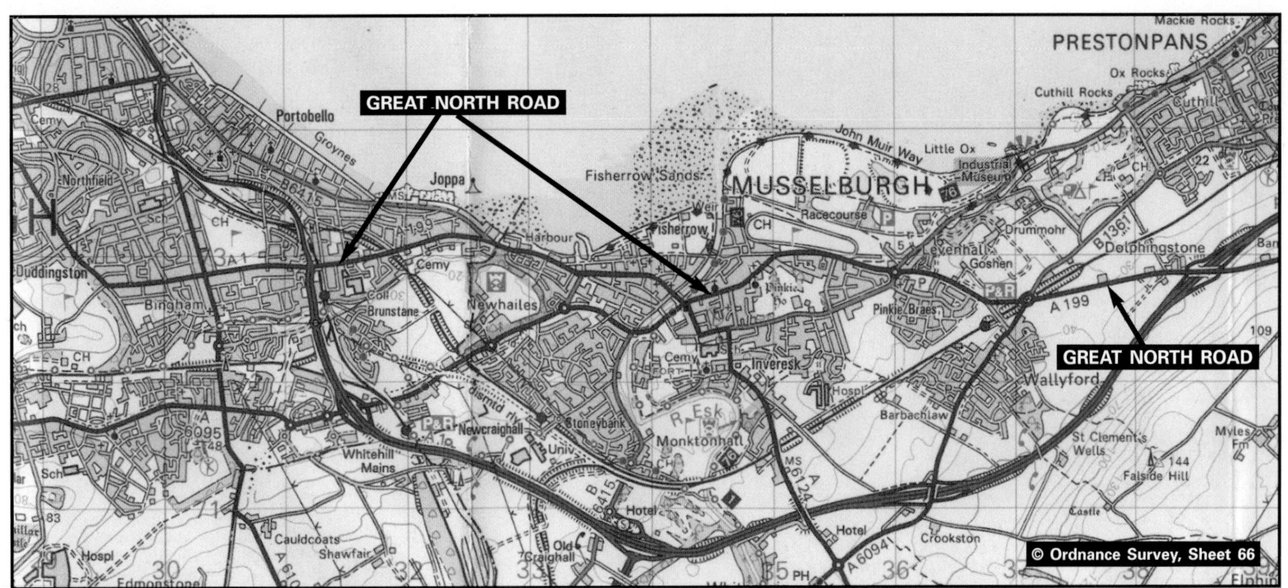

Moving on, we pass the site of the Battle of Prestonpans which was the first uprising in the Jacobite rebellion of 1745. A highly inexperienced government force was routed by a body of highlanders who cleverly attacked them from an unexpected direction. The rebellion ended six months later at Culloden. However, there would appear to be some recent evidence (2010) that the current battle site is not quite correct and that in fact the conflict took place some 500 yards further to the east.

This building in Musselburgh is one of the first we meet after passing the racecourse. It is known as the 'Ambassador's House' as it is generally believed to have been built for a French ambassador to Scotland. This view is looking east back towards the racecourse. The cobbled and tramlined nature of the Great North Road is clear to see.

racecourse is Musselburgh Links, a nine-hole golf course that has the distinction of being officially the oldest documented golf course in the world.

Linkfield Road becomes the High Street which crosses New Bridge over the Esk and becomes Bridge Street. Musselburgh is an old town having been settled by the Romans and a bridge that they built, although rebuilt a couple of times, still stands a few yards south of New Bridge. Thus being the Old Bridge!

We pass along Bridge Street into North High Street which becomes Edinburgh Road by the harbour. In Eastfield at the junction with Milton Road East it looks like we carry straight on, but the Great North Road took the left fork onto Milton Road East. We continue along the road across two railway bridges a couple of hundred yards apart. After the second one is a fairly large road junction, a traffic light controlled crossroads. To our left is the A1 coming round from where the dual carriageway has passed the Edinburgh city bypass and entered the suburbs. To our right is the continuation of the A199 but we follow it no longer. Here we go straight on, into the city, on the A1 Great North Road.

A little further along on the same side of the road is the Old Town Hall also known as the 'Tolbooth'. It was built out of the ruins of an abbey or chapel left vacant after the reformation, hence its size.

And barely half a mile down the road is the site of the Battle of Pinkie Cleugh between the villages of Walleyford and Pinkie Brae. In the 1540s the Scots were involved in a civil war between those who supported English rule and those who favoured France. Eventually Henry VIII decided enough was enough and declared war. Carried on by his son Edward VI, it culminated in the battle here between English forces and the Scots who were backed up by the French. Although they outnumbered the English two to one, it was a catastrophic defeat for the Scots who were routed and driven into the River Esk at Musselburgh. They lost half their force and all their artillery.

We too are approaching Musselburgh on the A199 Haddington Road. This becomes Linkfield Road which runs down the side of Musselburgh racecourse. In the centre of the

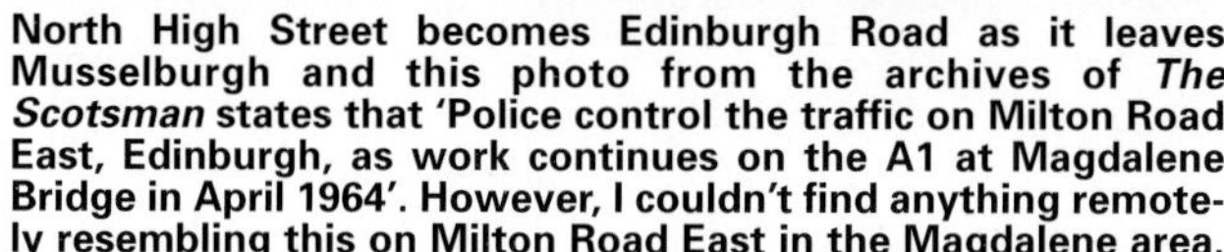

North High Street becomes Edinburgh Road as it leaves Musselburgh and this photo from the archives of *The Scotsman* states that 'Police control the traffic on Milton Road East, Edinburgh, as work continues on the A1 at Magdalene Bridge in April 1964'. However, I couldn't find anything remotely resembling this on Milton Road East in the Magdalene area.

On my return from Edinburgh, I just spotted the remains of the wooden sign on the left of the picture. I stopped for a look and decided I had stumbled across the place. It is Edinburgh Road on the outskirts of Musselburgh looking towards Edinburgh. Milton Road East is the left fork by the garage (the light coloured building in the background).

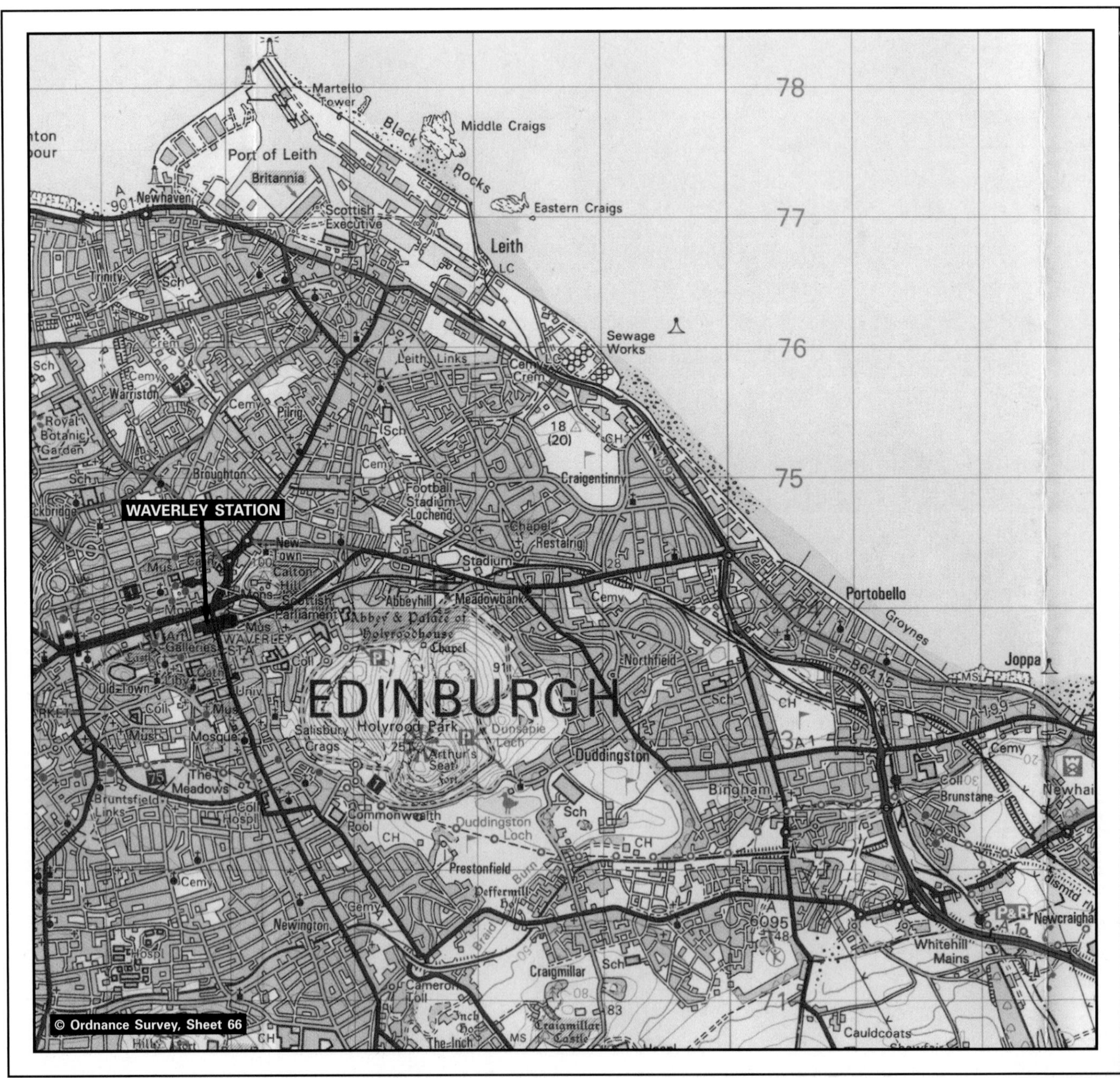
WAVERLEY STATION
EDINBURGH
Port of Leith
Britannia
Martello Tower
Black Rocks
Middle Craigs
Eastern Craigs
Scottish Executive
Newhaven
Leith
Sewage Works
Trinity
Warriston
Royal Botanic Garden
Leith Links
Pilrig
Broughton
Craigentinny
Football Stadium Lochend
Restalrig
Stadium
New Town
Calton Hill
Scottish Parliament
Abbeyhill
Meadowbank
Abbey & Palace of Holyroodhouse
Chapel
Portobello
Groynes
Joppa
Old Town
Northfield
Holyrood Park
Salisbury Crags
Arthur's Seat
Dunsapie Loch
Duddingston
Bingham
Brunstane
Newhaven
The Meadows
Bruntsfield Links
Commonwealth Pool
Duddingston Loch
Prestonfield
Peffermill
Braid Burn
Newington
Craigmillar
Craigmillar Castle
Cameron Toll
Inch
Whitehill Mains
Newcraighall
Cauldcoats
© Ordnance Survey, Sheet 66

The site of Jock's Lodge toll-bar was at the junction of Willowbrae Road and Portobello Road. The Great North Road comes in from the left, just past the tree in the illustration, and at the lights in the comparison. They merge to become London Road and head in to Edinburgh.

Unlike London, our journey through the suburbs is not one of a succession of high streets, in fact it is far shorter, it being only three miles from here to the end of our journey as opposed to the some 13 miles of built-up London between St Paul's and the M25.

Milton Road East becomes Duddingstone Crescent and then Milton Road West. As recently as the 1930s a lot of this area was still open fields, but by the 1950s the suburbs of Duddingstone and Willowbrae were springing up along the road. Milton Road West becomes Willowbrae Road which meets with Portobello Road to become London Road.

London Road is dead straight for quite a way until we reach Calton Hill where there is a fork with a road either side of the hill. Calton Hill is a rocky hill which stands close to the centre of Edinburgh. It is home to a number of buildings, including the Scottish Parliament, but it leaves us with a small quandary right at the end of our journey.

The road divides with Regent Road passing south of the hill and London Road to the north. That seems clear cut until you notice that it is Regent Road that keeps the designation A1. The oldest map I could find shows both roads although no numbers of course. I have to assume that London Road is the original.

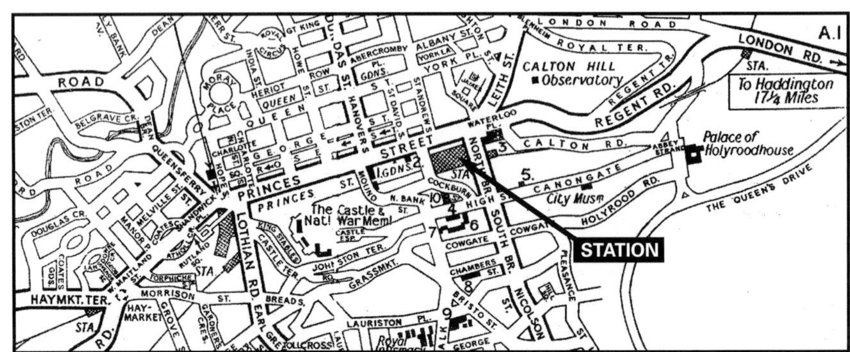

The last 200 yards of Regent Road is called Waterloo Place and is of great significance to us because it is the last few yards of the Great North Road. This photo was taken looking back up toward Calton Hill.

Waterloo Place pictured in 1880. The area in the foreground is where the A1, A7 and A8 all meet up.

Our epic journey ends at Waverley Station, which was claimed before the war to be the second largest station in Great Britain. Princess Street was also said to be one of the finest avenues in Europe.

Regent Road runs straight into Princess Street in the centre of Edinburgh while London Road meets Leith Walk which completes the journey around Calton Hill and meets the eastern end of Princess Street outside Waverley railway station. Again, unlike London, there are no doubts as to where the Great North Road finishes as the A1, A7 and A8 all meet up in Waterloo Place outside the station. To go any further would mean taking one of those other roads.

So we have finally ended our journey. A little short of 400 miles from St Paul's. We have passed through small and large towns and many a village. We have seen mighty highways and places where the road has become a footpath. We have seen moors and hills and fields and the sea. And what a journey. Me? I'd do it again tomorrow.

The end of a long and winding road. The A1 is directly ahead, the A7 is to my right, and the A8 (Princes Street) is behind me.

Give or take a mile or so, we have covered around 400 since we started. It has been a wonderful nostalgic trip, looking back to long-forgotten days, discovering past highways and byways, and the many faces of 'our' Great North Road.